Undergraduate Topics in Computer Science

Undergraduate Topics in Computer Science (UTiCS) delivers high-quality instructional content for undergraduates studying in all areas of computing and information science. From core foundational and theoretical material to final-year topics and applications, UTiCS books take a fresh, concise, and modern approach and are ideal for self-study or for a one- or two-semester course. The texts are all authored by established experts in their fields, reviewed by an international advisory board, and contain numerous examples and problems. Many include fully worked solutions.

More information about this series at http://www.springer.com/series/7592

Natalia Silvis-Cividjian

Pervasive Computing

Engineering Smart Systems

 Springer

Natalia Silvis-Cividjian
Department of Computer Science
Vrije Universiteit Amsterdam
Amsterdam
The Netherlands

ISSN 1863-7310   ISSN 2197-1781   (electronic)
Undergraduate Topics in Computer Science
ISBN 978-3-319-51654-7   ISBN 978-3-319-51655-4   (eBook)
DOI 10.1007/978-3-319-51655-4

Library of Congress Control Number: 2016963311

All figures made with MATLAB® are reprinted with permission of The MathWorks, Inc

This Springer imprint is published by Springer Nature
The registered company is Springer International Publishing AG
The registered company address is: Gewerbestrasse 11, 6330 Cham, Switzerland

To my students

Foreword

Computers have been getting smaller for decades. Back in the 1960s, we had mainframes, which filled large rooms and cost tens of millions of dollars. In the 1970s, we had minicomputers, which were the size of refrigerators and cost only tens of thousands of dollars. In the 1980s, we had personal computers, small and cheap enough for a person to buy in a store and take home. In 2007, the iPhone was introduced and you could hold a full-blown computer in your hand.

Now computers are about to disappear altogether. The next phase in computing is pervasive computing, with invisible computers everywhere, doing things for you without your even being aware of them. They will be embedded in door locks, clothes, medical devices, cars, banknotes, credit cards, thermostats, roads, toys, kitchen appliances, milk cartons, guns, cameras, light bulbs, drinking cups, pets, smoke detectors, blankets, pill bottles, toothbrushes, scales, lawn sprinklers, and a vast number of other things. They will interact with people, each other, and the cloud wirelessly and seamlessly, without people even being aware of them.

The idea of pervasive computing, also called ubiquitous computing, was dreamed up by the late Mark Weiser, a visionary and friend of mine, in 1991. When he wrote his classic paper about this idea, it was pure science fiction, not unlike a 1950s science fiction author writing about a device the size of a book that could summon up all the world's information. The latter remained science fiction, until the iPad came along. And Weiser's idea is not science fiction any more, either. It is happening right now. If you want to learn about the underlying technology that is making it happen, this is the book for you.

The book covers analog and digital signals, control systems, sensors, image processing, audio signal processing, and classifying patterns. The final chapter puts all the pieces together and discusses systems engineering, especially software engineering. The appendix contains some experiments you can try with readily available off-the-shelf parts. These are ideal for a lab course for computer science or engineering students.

Although the book is intended for computer science and engineering under-graduates, it should be accessible to anyone with a science background, a command of high school mathematics, and some programming experience.

Natalia's writing style is wonderfully refreshing. So many technical books are accurate and full of information, but dry and boring to read. This one is different. Throughout the book the author talks directly to the reader, often in amusing ways. The figures are clear and often fun to look at.

If you want to learn the technical details of how pervasive computing, the Internet of Things, or whatever you want to call it actually works, this book is a great place to start.

Amsterdam, The Netherlands   Andrew S. Tanenbaum

Preface

If you understand how the universe operates,
you control it, in a way.
Stephen Hawking, My Brief History

Pervasive computing describes ICT (information and communication technology) systems that seamlessly enable information and services to be made available everywhere. Other terms, used with approximately the same meaning as pervasive computing, are *Ubiquitous Computing, Internet of Things (IoT), calm computing, ambient intelligence, physical computing, smart spaces,* and *smart environments.*

You can write about pervasive computing in a million different ways. This book tells the story from a *systems engineering* perspective and focuses on smart systems that use pattern recognition to discover their context. My wish is to make you, the reader, feel confident that not only you *understand* how these systems operate, but you *can* also *build* such systems. While reading the book, you will realize, on the one hand, how simple the underlying principles are, and on the other hand, how difficult it is to implement them in practice. Learning how to ride a bicycle is also difficult. And yet, Dutch children learn this skill very early, usually before they reach four. What you have to do as a parent is to run along—over and over—and keep them in balance, until they suddenly get the trick and boost forwards, leaving you behind, out of breath, yet relieved. This book is a guide for exactly this period—of desperately running behind the bicycle. After that, I believe that imagination and talent will drive you toward building the most incredible systems.

This book is crafted around the lecture notes developed for the course *Pervasive Computing,* taught to computer science (CS) freshmen at the Vrije University in Amsterdam. Upon completion of this course, successful students will be able to:

- Design a realistic smart system with the potential to benefit human lives. The system acquires and processes data from video, audio, acceleration, or EEG sensors and uses pattern recognition to take decisions that affect the environment accordingly.

- Build a simplified version of the real system and program a software agent to control it.
- Work together in a team, collaboratively identifying not only the technical but also the safety or ethical issues with their designs, and then sharing their challenges and discoveries through reports, presentations, and in-class demonstrations.

Although mainly targeted for computer science undergraduate students, I believe this book will be interesting and readable for anyone wondering what happens behind the scenes of these fascinating systems. After reading it, the ones who dream of building their own system should feel one step closer to their goal.

Acknowledgements This book is a result of a collective effort. Maarten van Steen was the first who came up with the idea of designing a pervasive computing course. Countless brainstorm sessions on how to teach it followed, with valuable input from Melanie Rieback, Guillaume Pierre, Michel Klein, and Peter van Lith. The course followed a meandering evolution, toward the version described in this book. I am fortunate to work in the computer science department that owes so much fame to Prof. Andrew Tanenbaum and I am most grateful and honored that he kindly consented to contribute the foreword. We teachers are, in fact, story tellers. The engineering flavor in this book is inspired by my teacher, Mircea Ţăţulescu, who first told me the story of sensors, data acquisition and signal processing, and irreversibly influenced the way I see the world. Hans van Vliet pointed me out the importance of software testing, and Jaap Gordijn and Patricia Lago helped me to embed software modeling elements in this course. Many thanks go to Wan Fokkink and Spyros Voulgaris, for reviewing the original lecture notes, and to Anton Eliens and Herbert Bos for their encouragements during writing this book. Teaching this course could have been a disaster without my teaching assistants, who supported me over the years, for better or worse, with their awesome ideas, hardworking and enthusiasm. I am indebted to Alyssa Milburn, for her critical, perfectionistic eye set on my writing. Caroline, thank you for your interest in my book and for your time management lessons. I am grateful to my Springer editors, Beverley Ford and James Robinson, for their initial trust and efficient assistance during the manuscript preparation.

I collected many beautiful illustrations in this book. Grateful acknowledgment is made to all those who kindly granted me permission to use them: Roberto Brunelli, Diana Cook, Dariu Gavrila, Daniel Goehring, Horst-Michael Gross, Erico Guizzi, Alex Faaborg, Bob Fisher, Kees Hagen, Johan Hoorn, Mehdi Jayazeri, Phillip Laplante, Alisdair McAndrew, Jim McClellan, Steve McConnell, Thomas Moeslund, Niels Noordzij, Martin Pearson, Mauro Pezze, Dirk van der Pijl, Jozef Pucik, Hanna Reimers, Stuart Russell, Jan Schnupp, Chris Solomon, Ian Sommerville, Jakob Suckale, Sergios Theodoridis, Johannes Trabert, and Michal Young. Many thanks go to Naomi Fernandes and Joachim Levelt from Mathworks, Inc., for their speed in processing my permissions procedure.

Being able to teach and shape your own material is a blessing, and nobody understands this better than my parents. Thank you, *dragii mei*, for your unconditional love and for teaching me to respect and care about my students. Undergoing this writing project, especially in its final part, put some pressure on my home front, as well. Fortunately, we survived through all this turbulence, due to Peter, my guide and companion in the journey of life, who seamlessly took over my "ubiquitous" duties. *Oma en opa Silvis, dank voor het faciliteren van al die heerlijke, broodnodige rustmomenten.* Too often, my kids had to miss me without getting too many explanations. They only knew that mama writes a book. "About an adventure?" they asked. "No? Oh, then it must be very boring…" Fortunately, their cynical optimism and young spirit prevented the worst. I hope that one day they will find more answers and be able to forgive. *Dank, mijn liefste.*

Amsterdam, The Netherlands   Natalia Silvis-Cividjian
November 2016

Contents

Abbreviations

AC	Alternative current
ADC	Analog-to-digital converter
AI	Artifical intelligence
ANN	Artificial neural network
ASR	Automatic speech recognizer
AUC	Area under the curve
B	A formal specification language
B&W	Black and white
BGC	Blood glucose concentration
BLOB	Binary large object
BVA	Boundary value analysis
ConOps	Concept of operation
DAC	Digital-to-analog converter
DC	Direct current
DSP	Digital signal processing
EBID	Electron beam-induced deposition
ECG	Electrocardiogram
EEG	Electroencephalogram
EP	Equivalence partitioning
F1, F2	The frequencies of first two formants in the spectrum
FDA	Food and Drug Administration
FFT	Fast Fourier transform
FIR	Finite impulse response
FMEA	Failure mode and effects analysis
FPR	False-positive rate
FTA	Fault tree analysis
GPS	Global Positioning System
HMM	Hidden Markov model
IC	Integrated circuit
IDE	Integrated development environment

IFFT	Inverse fast Fourier transform
i-HCI	Implicit human–computer interaction
IIR	Infinite impulse response
IoT	Internet of Things
LED	Light-emitting diode
LIDAR	Light detection and ranging
MBT	Model-based testing
MEMS	Microelectromechanical systems
MFCC	Mel frequency cepstrum coefficients
MLP	Multilayer perceptron
MOSFET	Metal–oxide–semiconductor field-effect transistor
OCR	Optical character recognizer
PD	Proportional derivative
PID	Proportional integral derivative
PIR	Passive infrared sensor
PLI	Power line interference
RFID	Radio-frequency identification
RGB	Red green blue
ROC	Receiver operating characteristics
SRS	System (or software) requirements specification
STAMP	Systems-Theoretic Accident Model and Processes
STFT	Short-term Fourier transform
STM	Scanning tunneling microscope
STREL	Structuring element
TDD	Test-driven development
TN	True negative
TP	True positive
TPR	True-positive rate
UML	Unified modeling language
V&V	Verification and validation
VDL	Vienna definition language, a formal specification language
Z	A formal specification language

Chapter 1
Introduction

The most profound technologies are those that disappear.
Mark Weiser

Pervasive computing, also known as *Internet of Things*, or *Ubiquitous Computing*, describes the emerging trend of seamlessly integrating computing into the everyday physical world. Examples of pervasive computing systems include: self-driving cars, smart homes, navigation systems for disabled people, and environmental monitoring systems. In this chapter, we will take a first glance at such systems, and identify their properties and basic components.

An essential feature of these systems is their context-awareness, meaning that they determine circumstances (time, location, ambient temperature, emotions, seismic activity, etc.). In order to extract this context, a pervasive computing system must *sense* signals from the environment and then *process* them. Consequently, based on the inferred context and an internal process model, the pervasive computing system takes intelligent decisions and *acts* upon the same environment. Context inferring, reasoning, and decision making are the tasks of a *software agent*, or *controller*. In many cases, more computer systems work together behind the scenes, exchanging information in a transparent way, in order to deliver a service to the user.

To summarize, a generic pervasive computing system consists of sensors, actuators, software agents (controllers), and communication modules. Its core properties are context-awareness, implicit human–computer interaction, seamless networking, autonomy, and intelligence. The highest ideal of making computing naturally embedded in our lives cannot, however, be achieved by merely solving technical problems. Acceptance and trust of pervasive computing also requires solutions to legal, ethical and usability challenges.

© Springer International Publishing AG 2017
N. Silvis-Cividjian, *Pervasive Computing*, Undergraduate Topics
in Computer Science, DOI 10.1007/978-3-319-51655-4_1

1.1 Pervasive Computing—Past, Present, and Future

We all have a love–hate relationship with computers. They invade our lives; they watch, coach, assist, and entertain us, hidden inside smartphones, navigation systems, smart watches, medical devices, game consoles, and household appliances. We say that computing is becoming "*ubiquitous*" or "*pervasive.*" In this book, we consider exactly these embedded computers. Not the ones standing lonely on our desks, but the ones interconnected with cameras and microphones, radars and GPS, speakers and motors, and other computers, working together in a complex *pervasive computing system*, with the sole goal of making our lives easier.

The concept of "pervasive computing" is not new. The trend has its basis in a 1991 article [1], entitled "The Computer for the 21st Century," written by Mark Weiser of Xerox PARC (**P**alo **A**lto **R**esearch **C**enter). The PARC Laboratory in California is well known for other revolutionary inventions, like the laser printer, Ethernet technology, and mouse-driven graphical user interfaces (GUI). In this article, Mark Weiser expressed his vision on what he then called *Ubiquitous Computing* (*Ubicomp*). He described a world in which computing and applications are embedded in everyday objects, such as cars, televisions, and clothes, where "each person is continually interacting with hundreds of ... interconnected computers" that "weave themselves into the fabric of everyday life until they are indistinguishable from it" [1]. Ubiquitous Computing is considered to be the third wave in the evolution of computer science, where one person is served by many computers. It follows two previous periods of computing: the *mainframe era* (1960s–1970s), when many people were served by a single huge computer, and the age of *personal computers* (PC) (1980s–1990s), where one computer served just one person.

Mark Weiser predicted that the world will be populated by three basic forms of smart devices: *tabs* (wearable centimeter-sized devices), *pads* (handheld decimeter-sized devices), and *boards* (meter-sized interactive display devices). Unfortunately, at that time, device fabrication and wireless data communication were not so effective and affordable. Nowadays, we have much better news: All forms of devices envisioned by Weiser are already ubiquitously available! Think about smart watches and smartphones, RFID (radio-frequency identification) tags embedded in our clothes, books and smart cards (tabs), tablets and laptops (pads), and personalized advertisement boards that change their content to suit our preferences (boards). These achievements have been made possible by many technological advances, including device miniaturization, wireless communication, multimodal human–computer interaction, powerful artificial intelligence algorithms, new materials, and energy resources.

The key element in understanding how pervasive computing benefits from the miniaturization of electronic components is the *transistor*, the building block for all the integrated circuits (IC) such as logical gates, microprocessors, microcontrollers, and storage devices that eventually build up a computer. The type of transistor used over the past three decades in the computer industry is the metal-oxide-semiconductor field effect transistor (MOSFET). This type of transistor, shown in

Fig. 1.1, has three terminals: source (S), drain (D), and gate (G). The source–drain channel is isolated from the gate by a silicon-oxide layer. The transistor's main job in a logical device is to act as an on/off, binary switch. In a MOSFET, this is realized by varying the gate voltage that allows, or, respectively, blocks, electrical current to flow between the source and the drain.

An integrated circuit (IC) contains millions of MOSFETs. The more transistors the IC contains, the more computations it can perform. Thanks to miniaturization, all features including the critical source–drain distance, denoted by L in Fig. 1.1, have become smaller. As a result, the MOSFET structure as a whole has shrunk, allowing the integration density to grow, so that more transistors can be squeezed on one chip; as a result, the computational power of ICs has grown. Hopefully you understand now why miniaturization enables the creation of smaller and more computationally powerful electronic components. You might think: OK, I've got it, but how small is "small"? To put this in context, consider some facts about the present situation of miniaturization of electronic components. As of 2016, the highest transistor count in a commercially available processor is over 7.2 billion. Currently, industrially manufactured transistors exhibit minimum feature sizes of 20–30 nm. In comparison, a sheet of paper is about 100,000 nm thick. These features are continuously shrinking. An historical observation of this trend, known as *Moore's law*, claims that the number of transistors that can be placed on an IC chip will continue to double approximately every two years (see Fig. 1.2).

As mechanical devices are also becoming smaller, a new promising technology, called *MEMS* (microelectro-mechanical systems), is also rapidly evolving. MEMS are microns to millimeter-scale devices that integrate mechanical mechanisms together with the necessary electronic circuits, on a single silicon chip. MEMS can perform two basic functions: sensing and actuation. Examples of MEMS *sensors* are the accelerometers used to release safety airbags in modern cars, the gyroscopes

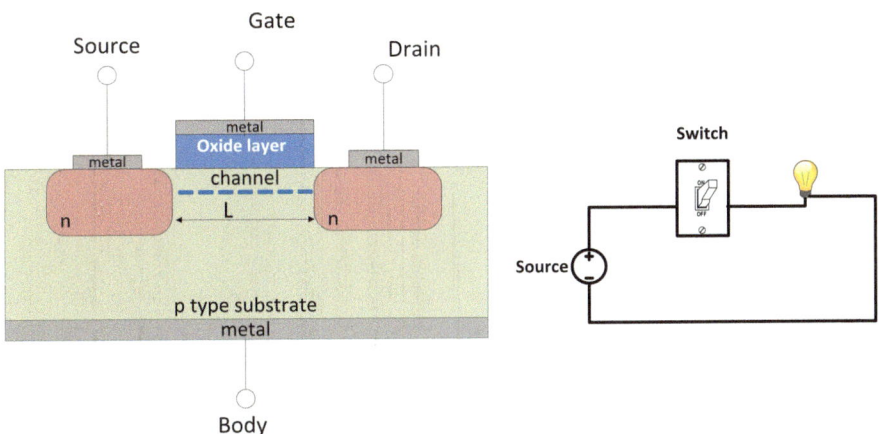

Fig. 1.1 An analogy between a MOSFET and an electrical switch

Fig. 1.2 An illustration of the historical evolution of device integration density and performance. From [5]. Used with permission

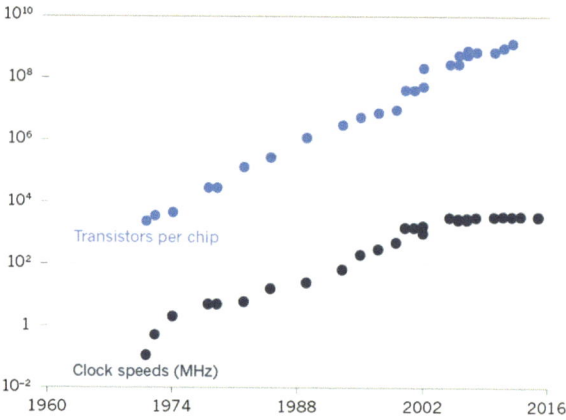

used to stabilize images in digital cameras and smartphones, the pressure sensors in microfluidic systems, and the Reed sensors in pacemakers.

Sensor nodes or *motes* are wireless devices that combine on one chip a MEMS sensor, a battery, a microprocessor, and a communication module. Some interesting ideas in this direction are the *smart dust, smart skins,* and *smart clay* technologies. They aim to fabricate motes as small as a sugar cube [2], to embed MEMS in the non-planar, flexible surfaces of aircrafts, vehicles, and clothes [3], or assembly MEMS in 3D artifacts, like *tangible interfaces* that give physical form to digital information [4], respectively.

Examples of MEMS actuators include the micropumps in implantable drug delivery devices, inkjet print heads, and micromirror optical actuators in overhead projectors. See the electron microscope image of a MEMS actuator shown in Fig. 1.3. It is really small, isn't it?

And this is still not the ultimate level of miniaturization. In nanotechnology laboratories, efforts are being made to push the fabrication size limits even lower,

Fig. 1.3 An electron microscope image of a MEMS nanoinjector for genetic modification of cells, built in 2014. Reproduced from [6] with the permission of AIP Publishing

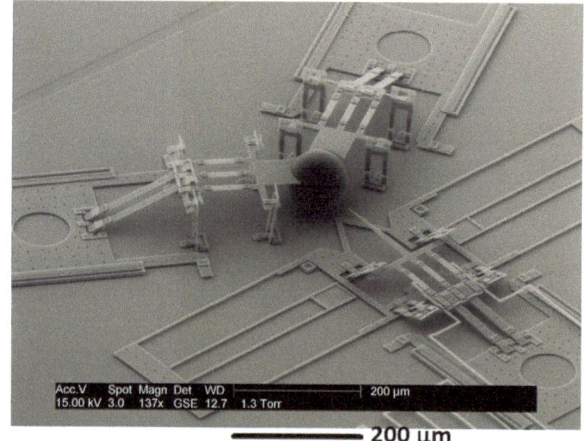

down to the 1–100 nm range. In the same way in which Mark Weiser inspired pervasive computing, nanotechnology has been instigated by the famous physicist Richard Feynman, and his lecture held in 1959, entitled "There is Plenty of Room at the Bottom" [7]. The images in Fig. 1.4 show that in laboratory settings, it is already possible to fabricate structures with features smaller than 20 nm.

Isn't this fantastic news? Atomic-scale devices are on the way, they will be easily embedded in the environment and out-of-sight, and they will be seamlessly wearable and implantable, keeping us company day and night. I think I can hear you worrying about this future. Where are we heading for? Is there a size limit that will stop miniaturization? Is there any device after all, if we cannot see it anymore? Can we inhale a smart dust mote by accident? Can police use invisible cameras to spy on us? Can we easily connect our smartphone to these tiny nanostructures? You are perfectly right, and you are not the only one to worry. Skeptic physicists also

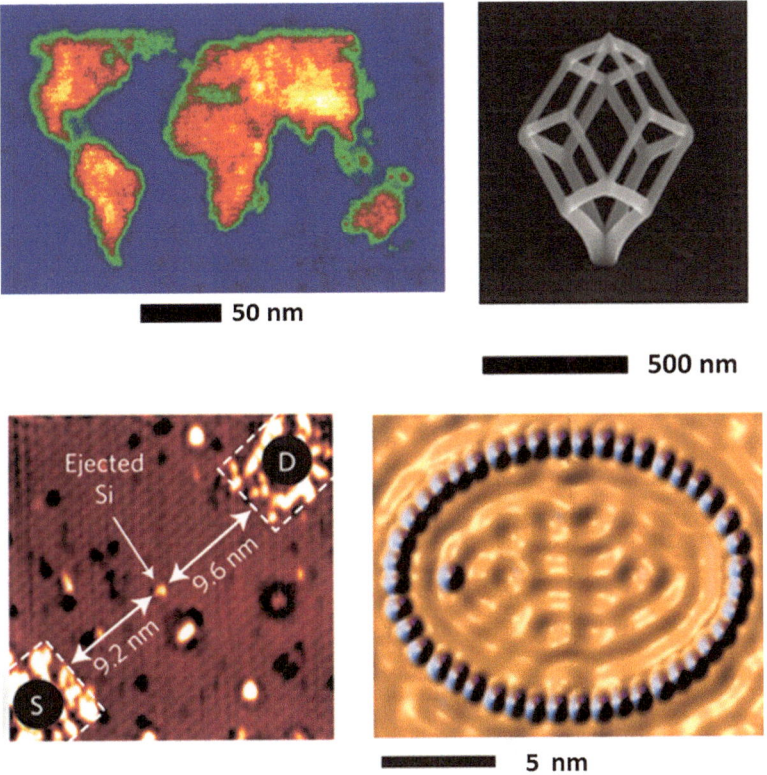

Fig. 1.4 Nanofabrication "on the edge." Clockwise, starting from top left. A 3D world map fabricated using electron-beam-induced deposition (EBID), where the Himalaya mountains have the lightest colour from [9]; a 3D structure fabricated with EBID, from [10]; Cobalt atoms manipulated in a quantum corral ring using a scanning tunneling microscope (STM), from [11]; a single-atom transistor, where the distance between the source and the drain is 18.8 nm, from [12]. All figures are used with permission

fear that the days of Moore's law might come to a close, because heat dissipation and quantum effects will become a problem when the chip size approaches atomic scale [5]. There are more issues that might turn pervasive computing to a "bleeding edge" experiment. First, there are still unsolved *technical* issues, concerning energy, scalability, and mobility management. For example, it turns out that battery technology does not follow Moore's law. In this field, a mere 5% increase in capacity for each year of development is considered good [8]. And no matter how much capacity a battery has, sooner or later it will have to be recharged or replaced. If you consider that many applications implant devices in human bodies or scatter them in remote or hazardous areas, you can see that this is not only inconvenient, but simply impractical. Moreover, heaps of ubiquitous discarded batteries may raise concerns about deteriorating effects on our health and environment.

Second, since pervasive computing systems work in human-centered environments, not only technical considerations, but also social and cognitive aspects become relevant. Intriguing questions arise, such as: Is a self-driving car such a good idea after all? Who will be responsible in case of a deadly accident? Should the car kill *you* to save others on the road since there are five and you are just one? Do we really want to be observed 24/7 by cameras? Is it ethically responsible to let an Alzheimer's patient get emotionally attached to a robot? Many such privacy, ethical, legal, and usability issues must be resolved before the last skeptics surrender, and pervasive computing gets unconditional trust and acceptance.

You probably understand by now that there is no crystal ball forecast for pervasive computing. Only time will tell. Either way, there is no doubt that since the beginning days of Ubiquitous Computing, technology has moved on with huge steps. It has made the tools for computing and communication much smaller, more affordable, more powerful than ever, bringing the vision of invisible computation that weaves into the fabric of daily life to a goal within reach. We can conclude that now, 25 years later, we are well positioned to carefully begin the quest for Weiser's vision.

1.2 Pervasive Computing Systems

When we begin building a pervasive computing system, we must first consider how this system is going to be used. Who will benefit from it? Who are the potential stakeholders? Why should we build it in the first place? All this because without a meaningful use, all the technological effort to build our system will be in vain. To begin, let us consider a few examples of use scenarios and envision the systems that could realize them.

Scenario #1. A Smart Home

You arrive at home, tired after a day's work. The house identifies you and unlocks the door. Recognizing the fatigue on your face, the home entertainment system starts playing your favorite relaxing music and replaces the artwork on the electronic wallboards with soothing images of nature. As you enter the bathroom, you are asked if a warm bath should be started. As you enter the kitchen, the display on the refrigerator door suggests a light meal and a specific recipe on the basis of the available ingredients in the refrigerator and fitting your mood. If you accept the suggestion, step-by-step instructions are displayed, helping you through the steps of the recipe. Once you place the bowl on the stove, the temperature is automatically adjusted to control the cooking time on the basis of your decision whether to take a bath [13].

Scenario #2. A Health Monitor

Your health monitor, possibly installed in your watch, notices that your blood sugar is suddenly elevated. It starts to monitor other conditions more closely, to uncover possible causes and potential problems. It contacts your medicine cabinet, to ensure that you have adequate medicine in your home and contacts the pharmacy for additional medicine if necessary. It reports the change to your electronic medical record and sends a short message to your doctor, informing the doctor of your current location and evening plans in case the doctor needs to contact you. Back at home, the kitchen modifies the refrigerator to mark all sweets in your home off-limit for you and suggests a healthy recipe for the evening [13].

Scenario #3. A Brain-Controlled Assistant

Your limbs are paralyzed after a recent car accident. You feel devastated, angry, and isolated. The good news is that you have a computerized assistant that can interpret the activity of your (fortunately not damaged) brain. You blink your eyes three times and a computer screen opens, displaying three windows: "Ask for assistance," "Play a game," and "Communicate." You decide to play a game. By thinking of the number 2, you click the appropriate window on the screen. A Tetris game starts, and you manipulate the falling tiles on the screen by thinking at left, right, rotation, and fall. The game starts at level 5, the one you achieved yesterday. Shortly after you started, the system realizes that today you are getting frustrated as you cannot keep up with the game. So it lowers the game level to 4. This feels less stressful. You play for a while and then stop the game by relaxing and lowering your attention. After a while, the system reminds you that today is the birthday of your grandmother. You select the communication menu window by thinking about the number 3 and compose an email to your grandmother. Yes, you can do it without using your hands. A P300 speller detects a peak in your brain activity, involuntarily produced 300 ms after you see the desired letter. You finish the email and ask the system to send it. You feel hungry and want to order your favorite pizza. You click with your brain on window #1, and the system notifies a caretaker about your wishes.

Let us analyze these three systems and try to answer the following questions. What do all these systems have in common? Which properties characterize them? Which basic components do we need to build such systems?

The most prominent feature is that these systems are aware of their *context*, meaning that they know their own state, the state of their user(s), and of their surroundings. Context is a very broad concept. The context can be simple like time, location, ambient temperature, noise level, or more complex like "the traffic light is red" or "the user is tired." In order to extract this context, a system uses *sensors* to capture environmental information, the same way we use our senses to feel how cold it is outside, how the food smells, or whether somebody loves us. The "raw" sensed data is then *processed*. By processing, we mean, for example, filtering the noise in an audio recording, detecting a peak of a certain frequency in brain activity, or recognizing a road traffic sign on a street image. This work of extracting context from sensor data is the task of a *software computation agent*, or *controller*. The software agent does more than just context inferring. It also reasons, takes decisions, and issues control actions, often making use of some form of artificial intelligence (AI). The actions related to these decisions are performed by devices called *actuators*. Think of motors, heaters, loudspeakers, buzzers, displays, and LEDs. Considering our examples, some possible control actions could be braking the car, playing quiet music, notifying the caretakers, and raising an alarm.

Moreover, pervasive computing systems are able to operate to some extend *autonomously*, with little, to no intervention from the human user. In the background, a *communication module* may be present, to collect data from the sensors, to send messages, or medical information about a patient, to obtain exact location from a GPS system, or to update software. In practice, in a pervasive computing system, tasks are distributed among many computers. Such a network of computers offers services to the user in a transparent way.

Summarizing, a generic pervasive computing system consists of sensors, actuators, a software controller, and optionally a communication module. This is illustrated in our first block diagram, shown in Fig. 1.5.

As discussed earlier, pervasive computing also comes with downsides. Threats to feasibility have to be taken into account, because it is unlikely that people like to be continuously monitored, governed, and overruled by machines. An ideal pervasive computing system should work seamlessly in the background, in a transparent way, such that the user does not even realize its presence. This discrete behavior was labeled by Weiser as *calm* or *disappearing computing*. For example, relaxing music could start when the system notices that we are tired, just by analyzing our face with a video camera; we do not have to explicitly announce that we are tired. Another example is a computer game controller that understands without words that the player is getting frustrated, only by analyzing his brain activity signals. This perfect man–machine symbiosis, where the system understands the situation without explicit actions at the user's end, is called *implicit human–computer interaction (i-HCI)*. Another typical feature of the interaction between pervasive computing systems and their users is that the communication happens via

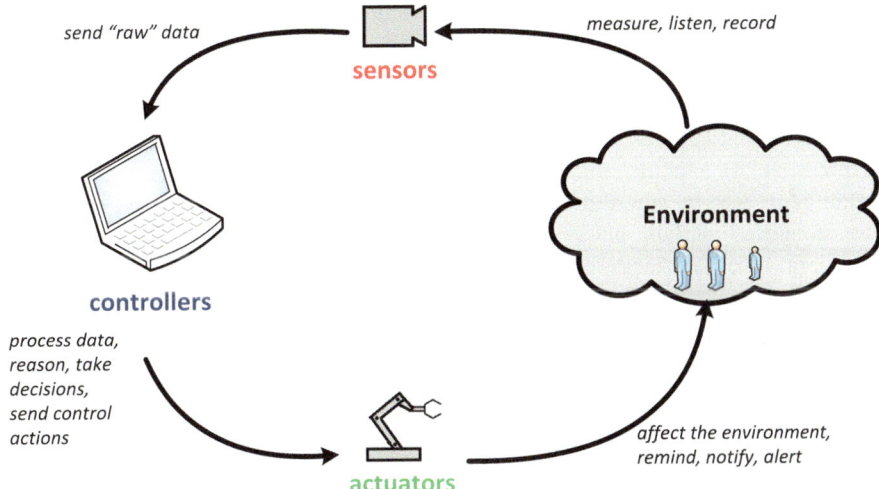

send "raw" data

sensors

measure, listen, record

Environment

controllers

process data,
reason, take
decisions,
send control
actions

affect the environment,
remind, notify, alert

actuators

Fig. 1.5 The main components of a generic pervasive computing system

many channels, beyond the keyboard, mouse, and display. This is known as a
multimodal human–computer interaction.

We conclude by stating a set of core properties that characterize any generic
pervasive computing system [14]. Note that concrete systems will to a certain extent
exhibit all of these properties.

(1) The system is context-aware.
(2) The system interacts with humans in an implicit and multimodal way.
(3) Behind the scenes, many computers are networked in a transparent way.
(4) The system exhibits some form of artificial intelligence (AI).
(5) The system can operate autonomously, without human intervention.

1.3   About This Book

The essence of pervasive computing is that we are surrounded by hundreds of
different types of intelligent computer systems. A comprehensive, yet gentle
introduction would run the risk of presenting an overwhelming collection of topics,
including embedded architectures, mobility management, sensor networks,
context-awareness, wearable computing, user interfaces, augmented reality, artificial intelligence, privacy, and security. This book mitigates this risk by addressing
only assistive pervasive systems that infer their context through pattern recognition.
Think about self-driving cars, multimodal wheelchairs, robotic social companions,
and smart homes. For example, the embedded computer system in a self-driving car
can *recognize* traffic signs, traffic lights, and pedestrians on the road and can notify,
take control, and act in critical situations. An advanced model of such a vehicle can

even prevent accidents by *recognizing* distraction *patterns* in driver's brain activity. A multimodal wheelchair could *recognize* brain activity EEG *patterns*, specific to the mobility wishes of its paralyzed user (drive, turn, slow down), or *recognize* spoken commands and act accordingly. A robotic social companion can *recognize* the mental and affective state of its lonely user from speech, movements, and facial expression. As a result, it adapts its behavior and succeeds in offering comfort and relief. An elderly smart home would monitor its users' well-being and *detect* abnormalities in their behavior *pattern*, such as high blood pressure, insomnia, wandering, forgetfulness, or fall incidents, and notify the caretakers.

Have you ever wondered about how all these systems work? If the answer is yes, then this book is for you. We will take you on a journey to explore these mysterious systems from a *data* perspective. And we will start from the very beginning—the data acquisition step. I know it sounds very much like engineering and maybe a bit strange for computer scientists who often take data for granted, but this is in my opinion the only way you can really understand, build, and control a pervasive computing system.

Let us investigate, as our final example, an autonomous car and in particular, its functionality to recognize traffic lights. This is realized by an embedded computer system, controlled by a software agent, as illustrated in Fig. 1.6. Our story starts with a windshield video camera that acquires an image of the road scene. This image is first interpreted by the software agent, and the status of the traffic light is classified. Subsequently, the software agent takes a decision, based on a process model. The process model in this example is very simple and consists of two rules, namely (1) "stop" the car when the spotlight is at the TOP and RED and (2) "drive" when the spotlight is at the BOTTOM and GREEN. Next, the decision is translated into a control action for the wheels' actuators that will break or accelerate the car accordingly.

This book aims to fully cover the model illustrated in Fig. 1.6. It follows the adventures of data, from the moment it gets captured all the way through the system, until it is sent back carrying a message for the same environment. Chapter 2 treats *Signals* and their life inside the system. This chapter builds a bridge between real-world signals, such as the 2D image of a street, and their mathematical representation in the computer, like, for example, a 2D array of integers. The basic principles of *Control Systems* that correlate sensing with actuation are treated in Chap. 3. Chapter 4 treats *Image Processing*, to show, for example, how to filter the noise in the street image, and how to identify the active traffic spotlight. For this traffic spotlight, one needs to determine its state, given by the position (TOP, MIDDLE, or BOTTOM) and the color (RED, YELLOW, or GREEN). This is the field of machine learning, and in particular of *Classification*, to which we dedicate Chap. 6. Other types of pervasive computing systems might use voice recognition, and this is why we added a separate Chap. 5 on *Sound Processing*, where typical concepts, such as spectral analysis and digital filtering will be discussed. It might come (again!) as a surprise for computer science students, the fact that building smart systems involves much more than programming alone. To demonstrate this, a substantial Chap. 7 on *Systems Engineering* is added, where we highlight the best practices in requirements elicitation and modeling, design, development, and testing

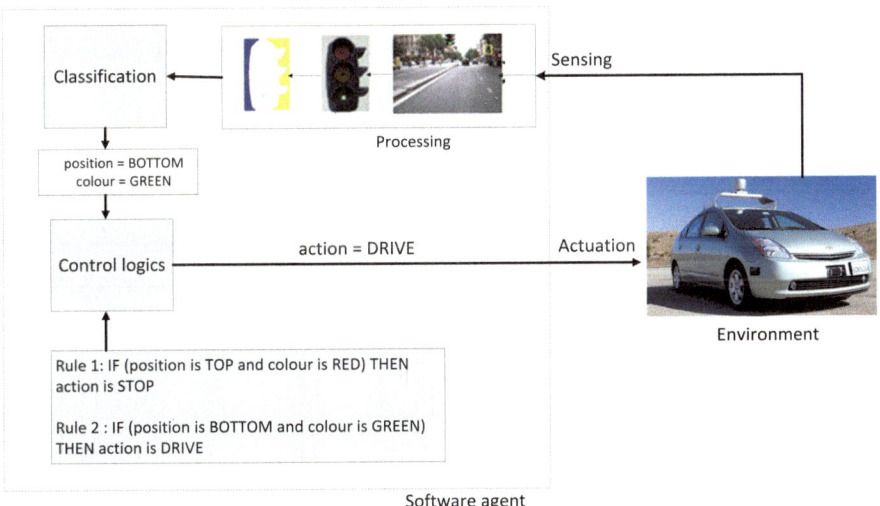

Fig. 1.6 The architecture of a traffic light recognition system in a smart car. The image of the Google car is reproduced from [22]. Used with permission

of software-based pervasive computing systems. Each chapter is accompanied by a list of recommended reading and a set of exercises.

The reward for reading this book is that you will get a fair good grasp of pervasive computing systems' underlying principles and even feel empowered to build one of your own. Of course, you will have to experiment first.

We recommend you craft your system using a LEGO® Mindstorms robotic kit [15]. Originally targeted for 8+ users, this framework is currently widely used in undergraduate computer science education. It is a robust, easy-to-program, and not too expensive, ARM microcontroller-based system, featuring a standard set of sensors (light, color, sound, distance, and touch), a few actuators (servomotors, a display, LEDs, and loudspeakers), and USB and Bluetooth communication. Blessed with mobility, scalability, and versatility, this toolkit is perfect to start modeling popular intelligent systems, such as cars, wheelchairs, wheeled robots, and other smart home appliances. Higher-quality external cameras and microphones can provide an even more accurate video and audio sensing. Depending on your project idea, you might want to build a 3D miniature world, to model streets and homes, traffic signs and traffic lights, tunnels and offices, walls and doors, people, etc.

As for software development, and linking the real world with math and programming, we warmly recommend Mathworks MATLAB® [16]. This is a relatively easy-to-learn scientific programming environment, with available and well-maintained libraries to control LEGO® Mindstorms NXT vehicles such as the RWTH toolbox [17, 18], and most importantly, powerful toolboxes for image and sound processing, pattern recognition and machine learning. All this makes it in our opinion an ideal, fast prototyping toolkit for software agents. For demonstration, two laboratory tutorials are included in the Appendix. The first one will guide

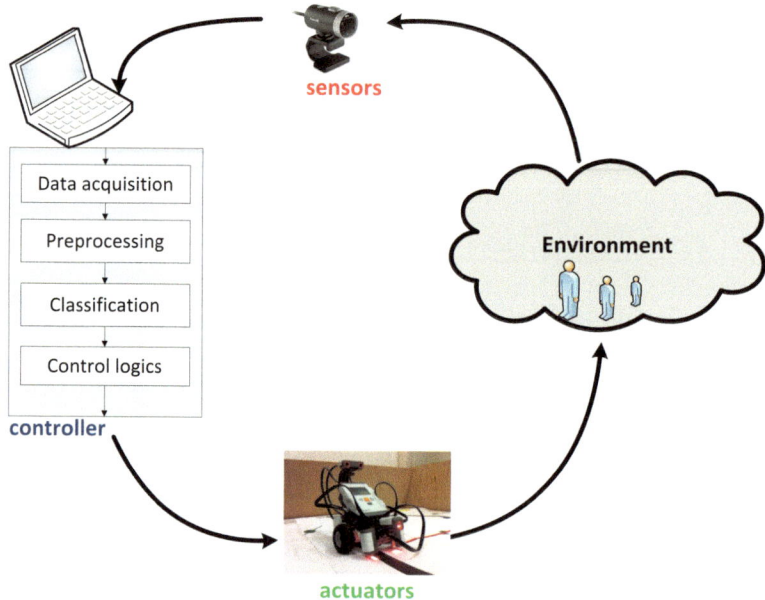

Fig. 1.7 A generic architecture of the pervasive computing system you are going to build

your first steps in audio and video signal acquisition and processing, and the second one will show you how to solve, in a very simple way, the traffic lights recognition problem. More tutorials, currently used in our course, are available on request.

As a result, you will be able to build a simplified, but realistic, pervasive computing system that uses pattern recognition of audio or video signals. The generic architecture of this system is illustrated in Fig. 1.7. Nevertheless, you should not by no means should you feel limited to this architecture. The skills you acquired, together with a healthy dose of curiosity, should give you wings to experiment with other sensors, such as accelerometers [19] or off-the-shelf commercial EEG headsets, such as Neurosky [20] or Emotiv EPOC [21], or with other classification techniques, not treated in the book. Only the sky is the limit!

Summarizing, this book offers a coherent mix of computer science and engineering topics, "glued" by a common goal: to engineer a smart pattern recognition system. In case you are worrying about this focus being too narrow, please don't! I deliberately left out typical pervasive computing topics such as embedded architectures, sensor networks, service discovery, human–computer interaction, privacy, and security. And believe me—I don't regret it. The experience of applying this teaching formula for a few times already, to roughly 200 CS freshmen per year, demonstrated that this theme *is* broad and challenging enough, leads to a wide range of interesting projects, and definitely has the potential to plant some seeds. Besides, this is an introduction for novices, remember?

Being aware that promises are not enough, I suggest to hit the road and move on to the next chapter.

1.4 Exercises

1. Estimate how many computers you have at home.
2. Explain Mark Weiser's vision of Ubiquitous Computing.
3. Enumerate and explain the core properties of a generic pervasive computing system.
4. What are the three waves of computing according to Mark Weiser?
5. What does MEMS mean? Give some examples.
6. Give an example of a pervasive computing system that uses pattern recognition. Identify its building blocks and explain their role. Quantify in what degree are the five core properties of pervasive computing manifested in this system.

References

1. Weiser, M.: The computer for the 21st century. Sci. Am. (Special Issue on Communications, Computers and Networks). September, 94–104 (1991)
2. Kahn, J.M., Katz, R.H., Pister, K.S.J.: Emerging challenges: mobile networking for "smart dust". J. Commun. Netw. **2**, 188–196 (2000)
3. Ahmed, M., Gonenli, I.E., Nadvi, G.S., Kilaru, R., Butler, D.P., Çelik-Butler, Z.: MEMS sensors on flexible substrates towards a smart skin. In: 11th IEEE SENSORS 2012 Conference. Taipei, 28–31 October (2012)
4. Ishii, H.: Tangible bits: beyond pixels. In: Proceedings of the 2nd International Conference on Tangible and Embedded Interaction, pp. xv–xxv. ACM, Bonn, Germany (2008)
5. Waldrop, M.M.: More than Moore. Nature **530**(11 February), 145–147 (2016)
6. Aten, Q.T., et al.: A self-reconfiguring metamorphic nanoinjector for injection into mouse zygotes. Rev. Sci. Instrum. **85**(055005), 1–10 (2014)
7. Feynman, R.P.: There's plenty of room at the bottom. Eng. Sci. **23**(5), 22–36 (1960)
8. Hodges, S.: Batteries not included: powering the ubiquitous computing dream. Computer **4** (April), 90–93 (2013)
9. van Dorp, W.F., Hagen, C.W.: A critical literature review of focused electron beam induced deposition. J. Appl. Phys. **104**(8), 081301 (2008)
10. Noordzij, N.: Reproducibility of Electron Beam Deposition in Electron Limited Regime. TU Delft, Delft, The Netherlands (2015)
11. Moon, C.R., Lutz, C.P., Manoharan, H.C.: Nat. Phys. **4**, 454–458 (2007)
12. Fuechsle, M., et al.: A single-atom transistor. Nat. Nanotechnol. **7**(April), 242–246 (2012)
13. Jazayeri, M.: On the way to pervasive computing. In: XVI Brazilian Symposium on Software Engineering (SBES'2002). Rio Grande do Sul, Brazil (2002)
14. Poslad, S.: Ubiquitous Computing: Smart Devices, Environments and Interactions. Wiley (2009)
15. LEGO Mindstorms NXT 2.0. Available from: https://education.lego.com/en-au/lego-education-product-database/mindstorms/9797-lego-mindstorms-education-base-set
16. MATLAB, the language of technical computing. Available from: http://www.mathworks.nl/products/matlab/
17. RWTH-Mindstorms NXT Toolbox for MATLAB. Available from: http://www.mindstorms.rwth-aachen.de/

18. Behrens, A., et al.: Key factors for freshmen education using MATLAB and LEGO Mindstorms. In: Jeschke, S., Liu, H., Schilberg, D. (eds.) Intelligent Robotics and Applications: 4th International Conference, ICIRA 2011, Aachen, Germany, December 6–8, 2011, Proceedings, Part I, pp. 553–562. Springer, Berlin, Heidelberg. (2011)
19. Hitechnic. Available from: https://www.hitechnic.com
20. Neurosky. Available from: https://www.neurosky.com
21. Emotiv EPOC. Available from: http://emotiv.com/epoc/
22. Guizzi, E.: How Google self driving car works. In: IEEE Spectrum (2011)

Chapter 2
Signals

Lasciate ogni speranza, voi ch'entrate.
Dante Alighieri, The Divine Comedy

We all send and receive signals. A letter or a phone call, a raised hand, a hunger cry—signals are our information carriers. Pervasive computing systems also send signals (to wheels, loudspeakers or displays), and sense signals (like speech, images, heart activity, or temperature). These signals are by nature *continuous*, meaning that their level is known always and everywhere, and they are *analog*, meaning that this level is an infinite-precision real number. The problem is that these properties are in conflict with the discrete and digital character of computers. The price the real-world signals have to pay to be admitted and processed by a computer is to undergo a process called *digitization*. Digitization happens in two stages. First, *sampling* periodically measures the signal's level and produces a finite-length sequence of *samples* of infinite precision. Next, *quantization* converts these samples into a sequence of finite-precision numbers. Digitization is the task of an electronic device, called *analog-to-digital converter* (ADC). The reverse process, needed by a computer system to decipher the carried message and send signals back to the real world, is called *reconstruction*. Reconstruction happens in another electronic device, called *digital-to-analog converter* (DAC). High-quality digitization and reconstruction are needed, in order to preserve the information the signal is carrying. This chapter is an introduction to signals and their representation in pervasive computing systems, with a focus on audio and video signals.

2.1 Signals in the Wild

2.1.1 One-Dimensional Continuous Time Signals

Signals are variations of a physical quantity that encode information. In some pervasive computing systems, these variations happen in *time*. A speech signal, for example, initially arises in the human vocal tract as a variation of air pressure. The

© Springer International Publishing AG 2017
N. Silvis-Cividjian, *Pervasive Computing*, Undergraduate Topics
in Computer Science, DOI 10.1007/978-3-319-51655-4_2

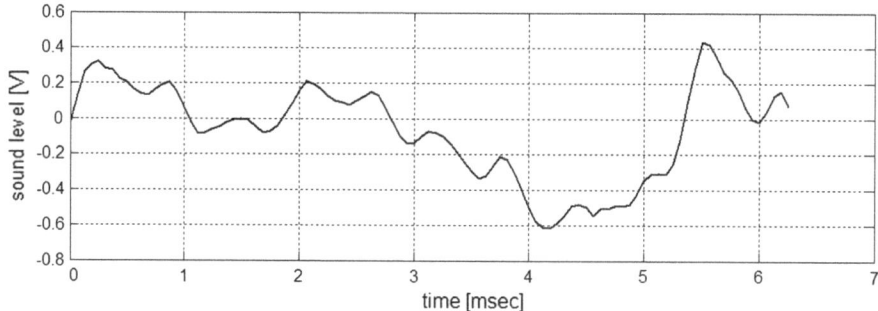

Fig. 2.1 Plot of a speech signal. The *vertical axis* represents the sound level, and the *horizontal axis* represents time

variation pattern propagates through air, until it eventually gets captured by a microphone, which transforms it in an electrical signal. Its level measured in volts (V), is proportional to the sound level, and can be plotted in a time waveform, as shown in Fig. 2.1.

The speech signal in Fig. 2.1 is an example of a *one-dimensional, continuous,* and *analog time* signal. Let us explain this long list of attributes. First, it is obviously a signal whose level varies in *time*. Second, it is *one dimensional,* because it can be represented mathematically as a function of a single independent variable, in this case the time. This mathematical function, denoted by s, assigns to each instant of time (denoted by t), a value, $s(t)$, equal to the signal level at that moment. Next, the signal is *continuous,* because this function is defined for *all* possible values of the variable t, $t \in \mathbb{R}$. Finally, because the signal level $s(t)$ can be any real number in a continuous range, $s(t) \in \mathbb{R}$, the signal is called *analog.*

Typical one-dimensional time signals encountered in pervasive computing are: speech, acceleration, pressure, temperature, and biomedical signals used for electroencephalograms (EEG), electrocardiograms (ECG), or electromyograms (EMG). The patterns of variation in these signals can take different shapes. For example, the signal shown in Fig. 2.1 is a short fragment of a "Hello" recording. It looks like one of many—its level varying quite chaotically in time. Luckily, other sounds exist in nature, displaying a more interesting and organized behavior. One such example is the tone emitted by the tuning fork, a device used to calibrate musical instruments (see Fig. 2.2a to the left). In the same figure to the right, you can see a time plot of this sound. This plot is telling a story. To start with, one can clearly identify the moment when the tone was initiated as effect of the fork struck. Further, one can follow the sound evolution during a few seconds, until it eventually fades out. Notice that during these few seconds, the sound level has been gradually decreasing. This phenomenon is called attenuation.

The story goes on, if we zoom in this plot. By looking at Fig. 2.2b, we can discover for example that the signal has a specific pattern that repeats over equal time intervals. A signal with such an organized behavior is called *periodic.* Its

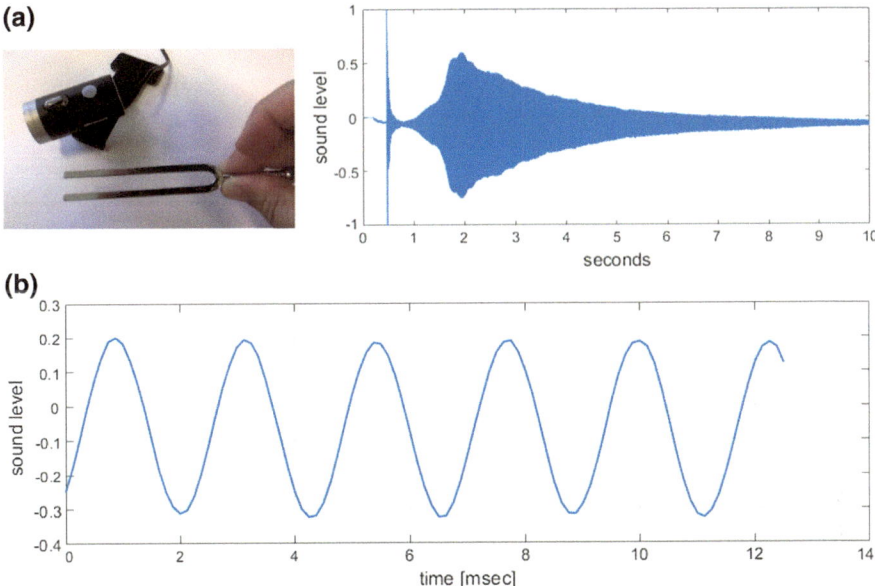

Fig. 2.2 **a** A 440 tuning fork experiment and a plot of the generated sound wave. **b** A zoom in the plot of the tuning fork signal

period, denoted by T, is defined as the length of this time interval. Mathematically, a periodic signal satisfies the condition $s(t + T) = s(t)$, for all $t \in \mathbb{R}$.

The *frequency* of a periodic signal, measured in Hertz [*Hz*], is defined as the number of identical patterns (cycles) contained in one second and can be calculated as:

$$f = 1/T \ [Hz] \tag{2.1}$$

where T is the period measured in seconds *[s]*. For example, a signal with the frequency $f = 10$ Hz will perform ten identical cycles each second.

Let us calculate the frequency of the tuning fork sound, using the formula (2.1). We measure on the plot that its period is approximately 2.3 ms, which corresponds to a frequency $f = 1/0.0023 = 435$ Hz. This is very close to 440 Hz, the frequency of the A note, as expected by any musician. Lucky us! We have just got a confirmation that the simple formula (2.1) does not lie; in contrary, it will save us in many situations, so try not to forget it.

The particular shape of the signal in Fig. 2.2b, which might look familiar from high-school math, is called *sinusoid*. *Sinusoidal signals* are one of the basic families of periodic signals, very useful in modeling common processes in nature. Therefore, they will deserve a special place in our story. Their name derives from *sinus*, or sine, a trigonometric function of a variable angle θ, plotted in Fig. 2.3. A few of its values for typical angles θ, expressed in radians, are:

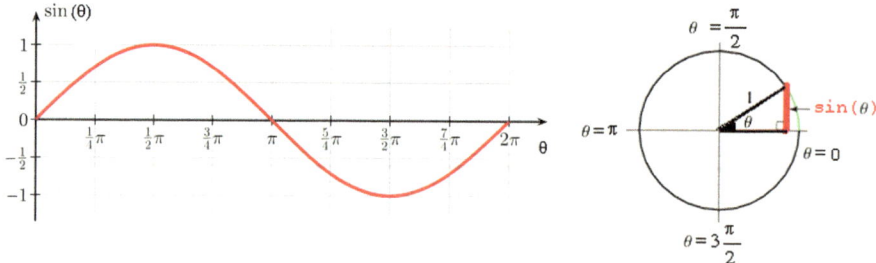

Fig. 2.3   Illustration of the sinus function

$$\sin(0) = 0$$
$$\sin(\pi/2) = 1$$
$$\sin(\pi) = 0 \quad\quad\quad (2.2)$$
$$\sin(3\pi/2) = -1$$
$$\sin(2\pi) = 0$$

This angle θ is in its turn, a function of time. A sinusoidal signal can be represented with the following mathematical formula:

$$s(t) = A \, \sin(\omega t + \varphi) = A \, \sin(2\pi f t + \varphi) \quad\quad\quad (2.3)$$

where A is called the *amplitude*, ω (pronounced omega) is the *radian frequency*, t is the *time*, f is the *signal frequency*, and φ (pronounced *phi*) is the *phase shift* that essentially depends on what moment in time we choose to call zero. All these parameters in this formula, except the time, are constant.

For example, Fig. 2.4 is a time plot of a sinusoidal signal, with an amplitude of 5 V and a period of $T = 2$. Its level oscillates between 5 and -5 V. The signal repeats the same pattern of oscillations every two seconds. Therefore, the frequency

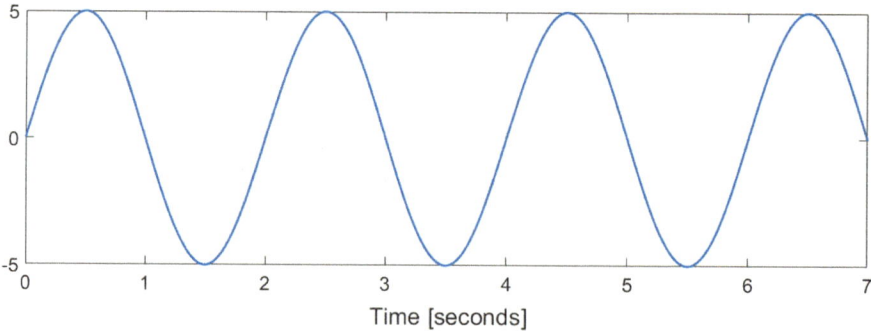

Fig. 2.4   A plot of a sinusoidal signal. Its parameters are: $T = 2$ s; $A = 5$; $\varphi = 0$; $S_0 = 0$

of this signal is $f = 1/T = 0.5$ Hz. The phase shift of this signal is zero ($\varphi = 0$), because the signal begins at time $t = 0$ with the value $s(0) = 0$.

Because at the initial moment $t = 0$, the signal level is not per definition zero. Therefore, the following formula describes a sinusoidal signal in a more general way.

$$s(t) = s_0 + A \sin(\omega t + \varphi) = s_0 + A \sin(2\pi f t + \varphi) \tag{2.4}$$

where s_0 is a constant component, called the *DC component* or *mean value* of the signal. The signal in Fig. 2.4 has a DC component equal to zero, meaning that the signal level oscillates between 5 and -5 V around the X axis, with a mean value equal to zero. If the DC component is for example 2 V, then the signal oscillates between 7 and -3 V.

2.1.2   Two-Dimensional Continuous Signals

We know by now how to mathematically represent continuous, time-varying signals. However, not all real-world signals are patterns evolving in time. Take for example a monochrome picture, also known as a black-and-white photo. Not the one that recently came out of a digital printer, but the one that dates back to the last century, developed in a darkroom, using traditional photography techniques, like the one in Fig. 2.5. This picture is a *spatial* pattern, represented mathematically by a *two-dimensional (2D) function*, denoted by $p(x, y)$. This function has two independent spatial variables, x and y, given by the position of each dot on the photo. The function assigns to each pair (x, y), the *brightness* at that position. Because this brightness value is known for each (x, y) in the continuous space on the photo, we say that the image signal p is *continuous*. The signal is also *analog*, because the brightness is represented by an infinite-precision real number, situated in the continuous range between 0.0 (black) and 1.0 (white). So now you can understand that

Fig. 2.5 An old black-and-white photo is a two-dimensional continuous, analog image signal

the photo in Fig. 2.5 is not exclusively black and white as its name would suggest, but can have any gray shade in between. Although this book will treat primarily 2D images, you should know that higher dimension image signals exist as well. Think of video camera signals, represented with a three-dimensional (3D) function of two spatial coordinates and time, or a tomographic movie of a beating heart, which is a 4D function of three spatial coordinates plus time.

2.2   Signals in the Cage

2.2.1   One-Dimensional Digital Signals

A time signal knocking at the computer's doors is blessed with two beautiful properties. First, the signal is continuous, meaning that its level is known at any time. Unfortunately, the computer is not particularly interested in this feature, because it does not have time nor space to record the signal at *every single moment*. In other words, "Big Brother" cannot watch you at all times. The only thing the computer can do is to poll the input signal from time to time. This process of measuring a continuous signal at isolated, equally spaced moments in time is known as *sampling*. The result is a sequence of *samples*, a *discrete-time* representation of the continuous input signal. Second, the input signal is *analog*, meaning that these samples are real numbers having an infinite precision. However, a computer, which is by nature digital, is unable to preserve this property, because it has only a limited number of bits available for data representation. In other words, "Big Brother" can by no means *precisely* know where you are. Instead, the samples are truncated to a finite-length digital representation. This process is called *quantization*. Sampling and quantization together are known under the name of *digitization*. This process describes the first thing that happens to the "wild" signal as soon as it gets captured by a pervasive computing system.

Digitization is a process that converts a continuous and analog time signal, s, into a *digital* signal, described by a discrete-variable, discrete-level function:

$$s[n] = s(n \cdot T_s) \tag{2.5}$$

where n is an integer between 0 and $N_s - 1$ representing the sample index, N_s is the total number of samples, and T_s is the *sampling period* defined as the distance in time between two successive sampling moments.

Formula (2.5) says in fact that the digital signal is a sequence (or vector) of finite-precision numbers, organized as follows. The first sample s[0] is the digital value of the analog signal at moment $t = 0$, $s(0)$; the second sample s[1] is the digital value of the signal at moment $t = T_s$, $s(T_s)$; the third sample is s[2], equal to $s(2T_s)$, and so on. Note that we use parentheses () to enclose the independent variable of a continuous–variable function, and square brackets [] to enclose the variable of a discrete-variable function.

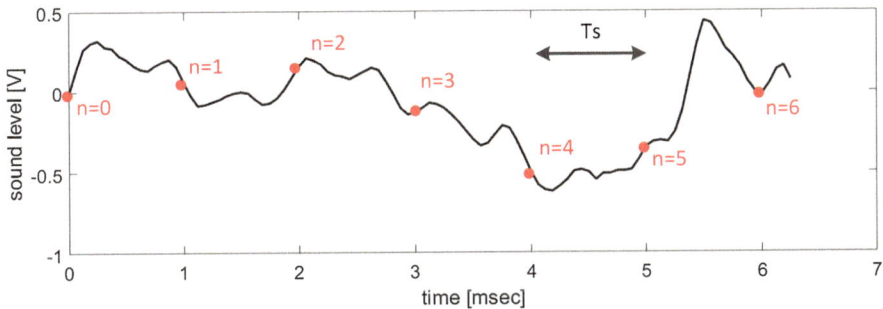

Fig. 2.6 Sampling the speech signal from Fig. 2.1. The *red bullets* represent the samples

Figure 2.6 illustrates the sampling process of the speech signal from Fig. 2.1. The samples, marked with red bullets, are taken every millisecond, meaning that the sampling period in this example is $T_s = 1$ ms $= 0.001$ s.

The *sampling frequency* or *rate*, defined as the number of samples taken every second, can be calculated as:

$$f_s = 1/T_s \ [Hz] \tag{2.6}$$

where T_s is the sampling period measured in seconds *[s]*. For example, the sampling frequency used to sample the signal in Fig. 2.6 is $f_s = 1/T_s = 1/0.001 = 1000$ Hz $= 1$ kHz.

Digitization of a one-dimensional analog signal is the task of an electronic device, called *analog-to-digital converter (ADC)*. Since it is not our intention here to dive into ADC details, we can describe it as just a black box, with two inputs and a few digital outputs, as shown in Fig. 2.7. One analog input is used for the voltage to be digitized, V_{in}, and another analog input expects a constant reference voltage, V_{ref}, that will define the input range. For example, an ADC with $V_{ref} = 8$ V can measure voltages in the range 0–8 V. An ADC has also N output pins, used to encode the result of digitization. The number of output bits N, also called *A/D resolution*, determines the number of alternatives that can be expected as output. For example, a 3-bit ADC can produce $2^3 = 8$ possible output values equal to 000, 001, 010, ... or 111.

An ADC works as follows. It *samples* the analog continuous input voltage, and obtains a value V_{in}. Next, it compares this instantaneous reading V_{in} to the reference voltage V_{ref} and quantifies their ratio. Finally, the ADC generates the digital output, D, according to the formula:

$$D = \left[2^N \frac{V_{in}}{V_{ref}} \right] \tag{2.7}$$

where [...] brackets mean truncation to N bits.

Figure 2.7 illustrates this mechanism for an ADC with a resolution of $N = 3$ bits and a reference voltage $V_{ref} = 8$ V. For example, if the input analog voltage is

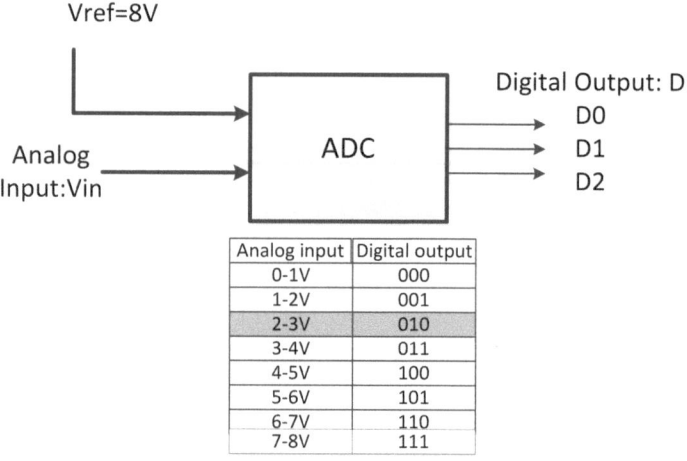

Fig. 2.7 A block diagram and the input/output (I/O) mapping for an ADC with a resolution of $N = 3$ bits, and a reference voltage $V_{ref} = 8$ V

$V_{in} = 2.7$ V, then the ADC output D is $[8 \times 2.7/8] = [2.7]$, which when represented using 3 bits, becomes 010.

The effect of quantization is visible in Fig. 2.7 from the fact that for example, *any* input voltage between 1 and 2 V, will produce the same output, D = 001. This is due to the relatively low number of bits used for quantization, equal to 3 in our case, that creates a staircase effect in the output digital signal. The higher the number of output bits, or A/D resolution, the better the digital signal will resemble its analog "brother" at the input, as illustrated in Fig. 2.8.

The reverse process, of reassembling an analog signal from its digital samples, is called *reconstruction*. This happens in another electronic device, called *digital-to-analog converter (DAC)*. This process is equally essential for pervasive computing systems, in order to extract the right information carried by the analog signal and to send commands to different actuators, such as motors, displays, or loudspeakers.

If you managed to follow the story until now, you could figure out that once entered in a computer, a real-world continuous and analog signal gets robbed of its beautiful properties as effect of digitization. The effect can be, in some cases, catastrophic. Take a look at the 19 MHz signal in Fig. 2.9, sampled with a frequency $f_s = 20$ MHz. If we measure the period of the sampled signal, marked with red bullets, we get $T = 1$ µs, meaning that the signal's frequency is equal to $f = 1/T = 1$ MHz. But wait a minute, this is not the real frequency of our signal! Something must have gone wrong. Did magic formula (2.1) suddenly fail on us? No. The reason is that we took too few samples. This effect of undersampling is called *aliasing*. The false frequencies resulted after reconstruction are called *alias frequencies*.

This example should be a warning that digitization is a powerful technique, but also a dangerous one. When performed wrongly, it can create a "broken telephone"

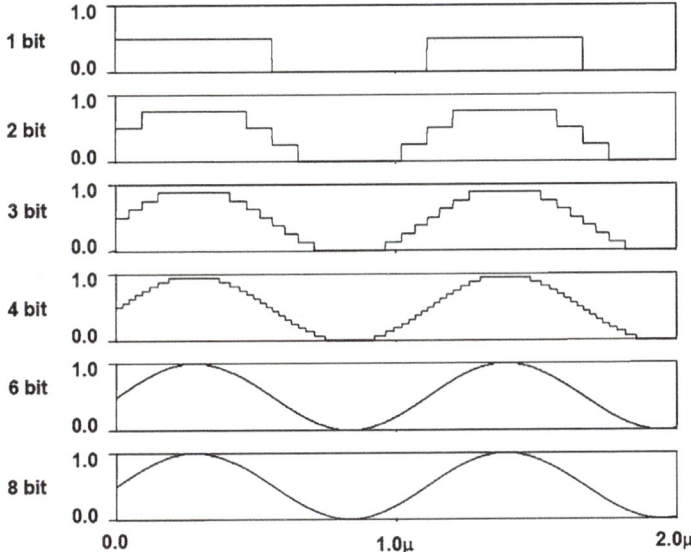

Fig. 2.8 Quantization of a 900 kHz sine wave with different resolution, varying from 1 bit to 8 bits. From [1]. Used with permission

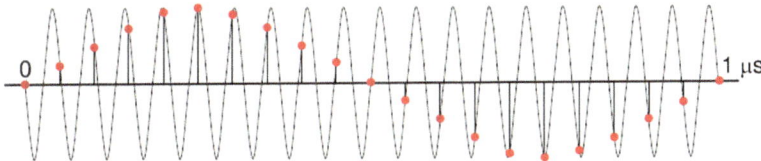

Fig. 2.9 A 19 MHz signal is sampled with a frequency $f_s = 20$ MHz. From [1]. Used with permission

effect, by corrupting the information carried by the signal. And this is the nightmare of any messenger, right? You might say: "OK, I understand the danger, but what can I do about it?" The solution is to perform a "good", careful digitization, that will distort the signal as little as possible. This can be realized by wisely controlling the digitization parameters, or more precisely, the sampling rate and the ADC resolution.

The proper ADC resolution is dictated by the smallest input variation that the system is required to "feel". In our example from Fig. 2.7, we saw that a 3-bit ADC with $V_{ref} = 8$ V was insensitive to input variation smaller than $V_{ref}/2^N$, in our case equal to 1 V. For some systems, this resolution limit might be acceptable. However, others, more sensitive systems, might require a higher resolution. Adding a few bits to the ADC resolution strongly improves the performance of quantization. For example, an 8 bits ADC can sense a minimal change in its input voltage of 8 V/2^8, equal to 0.03 V.

What of the ideal sampling frequency? This parameter depends on the frequency of the signal being measured. The goal is to obtain enough samples for an acceptable reconstruction of the signal, without too much information loss. But what means "acceptable"? For example, for a smart home, it might be acceptable to measure the room temperature once in a minute. A safety critical system, however, like an airbag control system, might need to measure the car's acceleration much more often, say one hundred times in a second. To ensure that there will be enough samples for reconstruction, it is required that the sampling period should not be greater that one half of the finest detail in the signal. This is known as the *Nyquist criterion* or the *Shannon sampling theorem* saying that:

A continuous analog signal s(t) with frequencies no higher than f_{max} can be reconstructed exactly from its samples s[n] = s(nT_s), if the samples are taken at a rate f_s, that is greater than $2f_{max}$.

This means in fact that the sampling frequency has to be *at least* twice the maximum frequency in the signal. This minimal sampling frequency given by $2f_{max}$ is called the *Nyquist rate*.

Let us consider, for illustration, the signal in Fig. 2.10 built by adding together three sinusoidal waves at frequencies of 1, 2, and 3 Hz. According to the Nyquist criterion, the signal must be sampled at twice its highest frequency. This highest frequency is in our case $f_{max} = 3$ Hz, meaning that a sampling frequency of 6 Hz (6 samples per second) should be just enough. However, for a good reconstruction, it is recommended to use a sampling frequency that is ten times higher than f_{max}.

Some best practice sampling rates commonly used are: 8 kHz, 8–12 bits for telephony, and 14–16 bits for mobile phones; 44.1 kHz, 16–24 bits for CD audio players; 8 kHz up to 20 kHz for analog speech signals, what makes sense, because 20 kHz is the generally accepted upper limit for human hearing and perception of musical sounds.

You might now ask a naughty question: "What happens if we do not obey the Nyquist criterion?" Sampling with a higher rate than the Nyquist rate, called *oversampling*, is not as bad. It will even improve the situation, creating a smoother

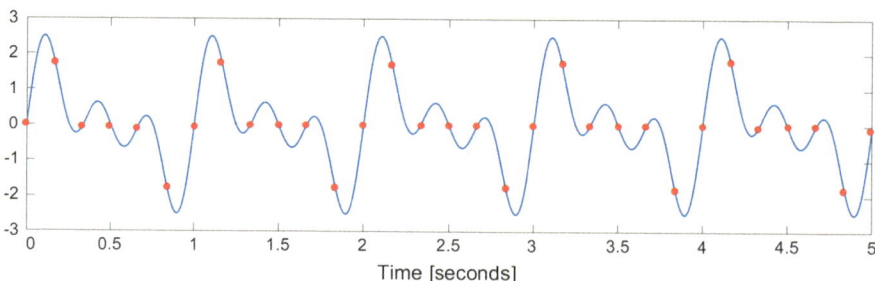

Fig. 2.10 Sampling with $f_s = 6$ Hz the sum of three sine waves of 1, 2, 3 Hz

reconstructed waveform. However, be careful with overdoing it, because a high sampling frequency means by definition more samples, that boosts up the storage and computational needs of the system. What might happen in case of *under-sampling* with a sampling frequency lower than the Nyquist rate, is known as aliasing, a phenomenon already demonstrated earlier in this section.

If we know the A/D resolution and sampling rate that are considered as acceptable for our system, we can choose an ADC device. The choice in doing this is large. ADCs are available for different market segments, with a range of resolutions varying from 8 to 24 bits, and maximum sampling rates between 100 Hz and 5 GHz. The choice is dictated by a trade-off between the application's required performance and available resources (memory, budget, etc.).

2.2.2 Two-Dimensional Digital Signals

We already know quite a lot about one-dimensional time signals, and how they are dealt with in pervasive computing systems. But how is the life of two-dimensional signals, such as 2D images? These signals are also continuous and analog, and therefore also need to be digitized. This again involves *sampling* and *quantization*. First, a spatial sampling takes place that converts the image into a 2D structure, where the brightness is known only at discrete positions in space. These discrete points in 2D space are called *pixels*, a mnemonic for "picture elements". If we denote by M an image size (number of pixels) in the horizontal direction, and by N the image size in the vertical direction, then we say that the *spatial resolution* of the image is $M \times N$. In practice, typical spatial resolution values are 640×380, 1072×640, etc. A high spatial resolution means that a large number of pixels are used, resulting in fine details in the image. Similar to the unidimensional case explained in the previous section, a low number of pixels results in a "blocky" effect in the image. The visual effect of different spatial resolutions can be seen in Fig. 2.11.

| 256 x 256 | 64 x 64 | 16 x 16 |

Fig. 2.11 Effect of spatial resolution. A 256×256 image has a higher resolution than a 16×16 one. From [2]. Used with permission

Fig. 2.12 Effects of spatial undersampling. Inspired from [3]

The same as with time signals, spatial oversampling is benefic and results in a higher quality image. However, huge amounts of data are created, that need to be processed and stored. Spatial undersampling, however, might create aliasing and false features, like the jagged edges in Fig. 2.12.

We are not done yet, because the pixel's brightness or color can be stored in a computer by using only a limited number of bits. Therefore, spatial sampling has to be followed by a quantization of the pixel color. The number of bits necessary to represent the color of a pixel is called *color resolution*. A higher color resolution results in a higher color quality.

The result of sampling followed by quantization, in one word known as digitization, is a digital image, carrying discrete-space and discrete-color information. A digital 2D image is mathematically represented by a two-dimensional discrete-space, discrete-color function that assigns to each pixel a color. A digital 2D image is stored in a computer as a two-dimensional array, denoted by p. Each element of this array, $p[x, y]$, stores the color of the pixel situated in position (x, y). This color is a finite-precision integer number.

Images can be stored in a computer in different formats, each having a specific color resolution (see Fig. 2.13). The simplest one is the *binary*, or *black-and-white* (*B&W*) format, where each pixel can be just black or white. The color resolution is in this case only one bit. Obviously, this is the most compact format that requires the least amount of memory space. A 100×100 binary image, for example, will need only $100 \times 100 = 10,000$ bits of memory storage.

In a *grayscale image,* each color is a shade of gray, varying usually from 0 (black) up to 255 (white). The color resolution is in this format 8 bits. A 100×100 grayscale image will need therefore more memory space, namely $100 \times 100 \times 8 = 80,000$ bits.

In a *true color,* or *red–green–blue* (RGB) image, each pixel has a color described by the amount of red (R), green (G), and blue (B) in it. Each of these three components is a value in the range of [0–255], giving us $2^8 \times 2^8 \times 2^8 = 2^{24} = 16,777,216$ possible color alternatives for each pixel. For example, a black

Fig. 2.13 Examples of digital image formats. An RGB color image, *upper left corner*; the same image in grayscale format *left under*; the same image in binary format, *upper right* corner

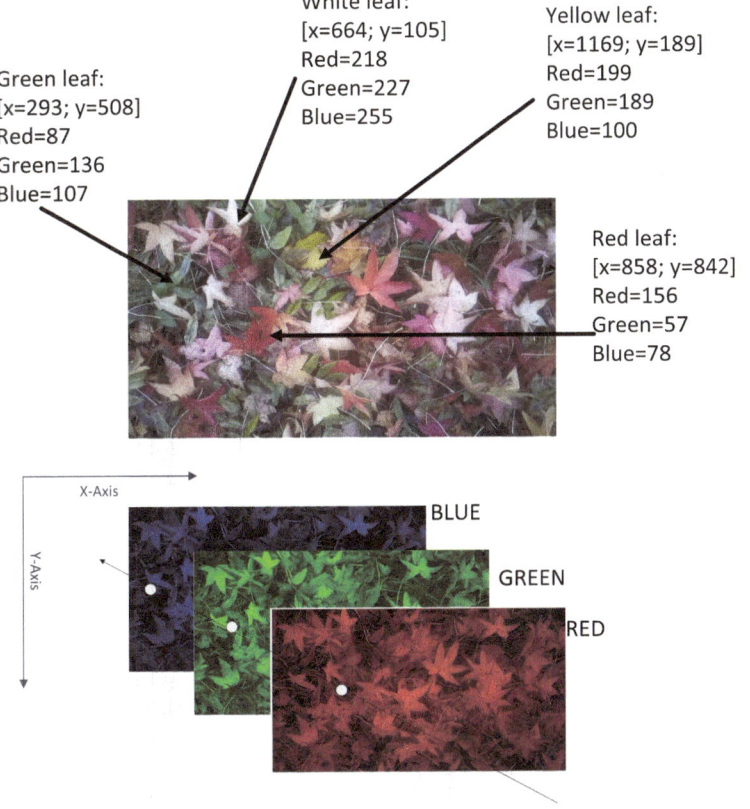

Green leaf:
[x=293; y=508]
Red=87
Green=136
Blue=107

White leaf:
[x=664; y=105]
Red=218
Green=227
Blue=255

Yellow leaf:
[x=1169; y=189]
Red=199
Green=189
Blue=100

Red leaf:
[x=858; y=842]
Red=156
Green=57
Blue=78

X-Axis

Y-Axis

BLUE

GREEN

RED

Fig. 2.14 Color decomposition of an RGB image

pixel is represented as (0, 0, 0), a pure red pixel is (255, 0, 0), and a white one is represented as (255, 255, 255). In Fig. 2.14, the pixel on the red leaf has a red value that is higher than the green and blue components. Likewise, the pixel on the green leaf has a higher green component. The color resolution is in this format equal to $3 \times 8 = 24$ bits. Images stored in this format are therefore also called 24-*bit color images*. Their storage requires also much more memory space. The 100×100 RGB image needs $100 \times 100 \times 24 = 240,000$ bits!

An $M \times N$ RGB color image is internally represented with three $M \times N$ arrays, one for each of the colors red, green, and blue. You can imagine an RGB image as a three-colored sandwich, made of three equally sized $M \times N$ slices of bread, containing Red, Blue, and Green information, respectively. The color of each pixel p[x, y] in the image is represented by a vector with three elements, p[x, y] = [Red (x, y), Green(x, y), Blue(x, y)]. To determine the values of these three elements, one can insert an imaginary toothpick through the three slices, at that selected position (x, y) and read the pure colors in the three punctures. These will give the three RGB values that together characterize the pixel's color, like illustrated in Fig. 2.14.

2.3   Conclusions

This chapter described the life of real signals, in their role of information messengers traveling between environment and pervasive computing systems. The systems use sensors to capture a signal from the environment and transform it into an electrical signal having the same pattern of variation. This electrical signal is continuous and analog, properties that are in conflict with the discrete, limited precision character of a digital computer. The solution for this conflict is a process called digitization. Digitization happens in two stages: sampling and quantization. If an analog continuous signal can be represented with a function of continuous domain and range, then sampling means discretization of the function's domain, and quantization means discretization of its range. Digitization is the task of an ADC. The result is a sequence of digital numbers, called samples. These samples are processed by the software controller and contribute to the making of appropriate decisions. These decisions must be translated in commands to actuators. Actuators, by nature, are devices that expect an analog electrical input signal. Therefore, before leaving the system, a signal reconstruction from its samples is needed, performed by a DAC. Digitization and reconstruction are processes of paramount importance for the quality of a pervasive computing system. Therefore, both must be performed with care, with minimal loss of information. The block diagram in Fig. 2.15 illustrates the findings of this chapter.

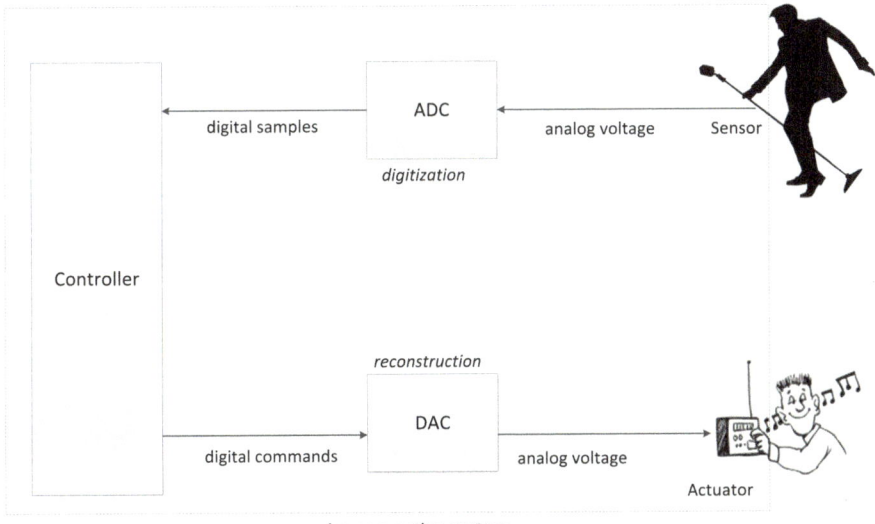

Fig. 2.15 A block diagram illustrating the life of signals in a pervasive computing system

2.4 Exercises

1. Draw a careful sketch for each of the following signals.

   (a) a sinusoidal signal with a DC component of 5 V, frequency $f = 0$ Hz, and amplitude $A = 5$ V (volts).
   (b) a sinusoidal signal with no DC component, the amplitude $A = 2$ V, frequency $f = 2$ Hz, and phase shift $\varphi = 0$.
   (c) a sinusoidal signal with no DC component, the amplitude $A = 2$ V, frequency $f = 0.2$ Hz, and phase shift $\varphi = 0$.
   (d) the sum of the signal from (a) and the signal from (b).

2. Figure 2.16 shows a plot of a sinusoidal waveform.

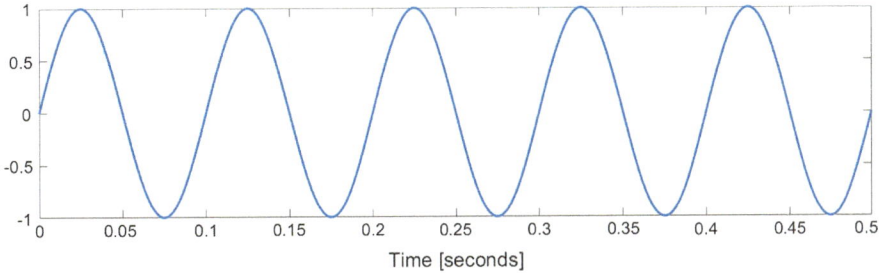

Fig. 2.16 A sinusoidal waveform

From this plot, determine its amplitude, frequency, and phase shift. Give the answers as numerical values and units. Justify your answers.

3. What sampling frequency would you recommend for the signal from Exercise 2? Justify your answer. How many samples will we get?
4. Imagine that the signal from Exercise 2 is sampled with a frequency of 100 Hz, for two periods. How many samples do we get and what is the time step between two consecutive measurements? Can you mark the samples on the plot?
5. What is an ADC, and why do we need it in pervasive computing? Answer the same question for a DAC.
6. Calculate the maximal quantization error for the ADC in Fig. 2.7. Make a new I/O mapping for a better ADC, with 8 bits and $V_{ref} = 8$ V. Show how a higher resolution improves quantization.
7. The note A above the middle C has a frequency of 440 Hz. What does the Shannon sampling theorem say about the frequency that we have to use to sample this sound properly? What will happen if we do not obey this criterion?
8. Define the concepts of spatial resolution and color resolution for a digital image. Give one example for each concept.
9. Explain how colors are represented in an RGB digital image.

References

1. Pelgrom, M.: Analog-to-Digital Conversion. (2010)
2. Moeslund, T.B.: Introduction to Video and Image Processing: building real systems and applications. Undergraduate Topics in Computer Science. (2012)
3. McAndrew, A.: Elementary Image Processing with Matlab. (2004)

Chapter 3
Control Systems

Watson,... if I can get a mechanism which will make a current of electricity vary in its intensity, as the air varies in density when a sound is passing through it, I can telegraph any sound, even the sound of speech.

Alexander Graham Bell

Pervasive computing systems are built around a controller that coordinates actuation with sensing. But which principles govern this coordination process? Is each system unique, applying its own principles? Or do all the systems have something in common, so that we can learn from successful examples how to build our own system? In this chapter, we will try to demonstrate that the latter is indeed the case. The range of sensors that can be used to discover context in pervasive computing is impressive. Luckily, most of these sensors are based on the same principle, saying that a physical quantity variation results in an electrical voltage at the terminals of the sensor. This allows us to restrict the scope here only to sensors that measure temperature, light, touch, and distance. The story starts with the analog voltage produced by a sensor and carrying information about the environment. This signal is digitized and processed by a software controller that usually makes use of machine learning to extract context. In this chapter, two types of control principles will be discussed: deliberative, which is slow, but strong in strategical searching and planning and reactive, that offers a fast reaction instead of deep thinking. Finally, the controller makes decisions that affect back the environment. In order to execute these decisions, the controller sends out commands that eventually reach the actuators. Examples of actuators are electrical heaters, motors, light sources, and simple screens and displays. The goal of this chapter is to demonstrate the principles behind the most commonly used types of control systems.

© Springer International Publishing AG 2017
N. Silvis-Cividjian, *Pervasive Computing*, Undergraduate Topics
in Computer Science, DOI 10.1007/978-3-319-51655-4_3

3.1   A Case Study: Computer-Based Navigation Systems

Modern navigation systems, be it in cars, personal assistants for cognitively impaired, or unmanned vehicles and aircrafts—are an example of pervasive computing systems, where computing facilities are embedded in an everyday object, for an everyday task. Basically, the functionality offered by an automotive navigation system is that given a start point A, and a final destination B, it guides the user to get from A to B. Although here we will discuss the most basic, static type of car navigation system, it is good to know that smarter systems exist, which are aware of problems on the road, such as traffic congestion due to events or roadwork, or highly polluted areas, and can suggest an alternative route to the user.

How does a navigation system work? First, the system has to determine its own geographical position. Subsequently, this position is matched to the known road network, which is stored in a digital map. Once the position of the car on the map has been determined, the system plans the best route from the current position to the destination, using the available road network. After a route has been found, the system provides the driver with spoken and/or visual instructions, to guide him to the chosen destination. The car's position is used in combination with the current route, to determine the necessary advice and the timing for giving this advice.

If we refine this functionality, we can identify some basic functionalities needed for navigation, such as self-localization (positioning), route planning, map building, map interpretation, and user guidance. Each functionality is provided by a certain building block, as shown in Fig. 3.1.

The positioning module computes the car's current location. This can happen for example, by using GPS receivers. Another, maybe less known method of positioning is called *dead-reckoning*. This method calculates the current position of a moving object based on its start position, speed, orientation, and time. For example, suppose that the car left from point A and travels *linea recta,* with an orientation angle θ, as shown in Fig. 3.2.

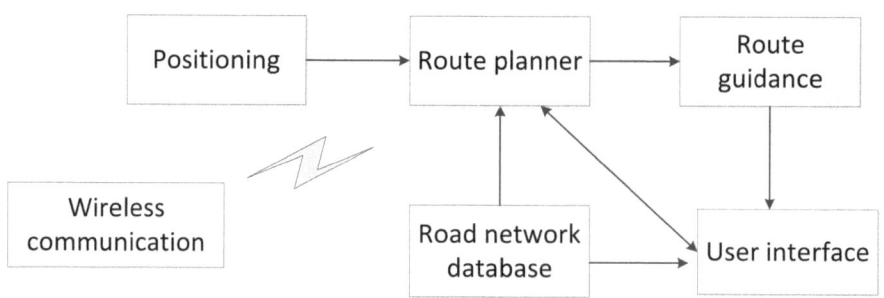

Fig. 3.1 The block diagram of a navigation system

Fig. 3.2 The principle of dead-reckoning

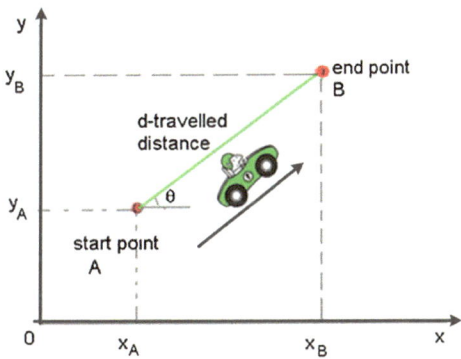

The current speed $v(t)$ is calculated by integrating acceleration over time.

$$v(t) = v_0 + \int a(t)\mathrm{d}t \qquad (3.1)$$

where v_0 is the initial speed at the start of the journey in point A.

The distance traveled from the departure is calculated by integrating speed over time.

$$d = \int v(t)\mathrm{d}t \qquad (3.2)$$

The coordinates of the current position B can be then calculated with:

$$\begin{cases} x_B = x_A + d \cdot \cos\theta \\ y_B = y_A + d \cdot \sin\theta \end{cases} \qquad (3.3)$$

This short math exercise demonstrates that the current position on a linear segment can be determined using two sensors: an accelerometer, to measure the acceleration $a(t)$, and a gyroscope, to measure the orientation angle, θ. In modern cars, an even higher accuracy in localization is possible, by using *sensor fusion* algorithms. These combine data coming from multiple positioning sensors based on different principles, such as GPS and dead-reckoning.

Let us analyze the route-planning module in more detail. This module plans a route from a starting point to a destination, based on a digital map of the available road network. The module answers the question: "*How do we get there?*".

In automotive navigation systems, the road infrastructure is usually represented using a directed valued graph. Figure 3.3 shows an example of a generic directed valued graph, where each edge from node i to node j has an associated real number, named *cost*. For example, ion Fig. 3.3 the edge from node 2 to node 1 has associated a cost equal to 3.

In a digital road map, the roads are divided into segments, and each road segment is represented by two edges in the graph. The cost associated with each edge is

Fig. 3.3 An example of a
directed, valued graph

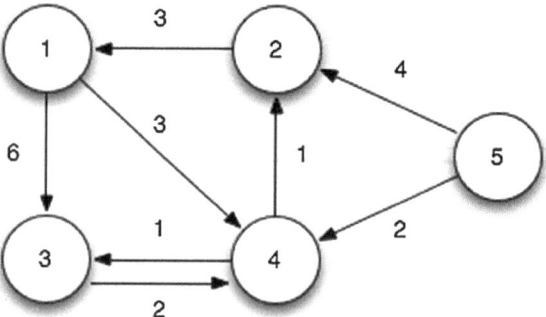

not per definition the distance between the nodes, as you might think, but can be the
expected travel time, the amount of money, fuel consumption, or number of traffic
lights encountered on the way.

Figure 3.4 shows a small example of a road network. If the cost is the distance
between two nodes, then the cost between Zurich and Andermatt is 110 km, the
same as for the edge between Andermatt and Zurich. However, if the cost is the
predicted fuel consumption, then we would expect the fuel consumption from
Zurich (400 m above sea level) up to Andermatt (1437 m above sea level), to be
higher than for the journey down the hill.

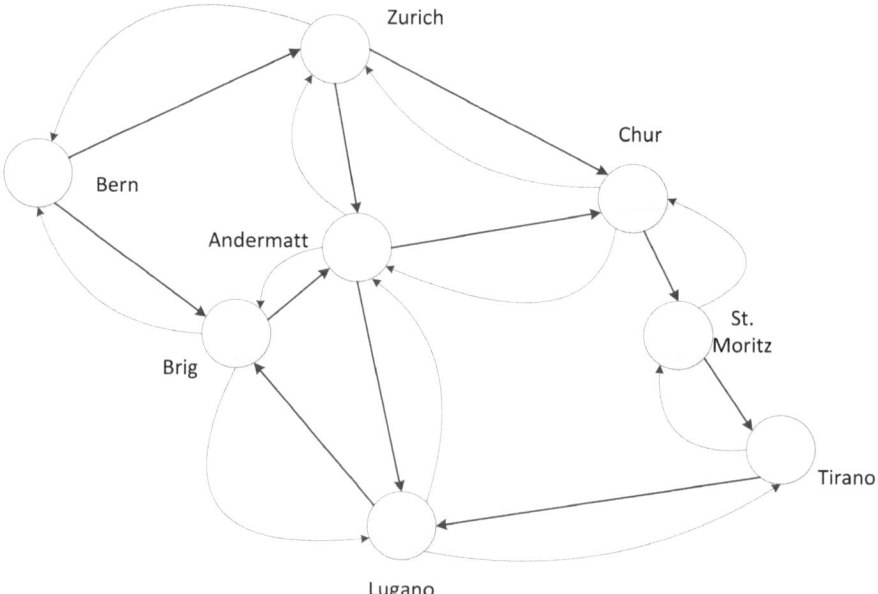

Fig. 3.4 A segment of the Swiss road map represented as a directed graph

Fig. 3.5 A shortest path example

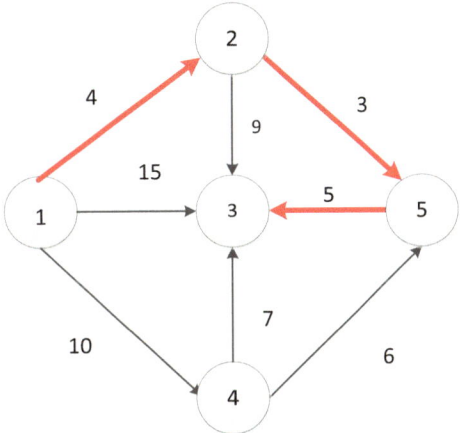

From the graph-theoretical point of view, the route planning in a navigation system is defined as a path-finding problem in a graph. Planning the optimal route from A to B is equivalent to finding *a shortest path* between the two nodes. *Shortest* means in this case a path with the lowest possible cost. In Fig. 3.5, the shortest path from node 1 to node 3 is not as you might think the path {1, 3}, but the path {1, 2, 5, 3}, with the total cost of 4 + 3 + 5 = 12 units.

The most well-known algorithm for computing shortest paths is the Dijkstra's algorithm. This algorithm works by visiting all nodes in the graph, beginning at the starting point. The search expands outward until it reaches the goal. Modern car navigation systems work based on faster variants of Dijkstra's algorithm. One example is the A* algorithm that uses heuristics, such as the current distance to the destination, and search only in the optimal direction.

Route-planning modules in navigation systems use a *deliberative* type of control. Deliberative control dates back to the early artificial intelligence (AI) years. It has been used to reason about actions in the first "thinking" mobile robot, called Shakey (1960s) and in chess software. Its principle is *"Think hard, Act later!"* [1]. The diagram in Fig. 3.6 shows the main phases in a deliberative control loop. The system takes all of the available sensory information (sense), together with all of the internally stored knowledge it has (maps), and it processes them, in order to create a

Fig. 3.6 The principle of deliberative control

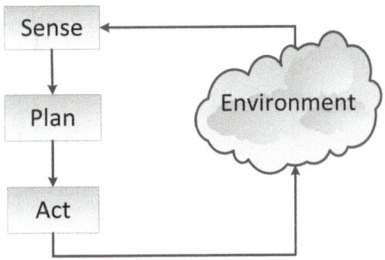

plan of action (plan). *Planning* is the process of looking ahead at the outcomes of the possible actions and searching for the sequence of actions that will reach the desired goal, for example, for the shortest path or chess mate. Planning might take a while, but after that, the decision is ready, and the actuators can execute it (act!).

3.2 A Case Study: Smart Homes

A smart home is a real home, yet augmented with all kinds of pervasive computing gadgets. Although there is so much to do to enhance the quality of life in such an environment, we select two challenges typical for this environment, and for each of them, we search for suitable sensing, control, and actuation solutions.

3.2.1 Let us Build Some Smart Curtains

Imagine that we are very lazy and want to build a smart system that makes life easier. We want the system to control our *curtains* without us needing to keep getting up and opening and closing them manually. As long as it is up and running, this smart curtains' system should work according to the following simple, daily scenario. The curtains are closed at night. At dawn, when it starts getting lighter outside, the curtains will open. At dusk, when it gets darker outside, the curtains will close, waiting in this state for a new day to come. Let us first sketch a system block diagram that will illustrate the way we imagined our system (see Fig. 3.7). We need a *sensor*, to sense the light intensity outdoors, *a software controller*, running on a computer, to read this sensor and decide when to activate the curtains, and finally, *a motor* to execute whatever decision might be taken, by pulling (open/close) the curtains. Next, we will show how to refine the design, by searching for the appropriate solutions for sensing, control, and actuation.

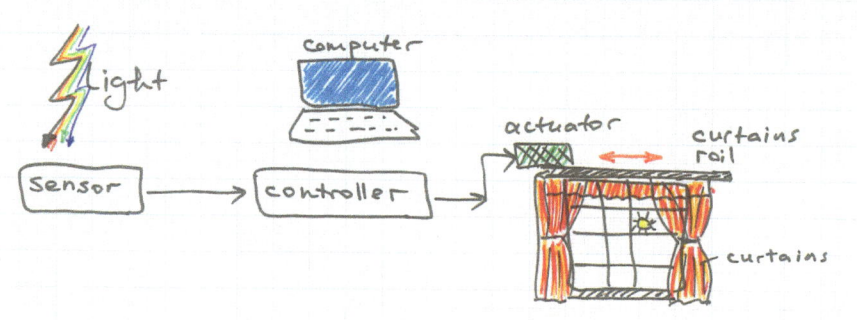

Fig. 3.7 A first sketch of our smart curtains' system

3.2.1.1 How to Sense?

The relevant environmental physical quantity is, in our case, the outdoor light intensity. This has to be measured by a sensor. Maybe it is a good moment to take a step back and first understand how sensors work in general. Think about the way we smell. Figure 3.8 shows a diagram of our nasal olfactory system. Our nose is a sensor that can detect small quantities of chemicals. The chemicals pass through the olfactory membrane to the olfactory bulbs, which contain biological receptors that sense the substance. The response is an electrical signal, which is transmitted to the brain via olfactory nerves. The brain transduces this response into a sensation we know as smell.

A *transducer* is a device that converts one physical quantity into another. For example, a thermometer converts temperature into a dilation of a mercury, or alcohol column. A *sensor is* a particular type of transducer that transforms the measured quantity into an electrical signal. All sensors work based on the same principle: Action from the measured quantity (called *measurand*) induces an effect somewhere (called *sensitive element*) in the sensor. This effect can be, for example, a change in the sensor's length, or its resistivity, a charge production, an induced voltage at the sensor's ends, etc. But what do we mean by *effect*? Let us take the very typical Dutch example of an open bridge on a hot summer day that cannot be closed anymore. Do you know why? Because the bridge is made of metal, and metal is a material with an interesting property, of expanding when heated. We say in this case that temperature has an *effect* on the bridge's length.

Let us suppose that we measure the temperature θ, with a so-called *resistive sensor*, which is basically a piece of metallic wire (see Fig. 3.9). What happens when the ambient temperature rises? This temperature gradient, denoted by $\Delta\theta$,

Fig. 3.8 The nose as a
sensor. From [2]. Used with
permission

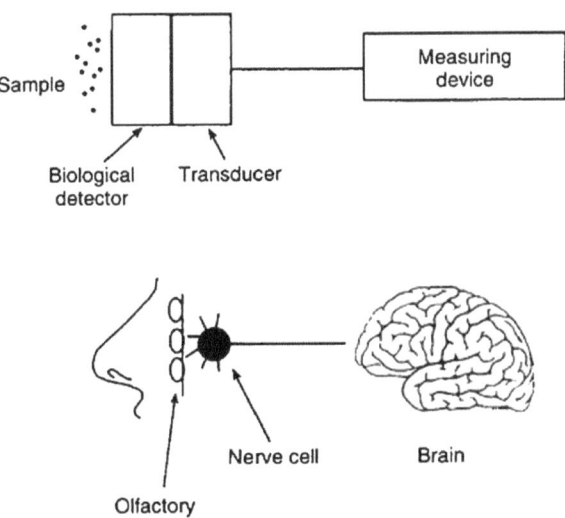

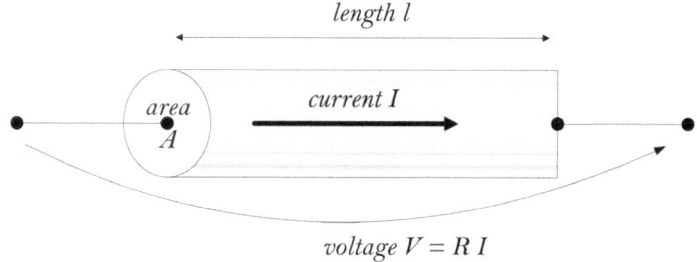

length l

area A

current I

voltage V = R I

Fig. 3.9 The resistive temperature sensor and the voltage produced at its terminals

results in a dilation of the metallic sensing element, meaning that its length will grow. By definition, the resistance of a conductor is given by:

$$R = \rho \frac{l}{A} \qquad (3.4)$$

where l is the conductor's length, A is its cross-sectional area, and ρ is its material resistivity.

If we assume that all these parameters, except for the length, remain constant, then Eq. (3.4) says in fact that a variation in the conductor's length, denoted by Δl, will result in a gradient in its *resistance*, ΔR. This is also the reason why this sensor is called *resistive*. If an electric current I flows through this conductor, then the electrical voltage V on its ends will vary too, according to Ohm's law, with $\Delta V = \Delta R \times I$. As the current I is constant, this change in voltage will be proportional to the change in resistance ΔR.

Summarizing, we have just demonstrated how a gradient in the environmental temperature, $\Delta \theta$, is converted by a resistive sensing element into a change in the electrical voltage at its ends, ΔV, following this chain:

$$\text{Environment } \Delta \theta \rightarrow \Delta l \rightarrow \Delta R \rightarrow \Delta V$$

For example, a temperature increase of 10 °C can generate a voltage gradient of 10 mV, at the ends of a temperature sensor. This voltage is an unidimensional signal, carrying information about the environmental temperature, ready to be captured and processed by a pervasive computing system. Hopefully, the rest of the story sounds familiar from Chap. 2.

Let us get back now to our smart curtains. You remember that we were searching for a sensor, able to measure the outdoors' light intensity, simply called illumination. The choice available is broad. One could use a *photocell*, also known as a photoresistor, as shown in Fig. 3.10. This is a semiconductor device that changes its resistance under the influence of light, based on the photoresistive effect. When placed and powered in an electrical circuit, the sensor will generate an analog voltage between its two terminals that will say something about the light intensity it is exposed to. Hopefully, here you recognize again the principle saying that the

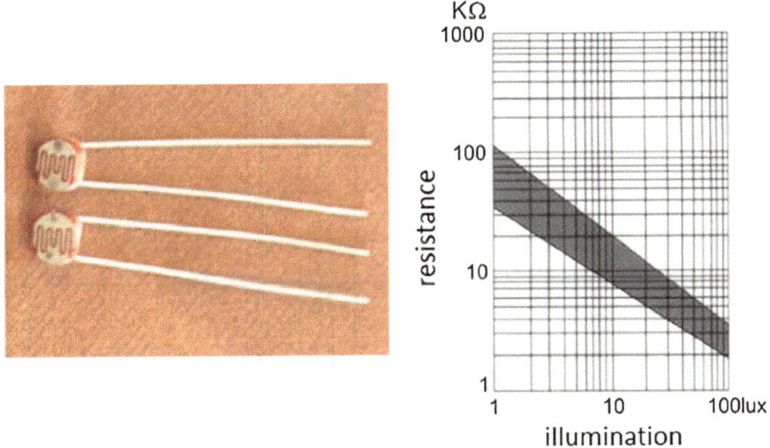

Fig. 3.10 A photocell and its sensitivity curve, showing the relationship between resistance and illumination. From [3]. Used with permission

measurand produces a voltage at the ends of the sensor. The relationship between this produced voltage and the measured quantity (illumination in our case) can be inferred from the a *sensitivity curve*. This is a graph provided by the sensor's producer in a data sheet. Figure 3.10 shows an example of a sensitivity plot curve for a photocell. This relation is very important for the software controller to correctly interpret the sensor reading. The electrical voltage produced by the sensor is actually a signal carrying illumination information. The level of this analog signal at a certain moment will be measured by the controller and converted by an analog-to-digital converter (ADC) into a digital number. This number, together with the sensitivity characteristic of the sensor, is what the controller software needs to calculate the digital value of the measured illumination.

LEGO® Mindstorms NXT robotic kits come with some light sensors, called *optosensors*. These optosensors can function in *passive mode*, measuring the ambient light, as well as in *active mode*, by producing a red light beam and measuring the intensity of the light reflected back from the illuminated surface. In this mode, the sensors can distinguish between surfaces of different colors. For example, the amount of light reflected from a white surface will be higher than the one reflected from a black surface.

3.2.1.2 How to Control?

We know by now how to obtain a digital number that quantifies the outdoor illumination. It is time now to focus on the smart curtains' control algorithm. The controller, or software agent, needs to decide how to activate the curtains, based on the measured light intensity. In other words, the controller coordinates sensing

Fig. 3.11 The principle of a reactive control system. Adapted from [4] with the permission from the author

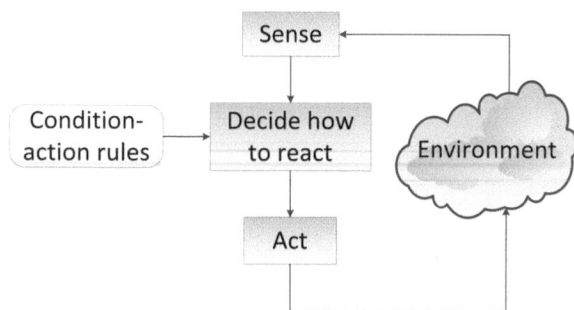

(light intensity) with actions (curtains motor). A deliberative type of control, like the one used for navigation systems, is not what we need here, since there is not much to think of. Instead, we want a quick reaction, based on the measured light intensity. In this case, a *reactive control*, with no planning phase, is a better choice. Based on the principle "*Don't think, react!*", this type of control algorithm does not need a map to represent the world, but directly relates the actions to certain sensor readings. Instead of a map, a reactive controller uses a set of condition-action *rules* that couple actions to specific sensed situations (see Fig. 3.11).

Human behavior is governed by many such connections; some are learned, like stopping in front of a red traffic light, and others are unconditioned reflexes, like closing your ears when there is too much noise.

One suitable rule for our curtains could be:

IF light_intensity > threshold **THEN** open the curtain

An experienced programmer will immediately complain about this rule being too abstract to be implemented. And with a good reason, because in order to do the job, a software controller must know *exactly* what is the value of the threshold between "daylight" and "dark." The values for "dark" and "daylight" are specific to each particular setting and can be discovered only through a series of measurements at location. The result is a table like the one in Fig. 3.12. Known as a *calibration table*, it shows the values of illumination at different moments of the day. This is exactly what was still missing. The tuning operation is called *calibration*. Based on this table, the curtains' control algorithm can be calibrated, for example, by assuming that a reasonable "dark" corresponds to an illumination level lower than 1 lux, and a reasonable "daylight" means an illumination level above 10 lux. This calibration can take some time, but it is a very important operation in control systems.

Now that we set both threshold values for "dark" and "daylight," we are prepared to write our first reactive controller in pseudocode. The code starts with an initialization phase. Next, an infinite loop follows that will continuously read the value of illumination and, based on two rules, will decide what to do with the curtains. We can also insert a waiting time in the sequence to simulate a sampling process with a period of say 10 min.

Condition	Illumination
	(lux)
Sunlight	107527
Full Daylight	10752
Overcast Day	1075
Very Dark Day	107
Twilight	10.8
Deep Twilight	1.08
Full Moon	0.108
Quarter Moon	0.0108
Starlight	0.0011
Overcast Night	0.0001

Fig. 3.12 A calibration table for the smart curtains system. From [5]

```
set initial curtains state to CLOSE
loop:

    measure light intensity level
    if (level > 10) then OPEN
    if (level < 1) then CLOSE
    wait (10 min)

endloop
```

Another way to classify control systems is by analyzing the type of connection between their output and input and; in other words, between the effect of actuation and the user's goals. If there is no connection whatsoever between the actuation effect and the user's goal, we are dealing with an *open-loop control system*. In an open-loop control system, whose principle is illustrated in Fig. 3.13, the controller only looks at its input signal in order to decide what to do with the actuator. Once an input demand has been made, the system is left to respond, in the hope that it will respond correctly.

Our smart curtains' system is in fact an open-loop control system, because the controller will activate the motor, which in its turn will open/close the curtains, without someone checking whether this really happened. The system relies only on a calibrated controller to achieve the desired goal. A programming mistake in the controller, or a defect in the motor, will be considered to be just bad luck. Another

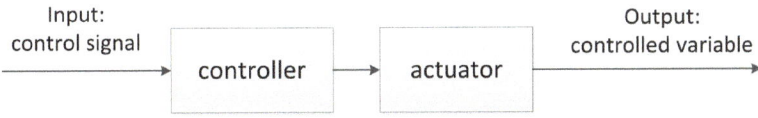

Fig. 3.13 The principle of an open-loop control system

example of open-loop control system is the traffic light recognition in an autonomous car. If the controller recognizes a red traffic light, it will give the stop command to the wheels' actuator, but will not check whether the breaks really worked. Other examples of open-loop control systems are microwave ovens, or programmable light switch timers that make a house look occupied to keep the burglars away.

3.2.1.3   Who Will Move the Curtains?

Now that the system is smart enough to know when to open or close the curtains, we need a so-called *actuator* to execute its decision. An actuator is basically also a transducer. In pervasive computing systems, it receives the electrical signal from the controller and uses it to vary another physical quantity. The effect of this actuation could be that something moves or changes in the environment or simply that information is provided via some form of display. Examples of actuators are electric motors, resistive heaters, lamps, LCD displays and LEDs, meters, and speakers.

In the smart curtains' example, we could use an electrical *motor* to activate the curtains. An electric motor is a device that converts electrical energy into mechanical energy that can be rotational or linear. There are a great variety of electrical motors that can be used in pervasive computing applications (see Fig. 3.14). *AC motors* are used in high-power applications, where high precision is not required. *DC motors* are used in low-power applications that require more precision. When powered, a DC motor just starts spinning its shaft, until the power is removed. Its rotation speed depends on the applied voltage. Most DC motors are pretty fast, with rotation speeds up to 5000 RPM (revolutions per minute). Examples are computer cooling fans and radio-controlled car wheels. *Servomotors* are a "smarter" type of motors that can control the position of the shaft more precisely than the standard DC motors. They are a combination of a DC motor and a position sensing and control system. *Servomotors* have three connectors, two for

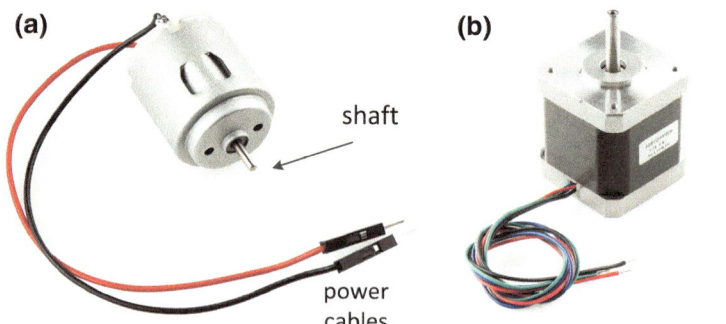

Fig. 3.14 Different types of motors. **a** A DC motor. From [6]. **b** A stepper motor. From [6]. Used with permission

power and one for the shaft position control. While the motor is always powered, the control loop reads the position of the shaft and adjusts it if needed. Servomotors are designed for more specific tasks, where position needs to be defined accurately, such as controlling the rudder on a boat or moving a robotic arm or robot leg within a certain range. The LEGO® Mindstorms robotic kit comes with three servomotors.

Stepper motors are a cheaper version of servomotors and do not require a complicated shaft position control system. Instead, the shaft reaches the desired position by moving in discrete steps. The controller needs to send a pulse signal to the motor, encoding the needed direction of rotation, speed, and number of steps. Stepper motors are used in a wide range of applications from robots, printers, projectors, cameras, medical equipment, and automotive devices.

Stepper and servomotors are both widely used in microcontroller applications. A *driver* device is needed to convert the digital signal produced by the controller into the right analog signal to activate the motor.

3.2.2 Efficient House Heating

The energy spent on house heating may reach 70% of the total residential energy consumption. The goal of this challenge is to save energy by heating the house only when necessary, with minimal discomfort for the inhabitants. Let us explore some possible solutions.

The simplest solution is to use a programmable thermostat. We could use, as sketched in Fig. 3.15, two temperature values: a lower *setback* point (15 °C) for situations when nobody is at home, and a higher *setpoint* temperature (20 °C) for situations when the house is inhabited.

A suitable obvious actuator will be an electrical heater. Because the chance is very small that at the moment the heater is turned on, the ambient temperature will be exactly at the desired value, we need a temperature regulation mechanism. More

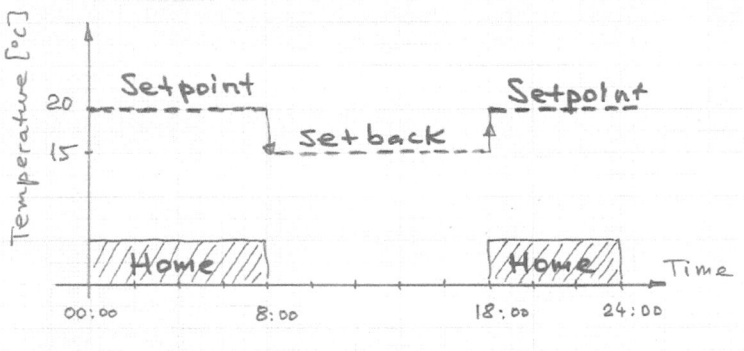

Fig. 3.15 A sketch of a schedule for the programmable thermostat

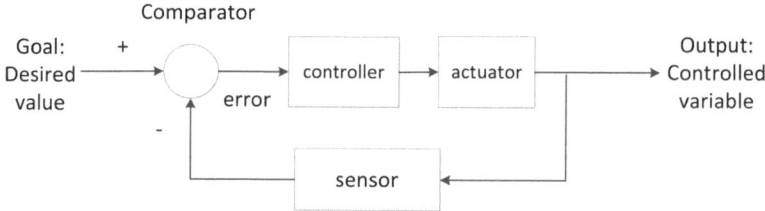

Fig. 3.16 The principle of the closed-loop feedback control system

generally, we are seeking a way to bring a physical value to a certain preset value and maintain that value, as long as necessary.

This goal can be realized with a *closed-loop* control algorithm, as illustrated in Fig. 3.16. In this case, the user inputs the desired goal directly into the system [7]. The control system continuously compares the current state to the desired state and calculates the error, by subtracting the output from the goal. Depending on the sign of this error, the current state is adjusted to minimize the error. For example, if the goal is an ambient temperature of 20 °C, and the currently measured output is 18 °C, the error signal is positive, and the heater will be turned on, to increase the output and reduce the error. If the sensor measures 22 °C, then the error signal is negative and the heater will be switched off. The process continues, until the desired state is achieved. This type of control is also called *feedback* control, because the output controlled variable—the room temperature in our case—is sensed and fed back to the input, and compared with the desired goal. The closed-loop feedback principle is ubiquitous in modern engineering. Examples are the cruise, climate, and transmission control systems in smart cars, fly-by-wire flight control systems, robotic surgery, but also network congestion and chemical processes control systems.

Feedback control is exactly what our thermostat needs to bring the house to a preset temperature.

In conclusion, our first solution for an efficient heating is to define the setpoint and setback temperature values, together with their corresponding time intervals, and use feedback control to maintain the temperature at one of these two values, according to the programmed time schedule.

This seems at first sight to be a pretty good, automatic solution. However, this solution has the disadvantage that it will not accurately match the house occupancy. For example, it might be that you arrive from work earlier one day and find a house that is still cold, or you leave on holiday and forget to reprogram the thermostat. As a result, the house will be needlessly heated for two weeks. A better solution is to somehow sense the house occupancy. Sensors such as Reed switches in the doors, RFID tags in the key holders, or passive infrared (PIR) motion sensors in the rooms can be used to sense the presence of persons in house. An even better solution is offered by a smart thermostat that combines occupancy sensing with occupancy prediction. Occupancy prediction uses machine learning and historical data to predict the probability of future occupancy. Machine learning prediction techniques will be discussed in detail in Chap. 6.

3.3 A Case Study: Autonomous Vehicles

Let us consider another example of pervasive computing systems, this time the autonomous vehicle. This can be a driverless car, an intelligent wheelchair, or an unmanned rover, exploring an area affected by an earthquake, or an unknown territory on Mars. In this section, we will reveal a few principles behind the most common functionalities of these autonomous vehicles.

3.3.1 Obstacle Detection

The first question is whether a smart navigation system that knows how to drive from A to B is capable of replacing the driver. In other words, is it enough to know how to drive from A to B? The answer is no, because the vehicle is not driving in a vacuum, and obstacles may occur on the way. These obstacles can be *positive*, such as other cars, pedestrians, animals, rocks, trees, shrubs, walls, and doors, or *negative*, such as potholes, craters, cliffs, gutters, and stairs. Obstacles must be handled by the system in different ways, depending on the application. In some cases, obstacles have to be detected and avoided (like in autonomous vehicles), detected and retrieved (like in earthquakes areas or fire sites), or detected and tracked (intruders tracking, guided museum tours, etc.).

The problem we want to solve here is obstacle detection while driving. The actuators are obviously the motors driving the wheels. For sensing and control, however, a few different technical solutions exist. Let us explore them!

The simplest solution would be to let the vehicle drive until it bumps into the obstacle. The collision can be detected with a *touch* or *switch* sensor. The principle of this binary sensor is very simple. Normally, the output of the sensor is 0, but when contact happens, an electrical contact is closed, and the sensor's output switches to 1. When contact disappears, the sensor's output flips back to 0. Examples of touch sensors used in robotics are the LEGO Mindstorms touch sensors or the biology-inspired whiskers, as the ones shown in Fig. 3.17.

Below, we show the pseudocode for a reactive controller that commands a vehicle, equipped with a touch sensor, to keep on driving until it collides with an obstacle.

```
while (no contact)
  drive-straight-forward
end_while
stop driving
```

Fig. 3.17 The Shrewbot, a
bio-bot that uses whiskers to
explore its surroundings.
From [8]. Used by permission
from Dr. Martin Pearson, at
Bristol robotics laboratory

Fig. 3.17 The Shrewbot, a bio-bot that uses whiskers to explore its surroundings. From [8]. Used by permission from Dr. Martin Pearson, at Bristol robotics laboratory

The previous solution is simple, but may cause damage in some cases. A more elegant way to detect an object is to use *ranging* sensors that can sense an object in their proximity, before they bump into it. *Ranging* means that these sensors measure the distance to the objects. While touch sensors had a binary output (0 or 1), a ranging sensor can produce an output with any real value situated in a continuous range. The first example of ranging sensors is the *ultrasound sensor*, or sonar. The name *sonar* comes from *so*und *na*vigation and *r*anging. Initially developed for underwater applications and Polaroid cameras, the sonar is widely used nowadays in robotics and automotive industry. Its underlying principle is called *echolocation*, the same principle bats and dolphins use, to locate obstacles, friends, and foes, as illustrated in Fig. 3.18. LEGO Mindstorms NXT robotic kit is equipped with one ultrasound sensor.

Echolocation works as follows. The sensor sends out a sound beam with a frequency that is beyond human hearing and measures the time needed to receive the echo reflected by the object, called *time of flight* (ToF). Since the sound speed is known and constant, ($c = 300$ m/s), the distance to the object d can be calculated with:

$$d = \frac{\text{ToF} \times c}{2} \tag{3.5}$$

Fig. 3.18 The sonar principle. From [9]

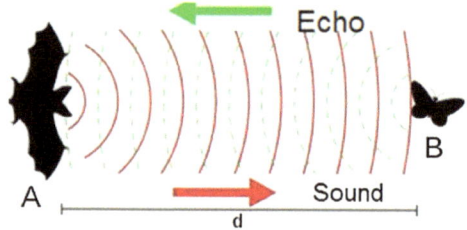

Ultrasound sensors are cheap, but not very accurate (ca 10–50 cm). Moreover, a shortcoming of ultrasound ranging is the sound *specular reflection*, a phenomenon that happens when the beam hits a smooth surface at a shallow angle. The problem is that the sound is then reflected outward and fails to reach back the emitter. This principle is exploited, for example, by stealth aircrafts.

Radar is a similar technology that uses radio waves instead of sound. Its name comes from Ra(dio) D(etection) A(nd) R(anging).

A third example of ranging sensors is the laser sensor, or LIDAR. *LIDAR* has its name from **LI**ght **D**etection **A**nd **R**anging and is in fact a laser radar; it also uses echolocation, but this time with light pulses instead of sound. A LIDAR can be static, when it measures distances in only one direction, or dynamic, when it scans across its field of view, to make an 3D image of the surroundings. LIDAR sensors are much more accurate and do not have any problems with specular reflection. Unfortunately, this laser beam ranging technology is also very expensive. Figure 3.19 to the left shows a Velodyne HDL-64E laser scanner, with 64 fast rotating laser light beams that can measure distance to obstacles with an accuracy of less than 2 cm.

All self-driving cars have at least one LIDAR laser scanner, mounted on their roof. Additional laser scanners and cameras are mounted elsewhere on the car (see Fig. 3.19). Altogether, by using sensor fusion algorithms, they provide the eyes of the autonomous car. Figure 3.20 shows examples of road images, detected by the laser scanners and cameras of different smart cars.

Regardless of the type of ranging sensor used, the pseudocode of a reactive controller that commands a vehicle to keep on driving until the distance to an obstacle is less than, for example, 20 cm, is presented below.

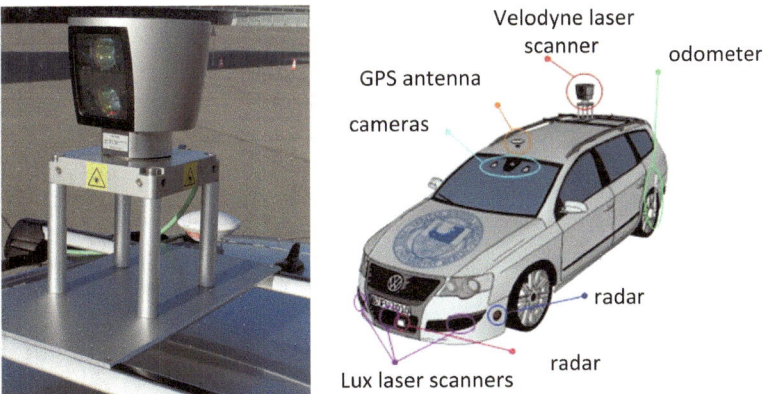

Fig. 3.19 An autonomous car, equiped with all kinds of sensors. From [10]. To the left, a detail of the Velodyne™ HDL-64E laser scanner mounted on the roof. Courtesy of AutoNOMOS-Labs, Freie Universität Berlin

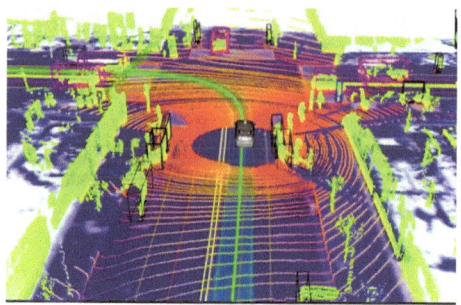

Another car in front of
the autonomous car

Fig. 3.20 Images of traffic situations "seen" by autonomous vehicles. Each color is the result of one laser beam measurements. The *top image* shows raw data obtained from the LIDAR in the Google self-driving car. From [11]. The *bottom image* shows images of traffic situations on the road, created by the FU Berlin autonomous car. The large caption shows a LIDAR image. The red blob is another car driving in front of the smart car. The small capture shows traffic lights in a roundabout as detected by a windshield camera. Courtesy of AutoNOMOS-Labs, Freie Universität Berlin

```
while distance > 20 cm
   drive forward
end_while
stop the motors
```

3.3.2   Let us Follow a Line

Many traffic accidents happen when the driver falls asleep for just one second behind the wheel, and the car leaves its designated lane on the road. The task of keeping a car in its lane is therefore crucial for safe traffic. A lane departure warning system, also known as a keep-in-lane assistant, is a technical gadget, currently incorporated in many modern cars that can save many lives. This system, based on

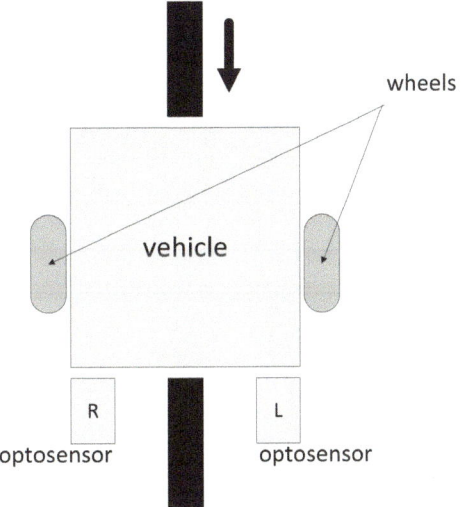

Fig. 3.21 A robotic vehicle that tries to follow a line R means Right and L means Left

a windshield camera or laser scanners, can alert the driver or even intervene as soon as the car drifts close to the lane markings. It works by detecting the line markers on the road view image and keeping the vehicle between these two lines.

Inspired by these real-life smart systems, line following is a classical challenge in robot engineering. A real car can be simulated with a robotic vehicle, equipped with two active optosensors, that keeps on driving over a black line on the floor, as shown in Fig. 3.21.

While driving, the following three situations can be encountered, as illustrated in Fig. 3.22.

A. both sensors sees white,
B. left sensor sees black, and
C. right sensor sees black.

Fig. 3.22 The vehicle in different positions relative to the black line

The reactive controller for this line follower could look like this:

```
position the robot with the black line between the two
optosensors.
while (true)
  while (both sensors detect white)
      drive straight forward
  end_while
  if (left sensor sees black) then turn left
  if (right sensor sees black) then turn right
end_while
```

3.3.3 Follow that Wall!

A known problem for advanced stage Alzheimer's patients is forgetting the location of their room and wandering disorientated and in panic through their residence. Let us imagine that in an augmented elderly home, a smart walker is guiding an old lady along the corridor, helping her to find her room. When they approach the right door, a familiar music and a message are spoken, announcing the lady that the destination has been reached.

Driving along a corridor can be simulated with a wall-following task in robotics, as illustrated in Fig. 3.23. The distance to the wall can be measured with an ultrasound sensor, facing toward the wall. A feedback controller can keep the vehicle at a particular distance from the wall, according to the following scenario. The system continuously measures the actual distance to the wall. By subtracting the actual distance from the desired one, an error is calculated. If the current distance is too large (negative error), the robot should turn toward the wall. In the opposite case, if the distance to the wall is too small (positive error), the robot should turn away from the wall. The pseudocode for this wall-following robot is then:

```
position the robot
while (true)
if distance-to-the-wall is the desired one
    then keep driving
if  distance-to-the-wall is larger than desired
    then turn towards the wall
    else turn away from the wall
end_while
```

If you carefully followed the story, you have probably noticed that in both line and wall follower examples, we did not specify how exactly to turn the vehicle. In other words, the car does not know what it means to turn left, turn right, turn toward the wall, or turn away from the wall. Let us investigate some different options we have to turn the vehicle toward or away from the wall. The simplest solution is to

Fig. 3.23 A robotic vehicle equipped with an ultrasound sensor that tries to follow a wall

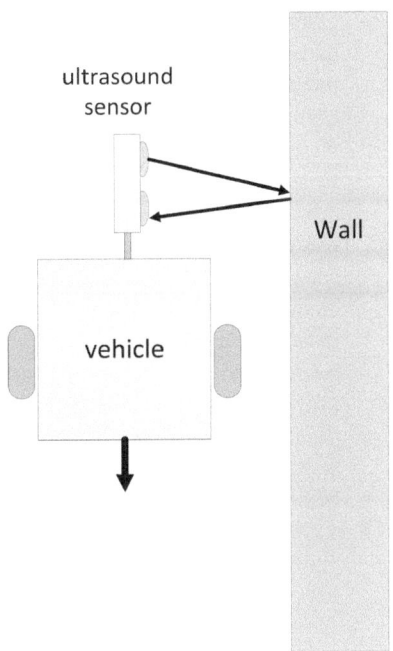

turn 45° each time, regardless of the distance to the wall. The problem is that when programmed in this way, the vehicle will have a very clumsy and silly walk. We can reduce these oscillations by *tuning* or calibrating the turning angle.

A few algorithms exist that tune parameters for an effective feedback control. The most simple is the so-called *proportional feedback control*, where the controller produces a signal proportional to the error. This means that when the robot is far from the wall, the turning angle is large, and when the robot is close to the wall, this angle is small. However, this solution is also not optimal. Practice learns that when the system is close to the desired state, it needs to be controlled differently than when it is far from it. Therefore, other types of controllers exist, such as *derivative* and/or *integral* control (PD, PI, PID), where the signal produced by the controller has a derivative component (D), depending on how fast the error changes, and an integrative one (I), reflecting the cumulative error. In a particular situation, you have to try different control solutions and chose the one that fits best.

3.4   Conclusions

- Any pervasive computing system endlessly executes the same sense-control-act sequence.
- Most sensors work based on the principle saying that a measurand causes an effect on the sensing element. In most pervasive computing systems, a change in the input causes a voltage gradient at the sensor's terminals.

- Controllers provide autonomy for pervasive computing systems. How *time* is handled distinguishes different approaches to control. Deliberative control has the principle Think first, act later! A deliberative system looks into the future before deciding how to act. It is highly intelligent, but slow, and needs a map. It is used, for example, in chess software and automotive navigation systems. Reactive control, on the other hand, is much faster and does not need an internal representation. It is based on simple rules and on the principle: Don't think, react! Reactive systems respond to the immediate requirements of the environment and do not look into the past or the future. The principle is used in for example cars dealing with obstacles. Reactive control can be open loop or closed loop. The latter, also called feedback control, might need tuning. This can be realized in different ways: proportional, proportional derivative (PD), and proportional derivative integrative (PID). Obstacle detection can be realized in different ways. The most common approaches use touch sensors and ranging sensors. Ranging sensors use ultrasound (sonar) radio (radar), or light (LIDAR) beams to measure the distance to obstacles.
- Actuators are transducers that receive the electrical signal from the controller and use it to affect back the environment. Examples of actuators are heaters, lamps, LEDs and displays, speakers, and motors.

3.5   Exercises

1. What does deliberative control mean? What is its principle? Where is it used?
2. How is a map represented in a computer-based navigation system?
3. What are the main modules in a navigation system?
4. How can we detect obstacles in a driverless car?
5. What is an ultrasound sensor? What does it measure and how does it work?
6. What is LIDAR? How does it work and where is it used?
7. What is a an optosensor? State the difference between an active and passive optosensor.
8. What is an actuator? Give a few examples.
9. What is a reactive control agent? Draw a diagram and explain its principle.
10. State the essential difference between open-loop and closed-loop control systems. Illustrate your answer by describing an example of each type.
11. Draw a diagram of a feedback controller for a cruise controller in a smart car.
12. Write in pseudocode a controller for a vehicle equipped with an ultrasound sensor that drives forward and stops in front of an obstacle.
13. Write in pseudocode a controller for a vehicle equipped with two optosensors that follows a black line and stops at a T-junction.

References

1. Mataric, M.J.: The Robotics Primer. MIT Press (2007)
2. Eggins, B.R.: Biosensors: an introduction. Teubner Studienbücher Chemie. (1996)
3. CdS Photoconductive Cells. Available from: http://cdn.sparkfun.com/datasheets/Sensors/LightImaging/SEN-09088.pdf
4. Russell, S.J. and Norvig, P.: Artificial Intelligence: a modern approach. Pearson Education (2003)
5. Illuminance—Recommended Light Levels. Available from: http://www.engineeringtoolbox.com/light-level-rooms-d_708.html
6. Motors and Selecting the Right One. Available from: https://learn.sparkfun.com/tutorials/motors-and-selecting-the-right-one
7. Storey, N.: Electrical and Electronic Systems. Pearson (2004)
8. Pearson, M., et al.: Biomimetic vibrissal sensing for robots. Philos. Trans. R. Soc. B: Biol. Sci. **366**(1581), 3085–3096 (2011)
9. Sonar. Available from: https://en.wikipedia.org/wiki/Sonar
10. Lange, S., Ulbrich, F., and Goehring, D.: Online vehicle detection using deep neural networks and lidar based preselected image patches. In Intelligent Vehicle (IV16). Gothenburg, Sweden (2016)
11. Guizzi, E.: How google self driving car works. In IEEE Spectrum. (2011)

Chapter 4
Image Processing

> *You see, but you do not observe, Watson. The distinction is clear.*
> Arthur Conan Doyle, "Sherlock Holmes—A Scandal in Bohemia"

In simple systems, the context can be easily extracted from the data coming directly from sensors, be it light intensity, distance, or temperature. This allows the right actuation decision to be easily taken, such as to open the curtains, drive straight, turn left, or start the heater. Unfortunately, context discovery from "raw" images is not as straightforward as that. The reason is that data produced by imaging sensors is only seldom perfect. Look at the image in Fig. 4.1. Suppose the goal is to simply count the miniature figures on it. You can say: "But even a child can do this!" Yes, that's true. However, there is high chance that a computer will come up with a different and wrong answer. Can you see why? One reason is the shadows; they can make the computer algorithm believe that there are only five objects in the image rather than seven. And we did not even mention more difficult tasks, such as recognizing the figures in the image.

Take a more serious, real-life example, and consider a traffic light recognition system in an autonomous car. Think about how the image taken by the vehicle camera will look, if there is mist, it is dark, and the red light is partially covered by dirt. The problem is that for different reasons, images are often corrupted by noise or blur; they suffer from uneven or poor illumination, poor contrast, or view obstruction. Hence, context information carried by image signals remains hidden, making classification and further reasoning impossible. An escape from this impasse is possible if one "cosmetically" enhances the image. This is called *preprocessing*, a process that encompasses a range of operations applied to a raw signal, with the purpose of extracting, against all odds, a reasonable context. This chapter will discuss different image preprocessing techniques, such as brightness and contrast optimization, thresholding, edge detection, noise filtering, and morphologic operations. The collateral damage that might be caused by these processing techniques is also exposed. Finally, automatic object counting is demonstrated using BLOB analysis.

© Springer International Publishing AG 2017
N. Silvis-Cividjian, *Pervasive Computing*, Undergraduate Topics
in Computer Science, DOI 10.1007/978-3-319-51655-4_4

Fig. 4.1 Shadows hinder
automatic object counting

4.1   Point Processing

In general, image processing can be summarized as taking an input image f and
converting it into a different, output image, denoted by g.

Point processing is an operation that calculates the new value of *each* pixel
$g(x, y)$, based on $f(x, y)$, the value of the pixel *in the same position*, and some
arithmetic operation (see Fig. 4.2). The values of other pixels in image f do not play
any role in such a transformation.

The arithmetic operation can be, for example, a simple addition with a constant
value, b. The new intensity of each pixel in the resulted image, $g(x, y)$, will then be:

$$g(x, y) = f(x, y) + b \tag{4.1}$$

If $b > 0$, the effect of the processing will be that the brightness of each pixel in
image f will increase, and the image will become lighter. If $b < 0$, the result of the
point operation will be a darker image. The effect of changing the brightness is
illustrated in Fig. 4.3.

But what does it mean for an image to be "too dark" or "too light"? Is there a
"good" brightness? This is an appropriate moment to introduce a simple, but
powerful image processing tool, called *image histogram*. A *histogram,* in general,
is a graphical representation of the frequency of events. An *image histogram* is a
plot of the relative frequency of occurrence of each of the permitted pixel values in
the image, against the values themselves. For a grayscale image, the histogram can
be constructed by simply counting how many times each gray value, a number
between 0 and 255, occurs within the image. The image histogram is actually a bar
graph, where on the x-axis, one represents the admissible range of intensity values
(e.g., from 0 to 255), and on the y-axis, we show the number of times each value
actually occurs. In Fig. 4.4, you can see a grayscale image showing some coins,
together with the corresponding histogram. This histogram was very easily

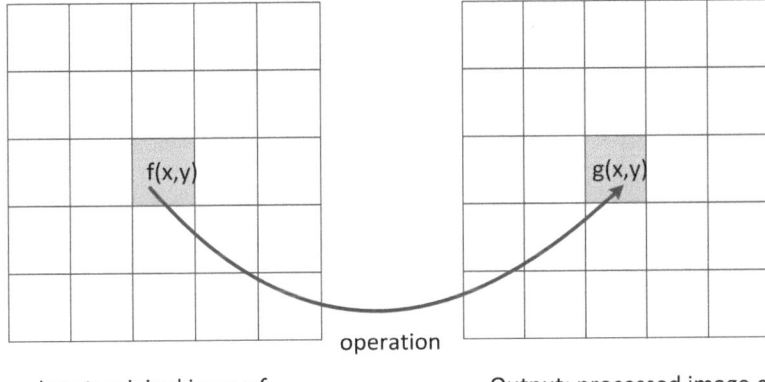

Fig. 4.2 The principle of point processing

Fig. 4.3 The effect of changing the brightness. The original image is in the middle, the image with a reduced brightness ($b < 0$) is to the *left*, and the image with a higher brightness ($b > 0$) is shown to the *right*

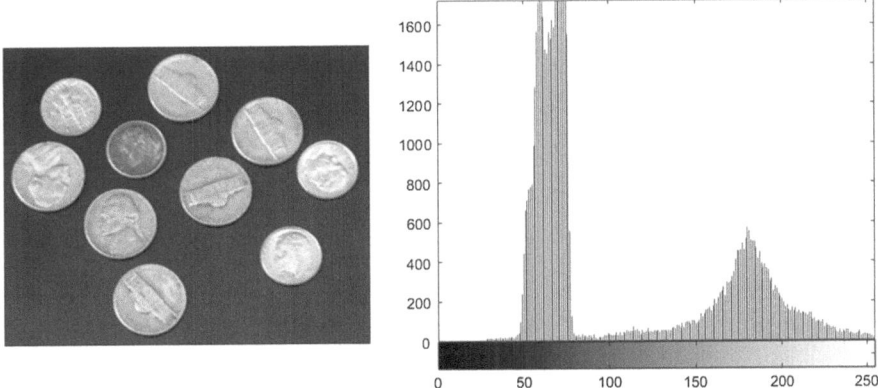

Fig. 4.4 To the *left*, a grayscale image with coins, from the MATLAB® image repository. Used with permission. Its histogram, to the *right*

obtained, by using the powerful MATLAB® Image Processing Toolbox. The histogram features two distinctive peaks: a peak in the lower range of brightness, corresponding to the dark background, and a peak in the higher range of brightness, corresponding to the foreground objects, the coins.

If the relevant intensity interval, corresponding to nonzero frequencies, is much smaller than the interval [0, 255], we say that the image has *a poor contrast*. In a poor contrast image, it is difficult to distinguish between dark and light. The contrast of an image can be improved by a point operation, called *histogram stretching*. Often called normalization or equalization, histogram stretching is a simple image enhancement technique that tries to "stretch" the range of intensity values to span a desired range of values, in our case [0, 255]. The new intensity value of each pixel in the new image is calculated with the formula:

$$g(x,y) = \frac{255}{f_2 - f_1} \cdot (f(x,y) - f_1) \tag{4.2}$$

where f_1 is the leftmost nonzero bin in the histogram, and f_2 is the rightmost nonzero bin in the histogram of the input image. In Fig. 4.5, you can see an

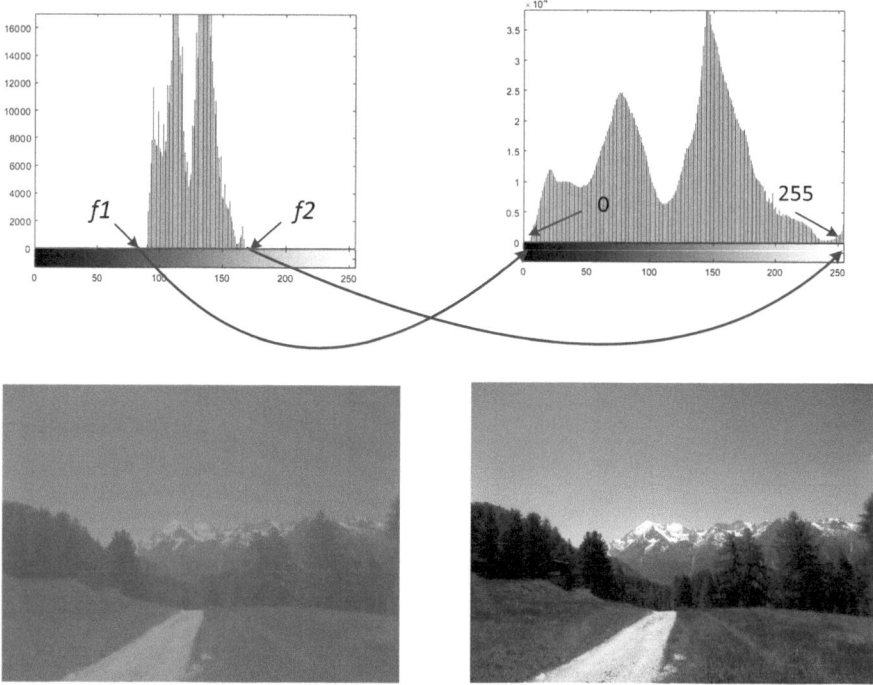

Fig. 4.5 The effect of histogram stretching. To the *left* is an image with poor contrast and to the *right* is the enhanced image

illustration of histogram stretching and the improved contrast effect on a grayscale image.

Thresholding is another, very useful, point-processing operation applicable to grayscale images. It transforms a grayscale image into a black and white (binary) one, by choosing a gray level T in the original image and then turning every pixel black or white, according to whether its gray value is greater than or less than T.

$$\text{A pixel becomes} \begin{cases} \text{white, if its grey level is} > T \\ \text{black, if its grey level is} \leq T \end{cases}$$

T is called the *threshold level*. Thresholding can be done very simply in MATLAB. Figure 4.6 shows the effect of thresholding. Notice some black dot noise on one of the white holes.

In many image processing systems, thresholding is a key step to a *segmentation* (separation) of the foreground (information) from the background (noise). By selecting a "good" threshold value between the two histogram peaks, one can successfully separate the foreground objects from the background. Take a look at the coins in Fig. 4.4. What would be a good threshold to separate them from their background? We can estimate it by just looking at the histogram and then select a brightness value of 100 ($T = 100$). MATLAB has a built-in function that automatically detects the optimal threshold. Segmentation by thresholding gives the best results if the image has a bimodal histogram. Bimodal means that the histogram has two prominent peaks, where one peak corresponds to the background pixels and the other peak to the foreground pixels. Such a good histogram, together with a problematic one are illustrated in Fig. 4.7.

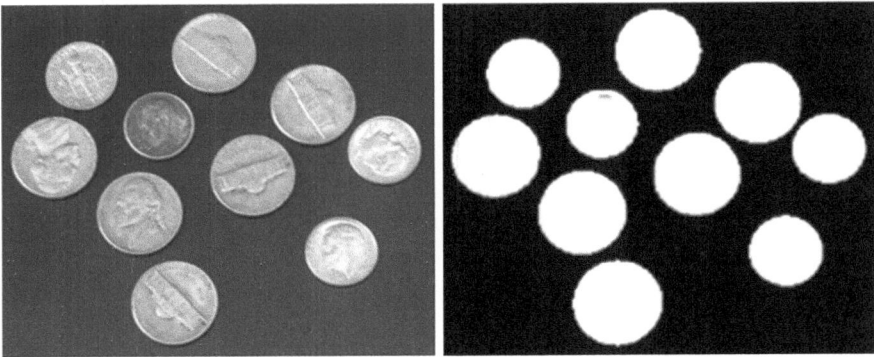

Fig. 4.6 Thresholded image of the coins

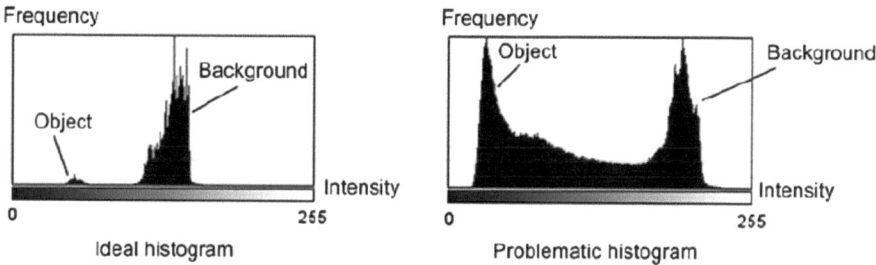

Fig. 4.7 A good histogram that easily enables thresholding, to the *left*, and a problematic one, to the *right*. From [1]

4.2   Neighborhood Processing

In neighborhood processing, the intensity value of each pixel in the output image g (x, y) is determined by the value of the pixel at the same position in the input image $f(x, y)$, together with its neighbors and a neighborhood processing operation (Fig. 4.8).

4.2.1   Filtering

A first example of neighborhood image processing is *filtering*, an attempt to improve image quality by reducing or even removing noise. Let us consider a corrupted image, as shown in Fig. 4.9, and try to filter the noise.

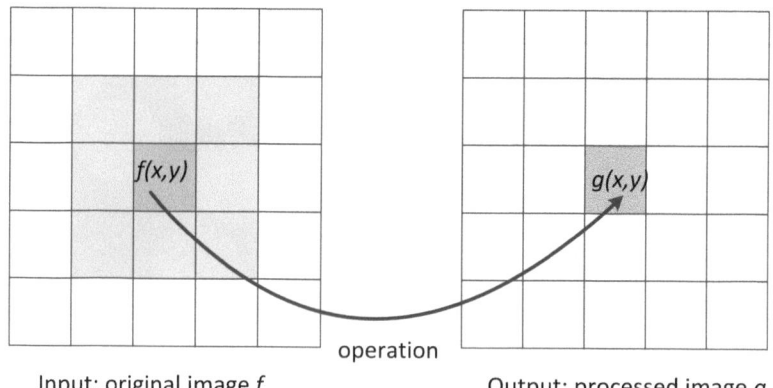

Fig. 4.8 The principle of neighborhood processing

Fig. 4.9 An image corrupted
by salt-and-pepper noise.
From [1]. Used with
permission

If we take a closer look at some particular noisy pixels in Fig. 4.9, we can see that this salt-and-pepper *noise* consists of isolated pixels, having a brightness of either 0 (black), or 255 (white). By isolated, we mean that the pixels have a brightness which is very different from their neighbors. We could improve this image quality, if we somehow identified such outliers and replaced them by a value which is more similar to their neighbors.

Let us consider the upper left black dot, pointed by an arrow in Fig. 4.10. This is a noisy pixel, because its intensity, $f(x, y) = 0$, strongly stands out from its neighbors. One idea could be to reduce this discrepancy, by changing its intensity to the *mean* value of its neighbors, including itself. Its new intensity value will become:

$$g(x, y) = (205 + 204 + 204 + 206 + 0 + 208 + 201 + 199 + 205)/9$$
$$= 181.3, \text{ rounded up to } 181.$$

This results in the noise pixel being replaced by 181, which is more similar to the values of its neighbors. If we perform this operation for each pixel in the image, then we say that "we apply a *mean filter* to the image." The result of this operation is the image shown in Fig. 4.11. You can see that applying mean filtering brings a visible improvement. However, the new image became unclear, and the noise has not been completely eliminated. Mean filtering in this particular case is good, but not exciting. Let us try another filtering technique.

Another possibility to filter that particular pixel is to replace it with the median value of its neighbors, including itself. The median value of a group of numbers is found by ordering the numbers in increasing order and picking the middle value. For example, ordering will give the following sequence: [0, 199, 201, 204, **204**, 205, 205, 206, 208]. The middle value is 204; hence, the median of the neighborhood is 204. The noisy pixel $f(x, y) = 0$ is now replaced by $g(x, y) = 204$, which does not stand out anymore.

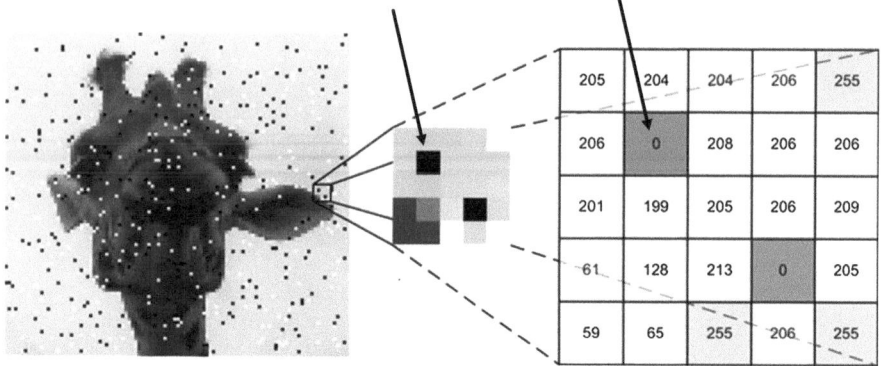

205	204	204	206	255
206	0	208	206	206
201	199	205	206	209
61	128	213	0	205
59	65	255	206	255

Fig. 4.10 The image with salt-and-pepper noise and a zoom in. From [1]. Used with permission

Fig. 4.11 The noisy image filtered with a mean filter. From [1]. Used with permission

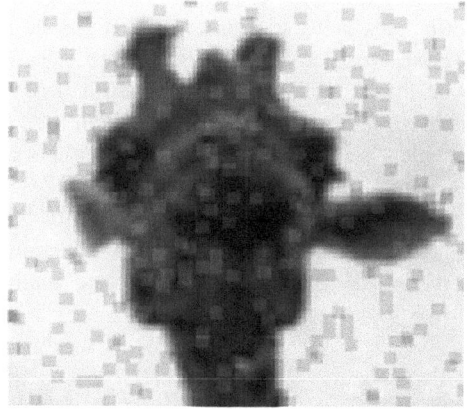

If we apply the median filter operation to every single pixel in the image, we say that "we filter the image using a *median filter*." The result of applying this median filter is shown in Fig. 4.12. The noise disappeared; however, there is now a slight distortion and blur in the image.

Filtering an image is equivalent to applying a filter to each pixel in the image. A *filter* is a N × N array (or image!), with all elements (pixels) equal to 1. For example, the filters used in Figs. 4.11 and 4.12 are 3 × 3 filters, because they took into consideration 3 × 3 = 9 neighbors. Since filters are centered on a particular pixel (the center of the filter), the size of the filter is always uneven, i.e., 3, 5, and 7. The size of a filter controls the number of neighbors included. The more neighbors are included, the stronger the image is filtered. Whether this is desirable or not depends on the application.

In conclusion, filtering is definitely a very helpful technique to enhance an image. However, as you have probably already noticed, there is no perfect filter,

Fig. 4.12 The noisy image
filtered with a median filter.
From [1]. Used with
permission

appropriate for all images. You should always try to apply different filters, with
different sizes, and see which one has the best effects. In any case, be aware that
filtering has the same effect as chemotherapy in cancer treatment. Since the processing applies to *all* pixels in the image, not only the noisy ones, there will be
always a price to be paid; the image might become better, but not the same
anymore.

4.2.2   Correlation

Correlation, or convolution, is another neighborhood processing technique that also
works by applying a filter to each pixel of an image. Here, the filter is called the
kernel, and it is filled with numbers not necessarily equal to 1, called *kernel
coefficients*.

Figure 4.13 shows examples of kernels, used for image filtering, blurring, and
edge detection.

Correlation between an input image f and a kernel h results in a new output
image, denoted by g. You can understand how correlation works, if you imagine the
kernel as a magnifying glass, or a mask, that scans over the image f as illustrated in
Fig. 4.14. As it scans over the image, the kernel alters the value of the pixel $f(x, y)$,
situated exactly under its center. When the scan is ready, a new image, denoted by
g, of the same size as the original image f is generated.

The intensity of each pixel $g(x, y)$ in the new output image is calculated as
follows. Suppose the kernel stopped with its center $h(0, 0)$ exactly above the pixel
$f(x, y)$, as shown in Fig. 4.14. First, the kernel coefficients are weighting the values
of original pixels they are covering. The new value $g(x, y)$ is the sum of these
weighted products. Mathematically, this is described with the following formula:

1	1	1
1	1	1
1	1	1

1	4	7	4	1
4	16	26	16	4
7	26	41	26	7
4	16	26	16	4
1	4	7	4	1

1	0	-1
2	0	-2
1	0	-1

3X3 Mean filter   Gaussian blur kernel   Sobel horizontal edge kernel

Fig. 4.13 Different correlation kernels

Fig. 4.14 The principle of
correlation

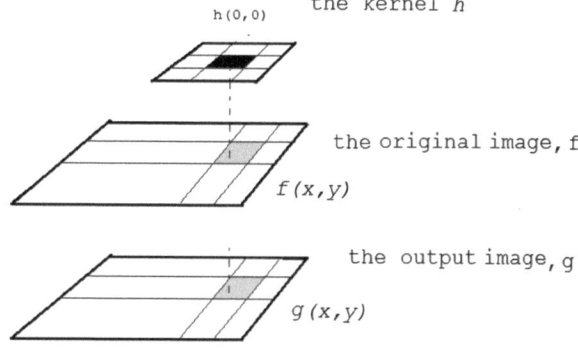

$$g(x,y) = \sum_{j=-R}^{R} \sum_{i=-R}^{R} h(i,j) \cdot f(x+i, y+j) \tag{4.3}$$

where R is the size of the kernel.

For example, let us say that we use a 3×3 kernel h that during scanning stopped above the pixel $f(2, 2)$ [1]. We want to calculate the intensity of the pixel at position (2, 2) in the new image $g(2, 2)$. If the kernel center $h(0,0)$ is above the pixel $f(2,2)$, then the pixel $h(-1, -1)$ is above the pixel $f(1, 1)$, $h(1, 1)$ above $f(3, 3)$, and so on, as illustrated in Fig. 4.15. First, the superimposed pixels are pairwise multiplied. In this way, we get 9 products, which are added, and give the value of the new $g(2, 2)$ pixel, calculated as follows:

$$\begin{aligned}
g(2,2) = &\, h(-1,-1) \cdot f(1,1) + h(0,-1) \cdot f(2,1) + h(1,-1) \cdot f(3,1) \\
&+ h(-1,0) \cdot f(1,2) + h(0,0) \cdot f(2,2) + h(1,0) \cdot f(3,2) \\
&+ h(-1,1) \cdot f(1,3) + h(0,1) \cdot f(2,3) + h(1,1) \cdot f(3,3)
\end{aligned} \tag{4.4}$$

Two typical image processing techniques make use of correlation: template matching and edge detection. Template matching can be used, for example, to locate a certain object on an image. When applying template matching, the kernel is

Fig. 4.15 This is how a particular value $g(2, 2)$ in the new output image is calculated

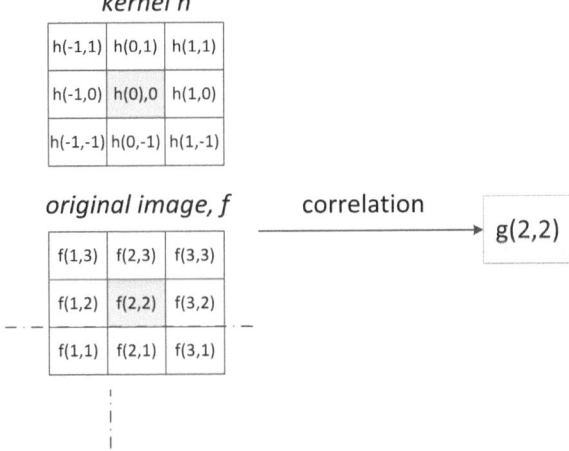

called a *template*, and it defines an image of the object we are looking for. By correlating an input image with this template, the output image will indicate *where* the object is. Each pixel in the output image will have a value, saying something about the similarity between the template and an image patch (with the same size as the template) centered at this particular pixel position. The brighter the value, the higher the similarity (see Fig. 4.16). We will come back and discuss template matching in Chap. 6.

An *edge* is a curve that follows a path of rapid change in image intensity. Edge detection is a very important process in image pattern recognition, computer vision, and medical imaging. Edge detection can be achieved by correlating the image with a kernel. There are many kernels suitable for edge detection, such as Sobel, Prewitt, Roberts, and Canny. Edge detection is extremely easy to obtain in MATLAB, using a built-in function that takes as parameter the type of kernel to be used and returns a binary image, containing 1s where the function finds edges in the input image and 0s elsewhere. Some examples of edge detection images obtained using MATLAB, are shown in Fig. 4.17.

4.3 Morphological Operations

Morphology is a branch of image processing, particularly useful for analyzing shapes in images. Morphology operates like the other neighborhood processing methods, by applying a kernel to each pixel in the input image. The kernel in a morphological operation is called *structuring element* (*STREL*) and contains only "0"s and "1"s. Normally, the pattern of "1"s forms a box or a disk. Structuring elements have a designated center pixel. In Fig. 4.18, different sized structuring elements are illustrated. The art of morphological processing is to choose the right shape of the structuring element that suits the particular application. Which type and

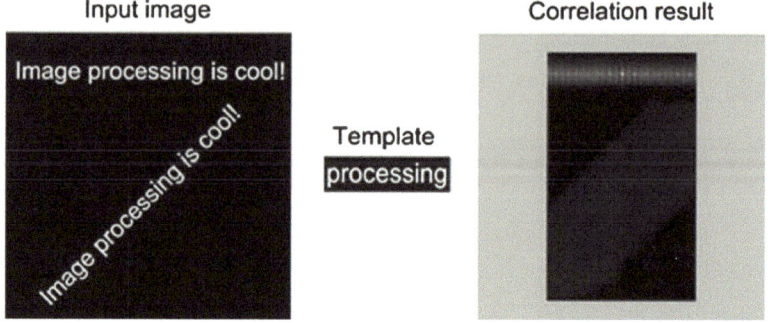

Fig. 4.16 Searching for an object in an image by template matching. In this case, the object is the phrase "image processing is cool." From [1]. Used with permission

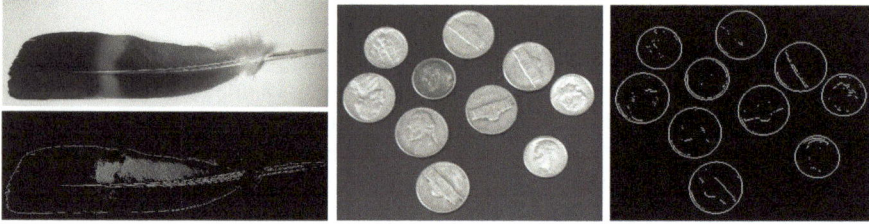

Fig. 4.17 Examples of edge detection using the Sobel kernel

Fig. 4.18 Different structuring elements. The center pixel is shaded

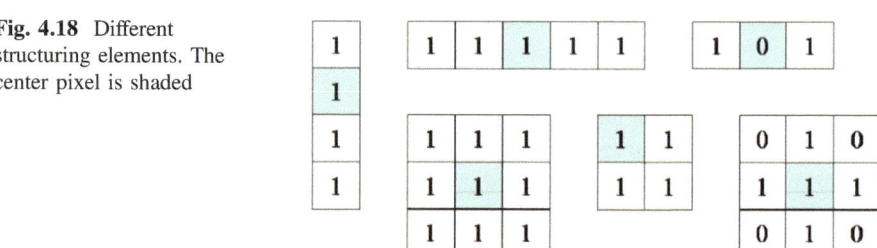

size to use is up to the designer, but in general, a box-shaped structuring element tends to preserve sharp object corners, whereas a disk-shaped structuring element tends to round the corners of the objects.

The most important morphological operators are *dilation* and *erosion*. All other operations can be defined in terms of these primitive operators. Morphological operators take a binary image and a structuring element as input and combine them using a set operator (intersection, union, inclusion, or complement). If we have an image A and a structuring element B, then we speak of the *erosion/dilation of A by B*. The procedure is similar to correlation. The STREL slides over the image A.

The center of the STREL is placed at the position of a pixel in focus, and it is the value of this pixel that will be calculated, by applying the structuring element.

However, a STREL is not applied in the same way as the kernel in correlation. Other operations (called Fit and Hit) are used instead of using multiplications and additions. To perform *erosion* of a binary image, we center the STREL on each "1" pixel in the image. If any of the neighborhood pixels is "0", then the pixel in question is switched to "0". Formally, the erosion of the image A by the structuring element B is denoted A $\ominus$ B.

To perform *dilation*, we center the STREL on each "0" pixel in the image. If any of the neighborhood pixels is 1, then the pixel in question is switched to "1". Formally, the dilation of image A by structuring element B is denoted A $\oplus$ B. Figure 4.19 shows the results of dilation and erosion on a simple binary image.

The term erosion refers to the fact that the object in the binary image is decreased in size. In general, erosion of an image results in objects becoming smaller, small objects disappearing, and larger objects splitting into smaller objects. Erosion might be useful, for example, if we want to count the coins shown in Fig. 4.20. This is not an easy task, since the touching coins form a single fused region of white, and a counting algorithm would have to first segment this region into separate coins before counting. The situation can be much simplified by eroding the image. The third image in Fig. 4.20 shows the result of eroding twice using a disk-shaped structuring element.

The term dilation refers to the fact that the object in the binary image is increased in size. In general, dilating an image results in objects becoming bigger, small holes being filled, and objects being merged.

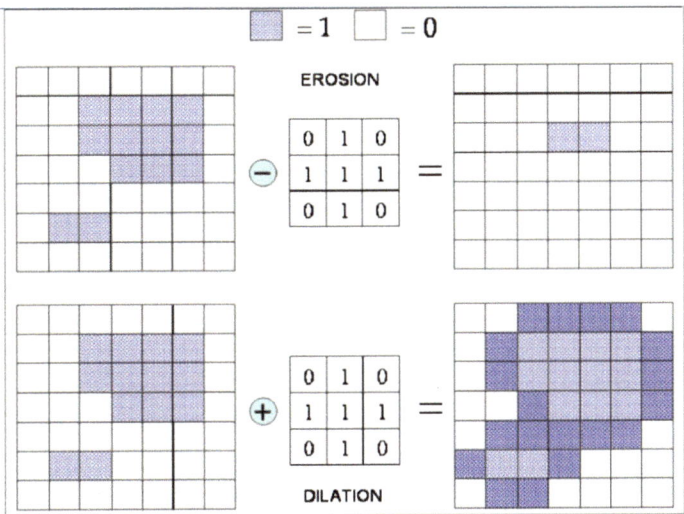

Fig. 4.19 The erosion and dilation of a simple binary image. From [2]. Used with permission

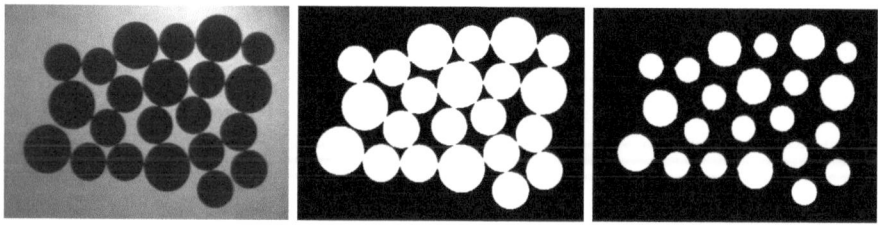

Fig. 4.20 Illustration of the erosion operation necessary to count objects. From [3]. Used with permission

Combining dilation and erosion in different ways results in a number of different morphological image processing techniques. These are called *compound operations*. Here, we present two of the most common compound operations, namely opening and closing.

Closing is the name given to the morphological operation of dilation followed by erosion, using the same structuring element. It deals with the problem associated with dilation, namely that as a result, the objects increase in size. This is a problem in situations where, for example, the size of the object (number of pixels) matters. Closing tends to remove small holes and to join narrow isthmuses between objects. We can see in Fig. 4.21 that the holes and convex structures are filled, and hence, the object is more compact.

Opening is the morphological operation of erosion followed by dilation, with the same structuring element. It deals with the problem associated with erosion, namely that as a result, the objects decrease in size. The decreasing object size is a problem in situations where, for example, the size of the object (number of pixels) matters. The general effect of opening is to remove small, isolated noisy objects while the main object preserves its original size (see Fig. 4.22).

An opening can be also used for segmentation of objects of the same shape in an image. Consider, for example, the binary image in Fig. 4.23 to the left, containing a

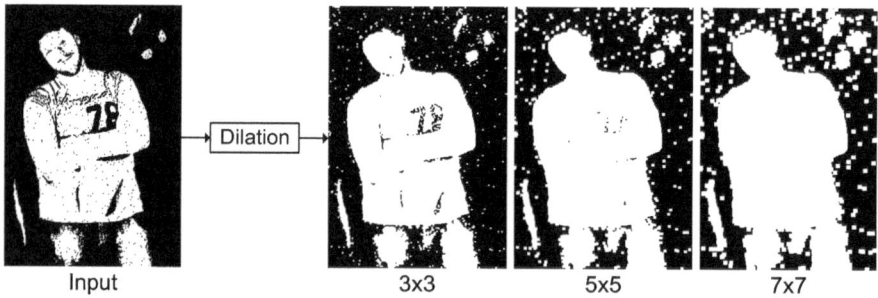

Fig. 4.21 Closing performed using 7×7 box-shaped structuring elements. From [1]. Used with permission

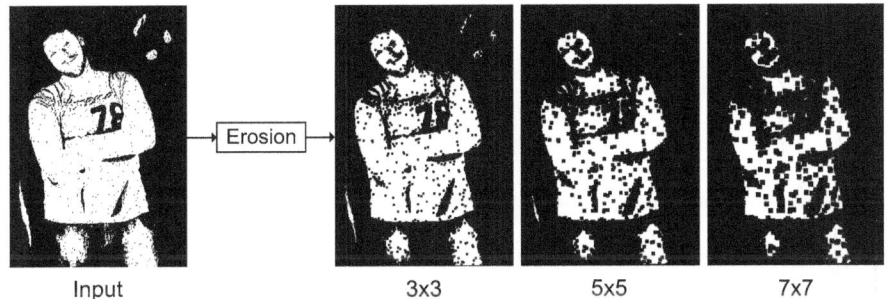

Input | 3x3 | 5x5 | 7x7

Fig. 4.22 Opening performed using a 7×7 box-shaped structuring element. From [1]. Used with permission

mixture of circles and lines. Suppose that we want to separate out the circles from the lines, so that they can be counted. In other words, we want to filter out the lines. If we apply an opening with a STREL as a disk, we obtain the image in Fig. 4.23, to the right. We can see that some of the circles are slightly distorted, but in general, the lines have been almost completely removed, while the circles remain almost completely unaffected. Figure 4.24 shows the processing of a microscope image to retain only the large cells. MATLAB supports morphological operation and has built-in functions to generate a structuring object and to apply opening and closing operations.

In conclusion, morphologic operations are powerful tools that can improve the quality of an image by correcting imperfections, eliminating noise, or retaining objects with a certain shape or size. In a particular situation, you should always try to adjust the size of the structuring element until the best effect is obtained. Remember to save the original image, because the effect of morphologic operations can change the image drastically.

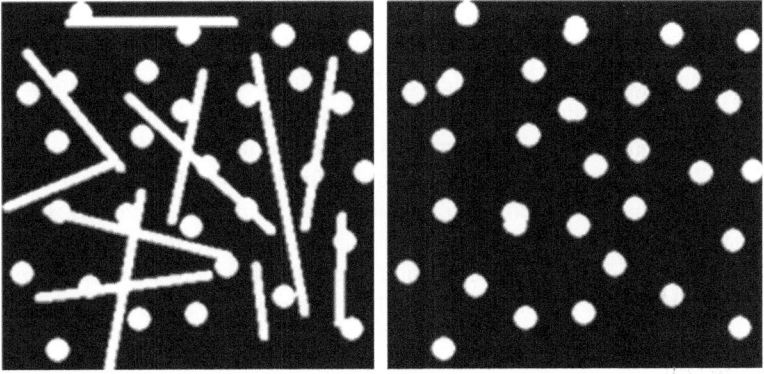

Fig. 4.23 An image with *circles* and *lines*, to the *left*. The same image after the opening with a disk-shaped structuring element, to the *right*. From [3]. Used with permission

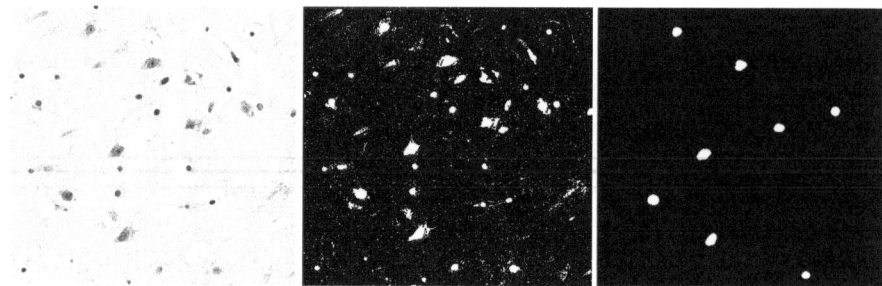

Fig. 4.24 An microscope image showing small and large cells, to the *left*. Thresholding transforms it in a binary image, in the *middle*. An opening was applied with disk-shaped structuring elements to retain only large cells, to the *right*. From [3]. Used with permission. We thank R. Aguilar-Chongtay of the Department of Artificial Intelligence, University of Edinburgh, for the use of this image

4.4   Let us Count Objects!

The object counting problem is the estimation of the number of objects in a still image or video frame. It arises in many real-world applications, including computer games, cell counting in microscopic images, monitoring crowds in surveillance systems, highway vehicle counting, performing wildlife census, or counting the number of trees in an aerial image of a forest (Fig. 4.25). The typical scenario consists in having a large number of objects of different size, but approximately of similar shape. From the image processing point of view, object counting can be solved through BLOB extraction, where BLOB stands for ***Binary Large Object***, and refers to a group of connected pixels in a binary image, also called *connected components*. The term "Large" indicates that only objects of a certain size are of interest and that "small" binary objects are regarded as noise. The purpose of BLOB extraction is to isolate the BLOBs (objects) in a binary image. As mentioned above, a BLOB consists of a group of connected pixels. Whether or not two pixels are connected is defined by the *connectivity*, that is, which pixels are neighbors and which are not. The two most often applied types of connectivity are 4-connectivity and 8-connectivity, both illustrated in Fig. 4.26. 8-connectivity is more accurate than 4-connectivity, but 4-connectivity is often applied since it requires fewer computations, and hence, it can process the image faster.

A number of different algorithms exist for finding the BLOBs in an image. Such algorithms are usually referred to as *connected component analysis* or *connected component labeling*. These algorithms search for connected pixels and assign a label to each found BLOB. Background is usually labelled with 0, the first BLOB gets the label 1, the second gets label 2, and so on. The label can be further translated into a color.

MATLAB has a built-in function that takes a binary image and returns a labeled matrix, where all the pixels belonging to one connected BLOB get the same label. The function also returns the number of labeled BLOBs found. This number is very

Fig. 4.25 Examples of object counting problems

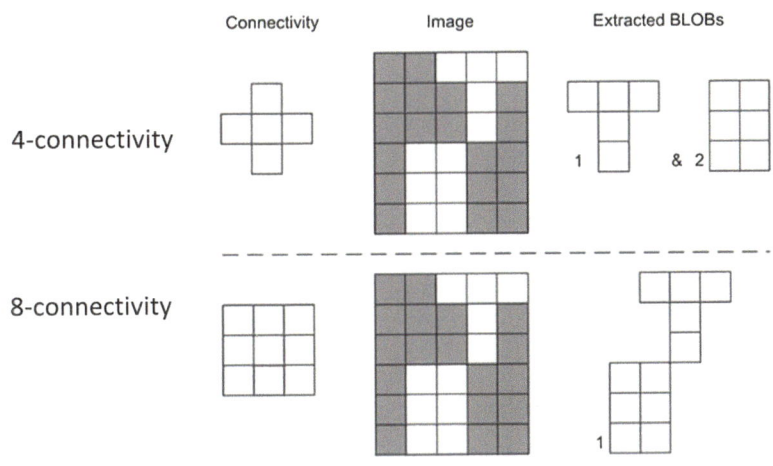

Fig. 4.26 Connected components for different types of connectivity. From [1]. Used with permission

useful information, because it gives us actually the number of BLOBs, the answer to the object counting problem.

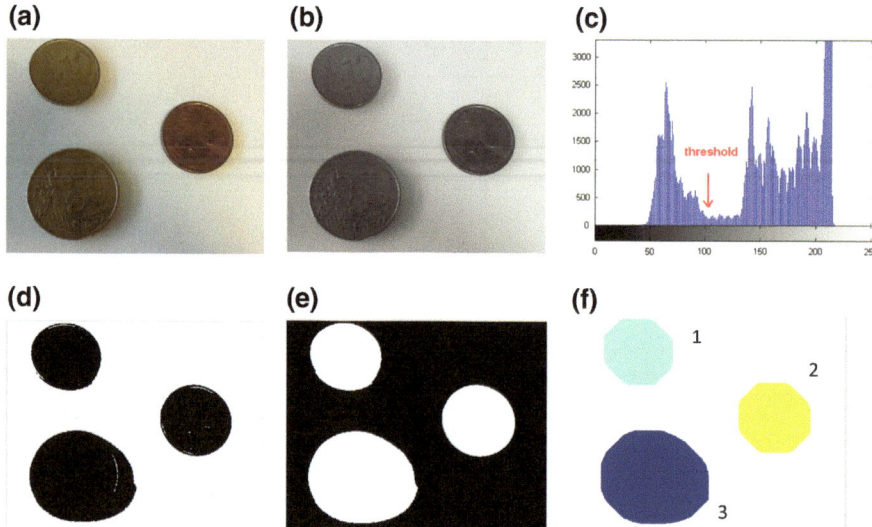

Fig. 4.27 An example of object counting using connected component labeling. **a** Original RGB image; **b** the grayscale image; **c** the image histogram; **d** the thresholded image; **e** the image after morphologic operation; and **f** the BLOB extraction using connected component labeling, where each BLOB (coin) got a different color. You can see that the system has found three objects

In Fig. 4.27, we show as illustration an original RGB image with coins, followed by a series of intermediate, processed images. Finally, the last image shows the labeled BLOBs, from which it becomes evident that three objects have been automatically found. Object counting problem was solved. By the computer!

4.5   Conclusions

- Very often and for many different reasons, the images coming directly from sensors cannot directly provide context information. Therefore, processing of acquired images is needed, to improve their quality and make the context easily accessible.
- We have presented a few image processing techniques, such as brightness improvement, contrast enhancement, thresholding, filtering, and morphological operations.
- We have also shown some methods to extract useful context information from an image, such as template matching using correlation and BLOB extraction through connected component labeling.
- As a demonstration of practical context extraction, we counted the number of similar objects in an image.

4.6 Exercises

1. What is an image histogram? Sketch an example.
2. What is histogram stretching? When do we need it?
3. What is thresholding? Where do we need it? How does it work?
4. Explain how the mean/median filter works.
5. What is the big disadvantage of filtering?
6. Define the following concepts: neighborhood processing, kernel, correlation, image edge, and BLOB.
7. What is a structuring element? Give some examples.
8. What are morphological operations? Give some examples where we need them.
9. Explain how connected component labeling works.

References

1. Moeslund, T.B.: *Introduction to Video and Image Processing: Building Real Systems and Applications*. Undergraduate Topics in Computer Science (2012)
2. Solomon, C., Breckon, T.: *Fundamentals of Digital Image Processing: A practical Approach with Examples in MATLAB®*. Wiley-Blackwell (2012)
3. Fisher, R.B., Koryllos, K.: Interactive textbooks; embedding image processing operator demonstrations in text. Int. J. Pattern Recogn. Artif. Intell. **12**(8), 1095–1123 (1998). Images obtained from: http://homepages.inf.ed.ac.uk/rbf/HIPR2/

Chapter 5
Sound Processing

C'est le ton qui fait la musique.
French proverb

A pervasive computing system is considered extremely "cool" if it can recognize speech, understand a baby cry, identify daily activities from recorded noises, or name the composer of a famous music passage and, in other words, if it can find patterns in sound recordings. But prior to that, the system needs to know more about the recorded sound. Sound is a one-dimensional time-varying signal, created by a mechanical oscillation of pressure transmitted through air. Information is normally encoded in this signal through intensity or frequency patterns of variation. Measuring sound's intensity is a relatively straightforward operation. However, extracting *frequency* information from a raw sound signal is far from being easy. First, because real-world sounds are a Tower of Babel of different frequencies and amplitudes. There is not one frequency, but a whole spectrum of frequencies involved in making a sound waveform. Second, because the raw sound captured by the system is often contaminated by predictable, like the 50/60 Hz power hum, or less predictable random noise, coming, for example, from an airplane flying in the neighborhood. Some processing of the recorded signal is therefore highly needed.

This chapter starts by introducing Fourier analysis, a versatile and powerful mathematical tool, used to understand sound. Moreover, two types of digital filtering techniques are presented, without getting too far in mathematical details. These are (1) the moving average filters, suitable for suppression of random noise, and (2) the frequency-selective filters, used when a priori information about the spectral characteristics of noise is available. These techniques are not restricted to sound processing. They can be applied to any one-dimensional time-varying signal, such as acceleration, temperature, pressure, and bioelectrical signals (EEG, ECG, or EMG).

© Springer International Publishing AG 2017
N. Silvis-Cividjian, *Pervasive Computing*, Undergraduate Topics
in Computer Science, DOI 10.1007/978-3-319-51655-4_5

5.1 Frequency Spectrum Analysis

Frequency spectrum analysis aims to identify which frequencies are present in a time-varying signal, at a given moment. We actually solved this problem in Chap. 2, for the particular case of a sinusoidal signal. We started by plotting the signal versus time, as shown in Fig. 5.1. By measuring its period T, we could calculate its frequency with the following simple, "magic," formula:

$$f = \frac{1}{T} \tag{5.1}$$

If this formula always held, we could have closed this chapter here. But take a look at the speech signal plotted in Fig. 5.2.

Obviously, this signal is not sinusoidal. And the painful truth is that the world is by no means a sinusoidal place, with the exception of some pure, one-frequency sounds, generated, for example, by a tuning fork. Should we start worrying about our magic formula? Yes. But we should also seek for another way to extract some frequency information from this signal. Think, for example, of an orchestra. It consists of many instruments, sounding different notes together. If each instrument produced a pure sinusoidal tone at the frequency of the note that is assigned to it,

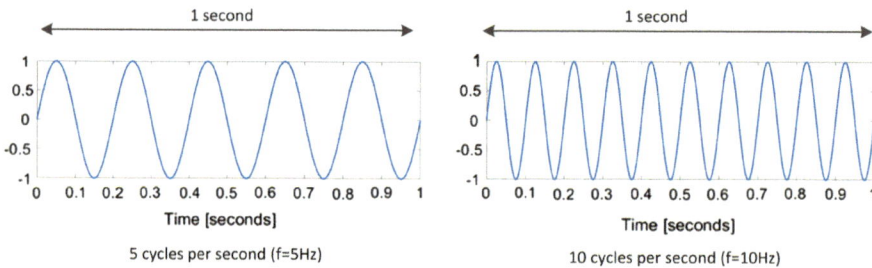

Fig. 5.1 The frequency of a sinusoidal signal is defined as the number of cycles per second

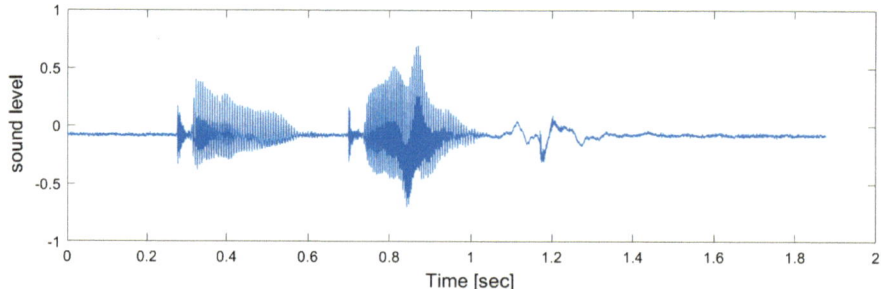

Fig. 5.2 A speech signal (the word "compute") plotted in time domain

then the composite orchestra signal would be simply a sum of sinusoids with different frequencies and amplitudes. Even if a real instrument is far from this model, this is actually a highly appropriate way to think about the orchestra signal.

We can apply the same approach to a speech signal. Mathematics gives us very good news, when it says that any signal can be decomposed into a series of sinusoidal waves, with different frequencies, amplitudes, and phase shifts. This decomposition is called *Fourier analysis*, introduced by the French mathematician Jean-Baptiste Fourier, in 1807.

To use Fourier analysis on a sinusoidal signal would be an overkill, since it will find only one component, with one frequency. However, real-life signals consist normally of a mix of components with different frequencies, belonging to a *spectrum of frequencies*. And in this case, Fourier analysis can help. A *frequency spectrum plot* of a signal is a graph showing frequency on x-axis and amplitudes on the y-axis. If you ever looked at a stereo equalizer, you actually watched the Fourier frequency spectrum plot of the produced sound of music.

Fourier analysis provides an alternative representation of a signal, not in the time domain (with time on the x-axis), but in the *frequency domain* (with frequency on the x-axis). This representation is equivalent to the one in the time domain, and in our case, as we will see in a minute, even more useful. We say that the Fourier analysis turns a *time-varying* signal into a *frequency-varying* signal. Figure 5.3 illustrates the frequency spectrum plot of the word "compute".

5.2 The Frequency Spectrum of a Periodic Signal

Let us consider a time-varying, continuous and analog signal $x(t)$, which is not sinusoidal, but nevertheless *periodic*, with a period of T_0. In this case, the Fourier analysis can break or decompose the signal in a set of pure sinusoids, called a *Fourier series*, described by Eq. (5.2)

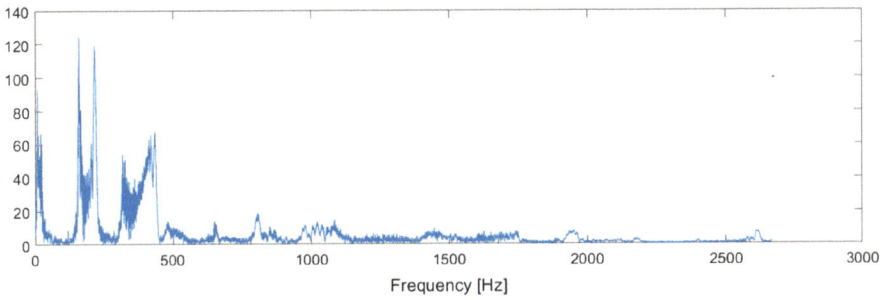

Fig. 5.3 A speech signal (the word "compute") represented in the frequency domain

$$x(t) = a_0 + \sum_k a_k \, \sin(2\pi f_k t + \varphi_k) \qquad (5.2)$$

Each sinusoidal component in the signal has an index number k, an amplitude a_k, a frequency f_k, and a phase shift φ_k, where k is an integer number that goes from 1 to even infinity.

The amplitudes a_k are called *Fourier coefficients*. We are especially interested in these coefficients, because they will say which frequency is present in the signal and to what extent.

Because the signal is periodic, its sinusoidal components have an interesting property. Their frequency is a multiple of a frequency f_0, called *fundamental frequency*, defined as:

$$f_0 = \frac{1}{T_0} \qquad (5.3)$$

As a result, the stems or impulses in its frequency spectrum plot are equally distanced and separated by a step equal to f_0, as shown in Fig. 5.4. These sinusoidal components are called *harmonics*. We say that the signal is "broken into a set of harmonic components." The frequency of each harmonic with index k, f_k, is calculated with:

$$f_k = f_0 k \qquad (5.4)$$

where $k = 1 \dots N$.

The first Fourier coefficient with the index $k = 0$, $a0$, has a special status and is called the *average value* of the signal $x(t)$ or its *DC* (direct current) component. Hopefully, you do remember this component from Chap. 2.

When the Fourier analysis is performed on a digital signal, represented by a vector $x[n]$ with N samples, the spectrum assigns to each discrete frequency f_k an amplitude a_k of the corresponding sinusoidal component. These amplitudes a_k are calculated using the following formula:

$$a_k = \frac{1}{N} \sum_{i=0}^{N-1} x[i] e^{-j\frac{2\pi k i}{N}} \qquad (5.5)$$

Fig. 5.4 The frequency spectrum plot for a periodic signal

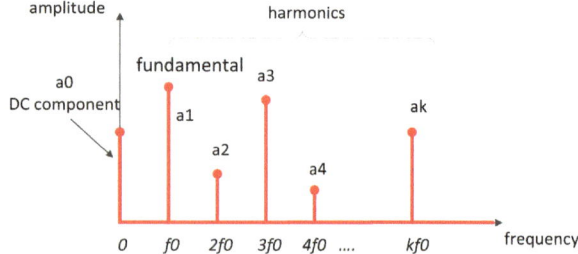

Note. You do not have to understand or remember this formula. All we want to show here is that there *is* a formula to calculate a_k that depends on the values of the digital signal.

The Fourier analysis of digital signals is realized in practice by using the discrete *Fourier transform (DFT)*, an algorithm to transform a time-domain representation of a digital signal into a frequency-domain one. For us, this algorithm is very helpful, because it can calculate the frequency components within a time series of data. The *fast Fourier transform (FFT)* is as the name suggests a widely used, fast, and efficient algorithm for the DFT. All signal processing software packages, MATLAB(R) included, implement the FFT algorithm in a built-in function.

You should be aware that FFT is very similar to nuclear power—although powerful, it should be used with care. Experience shows that it is dangerous to blindly apply a FFT function, without a very good understanding of what it really does. Therefore, let us take a step back and explain thoroughly the ins and outs of this seductive function.

The FFT function can be imagined as a black box, with two inputs: a vector containing the digitized signal samples, denoted by $x[n]$, and the number of samples, N, as illustrated in Fig. 5.5.

The output produced by the FFT function is also a vector. This FFT vector contains *some* amplitudes denoted by a_k, where k is an integer running from 0 to N. But whose

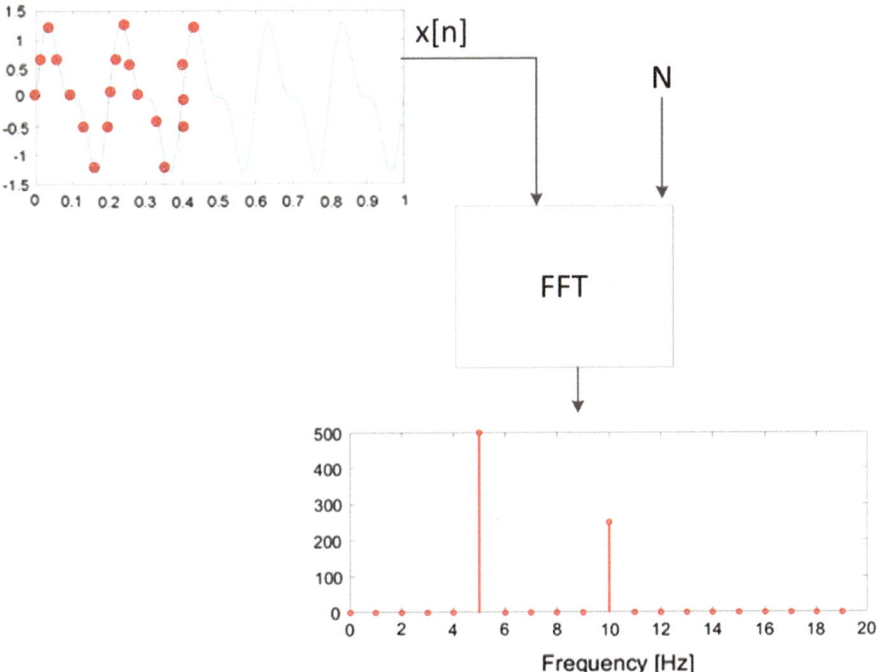

Fig. 5.5 This is how the fast Fourier transform (FFT) works

Fig. 5.6 The vector returned
by the FFT function

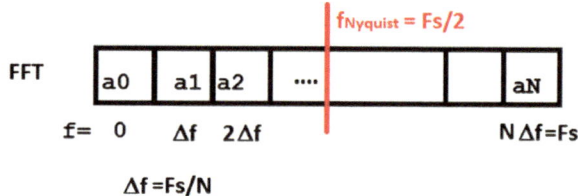

$$\Delta f = Fs/N$$

are these amplitudes? This is the key question. If you understand this part, then you tamed the "beast".

Let us explain the architecture of this FFT output vector, without getting in too many mathematical details. See Fig. 5.6. The length of this vector is $N + 1$. Each element a_k corresponds to a certain frequency f_k that goes from 0 to F_s (Hz), where F_s is the frequency used to sample the input signal x. Knowing this, we can calculate the frequency step between two neighbor elements in the FFT vector, with:

$$\Delta f = \frac{F_s}{N} \tag{5.6}$$

This frequency grain size is also the distance between two stems in the frequency spectrum plot. The frequency corresponding to each amplitude a_k in the FFT output vector can be calculated as follows:

$$f_k = k\Delta f = \frac{kF_s}{N} \tag{5.7}$$

For example, the first element in the FFT output vector, with the index $k = 0$, is the amplitude of the DC component a0, with the frequency $f = 0$; the second element is a_1, the amplitude of the component with the frequency $f_1 = \Delta f$; the third element is a_2, the amplitude of the component with the frequency $f_2 = 2\Delta f$; and so on.

According to the Shannon sampling theorem, only the first half of the FFT vector can be used. The second half of the spectrum is a mirror copy of the first, because the maximal frequency that can be extracted with FFT is the Nyquist frequency $= F_s/2$. This means that the last useful amplitude returned by FFT is corresponding to the frequency $f_{N/2} = N/2 \ \Delta f$.

For example, for a signal sampled with the frequency $F_s = 8000$ Hz, the highest useful frequency identified by the Fourier analysis will be $8000/2 = 4000$ Hz. If we perform FFT on $N = 1000$ samples, then the frequency grain size will be $F_s/N = 8$ Hz. This is the reason why it is more convenient to choose an even number of samples, N. Moreover, the FFT algorithm works most efficiently if N is a power of 2. Typically, N is selected between 32 and 4096.

Now, we know how to interpret the vector produced by the FFT function. Normally, we do not have to plot it all. Depending on the application, we can zoom in and show only a particular frequency interval. For example, suppose we sampled a 440 Hz tuning fork signal with $F_s = 8000$ Hz. In this case, FFT will return the spectrum from 0 to 4000 Hz. However, we are interested only in visualizing the frequency interval of say [0, 800 Hz].

Enough with the theory. We want to show now some examples to demonstrate the power of FFT. Let us apply FFT to a "nice" segment of the 440 Hz tuning fork sound. Try to first sketch its frequency spectrum. Compare it now with the frequency spectrum shown in Fig. 5.7. Hopefully, they look alike. Can you see a peak around the frequency of 440 Hz? This peak belongs to the only sinusoidal component of the signal. In our example, there is also a DC component, corresponding

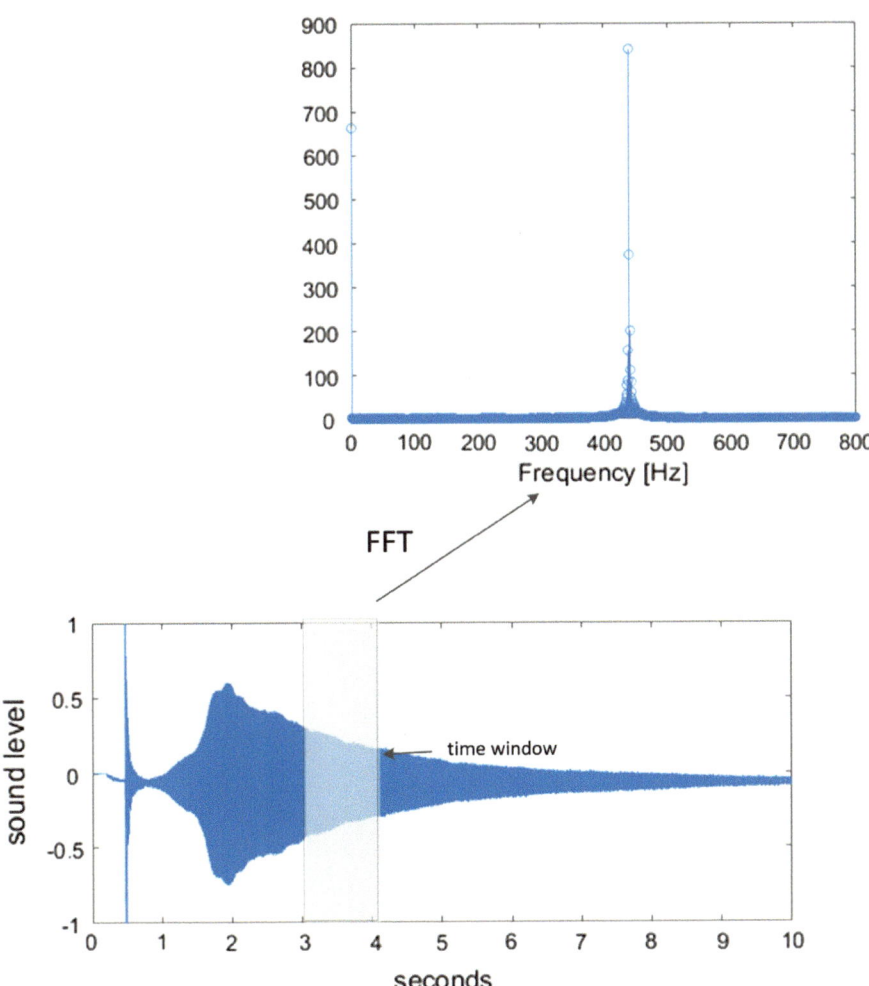

Fig. 5.7 The tuning fork signal in time domain to the *left* and its frequency spectrum calculated using FFT, to the *right*. A peak around 440 Hz can be clearly observed

to frequency $f = 0$, because as you can see, there is a small offset in the signal. Other frequencies are not present in the spectrum, and therefore, their amplitudes in the spectrum plot are equal to zero.

So far so good. You can say, "OK, but this is a simple case we've already solved in Chap. 2".

Let us try the trick with a more general example of a non-sinusoidal, periodic signal. The best way to test FFT is to fabricate our own signal. Let us prepare a signal by adding two sinusoidal signals, with frequencies of 5 and 10 Hz, respectively, as shown individually in Fig. 5.8. To make things even more complex, we take the amplitude of the 5 Hz signal to be two times higher than the amplitude of the 10 Hz signal. The resulted compound signal is shown in Fig. 5.9. Notice that the fundamental frequency of the sum signal is the greatest common divider of the two frequencies, equal to 5 Hz.

If FFT really works, then we should be able to read out the individual components from its frequency spectrum, right? Let us give it a go. We apply FFT, and we show the resulted frequency spectrum in Fig. 5.10. We distinguish on it exactly as expected, two stems: one at the frequency of 5 Hz and another one at the frequency of 10 Hz, the latter having a two times smaller amplitude. Quod Erat Demonstrandum.

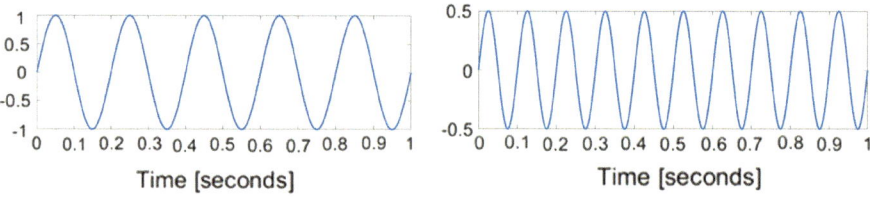

Fig. 5.8 The sinusoidal components of the signal from Fig. 5.9 ($f = 5$ Hz to the *left*, $f = 10$ Hz to the *right*)

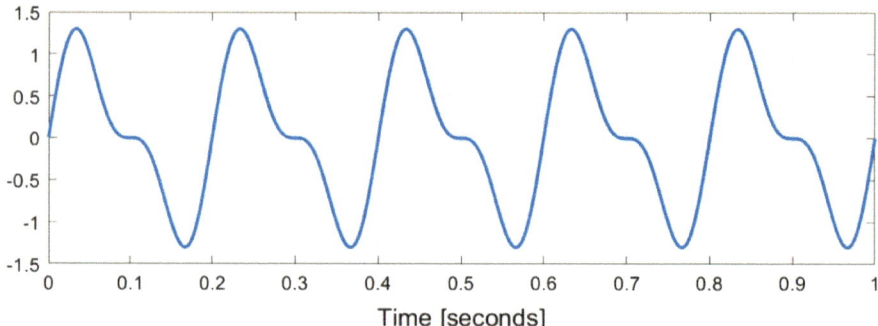

Fig. 5.9 This signal is a sum of two sinusoidal signals of 5 Hz and 10 Hz, respectively

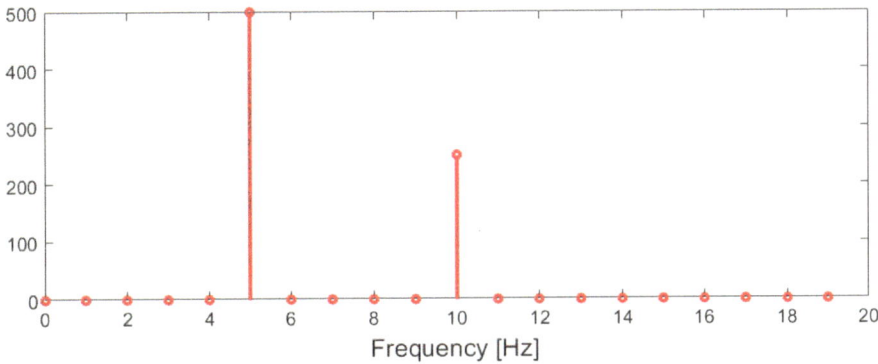

Fig. 5.10 The frequency spectrum of the compound signal from Fig. 5.9

5.3   The Frequency Spectrum of a Non-periodic Signal

For a brief moment, it seemed that we have finally might solved the frequency spectrum problem. However, it is (again!) too early to celebrate. The bad news is that most real-life signals are not periodic. They are continuously changing in time, and the same does their frequency spectrum. We say that the signals are *not stationary*. Of course, nobody can stop us to apply FFT to these signals, but the result will not have much sense, because the spectrum will be continuous, containing almost all frequencies, since there are no harmonics. It seems again like a dead end.

Fortunately, there is an escape also from this situation. What we have to do is to cut the signal in short time chunks, called *windows* or *frames*. If during these short time windows, the signal can be considered reasonably stationary, and almost periodic, as illustrated in Fig. 5.11, then there is again hope. Because then it makes sense to apply the FFT theory, as we did in detail in Sect. 5.2.

This splitting of the signal in time chunks is called *segmentation* or *windowing*. The problem with windowing is that by cutting a signal in time frames, certain features might be lost, because a part of the signal might belong to one segment and the other part to the next one. The solution is to overlap successive frames, as shown in Fig. 5.12.

Usually, for speech processing, windows of 20–30 ms are taken, with an overlap of 10 ms (50%).

Fig. 5.11 A short segment of orchestra music plotted in time domain. From [1]. Used with permission

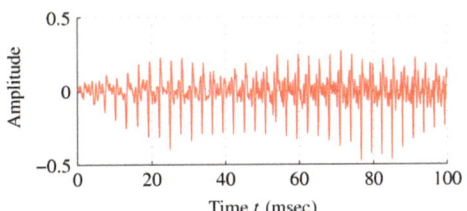

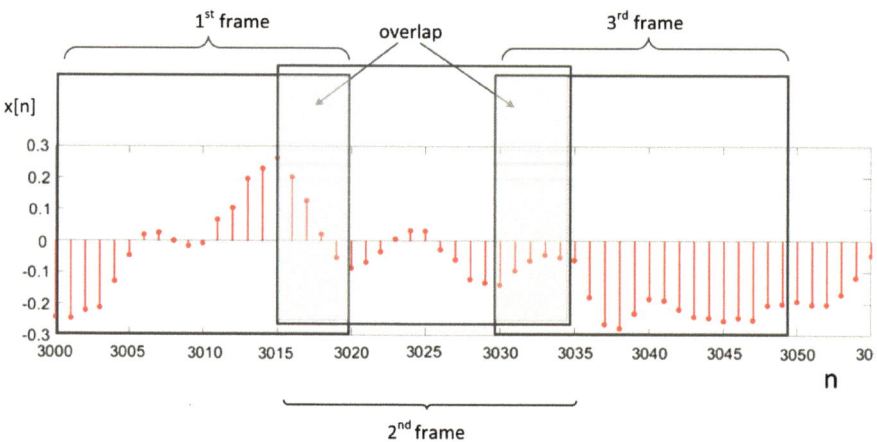

Fig. 5.12 Overlapping time windows. Three successive frames, each of length $N = 20$ samples. The overlap between successive frames is 5 samples. Adapted from [2] with permission

If the sound is periodic in each time window, then we can compute the frequency spectrum for that window, called the *short-time Fourier transform (STFT)*. Figure 5.13 shows a short segment from the time wave of the vowel "a" as in "father." Figure 5.14 shows its corresponding SFTF. Although the fundamental frequency is 100 Hz, only the harmonics nr. 2, 4, 5, 16, and 17 are present.

If we consider the next time frame, calculate its STFT, and repeat this process while displaying the spectra against time on one and the same plot, we will eventually obtain a so-called *spectrogram*. A spectrogram is a visual rendering of the signal's frequency spectrum as a function of time. It is basically a set of short-time Fourier transforms, plotted in parallel. The resulted spectrogram is a 3D plot, with frequency on y-axis, time on x-axis, and amplitude on z-axis, given by the color of the pixel. Spectrograms can be grayscale or RGB color images. In grayscale spectrograms, louder sound components are shown in a darker shade of gray, whereas lower amplitudes are shown in a lighter shade. In color spectrograms, the colors represent the most important acoustic peaks for a given time frame, with red representing the highest energies, then in decreasing order orange, yellow, green, cyan, blue, and magenta. Spectrograms are excellent instruments to visualize and interpret speech, noise, and music. Figures 5.15 and 5.16 illustrate examples of spectrograms.

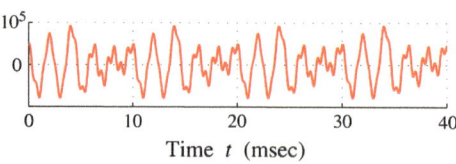

Fig. 5.13 A short segment of a spoken vowel "a" as in "father," plotted in time domain. From [1]. Used with permission

Fig. 5.14 The short-time frequency spectrum (STFT) of the vowel "a" as in "father." From [1]. Used with permission

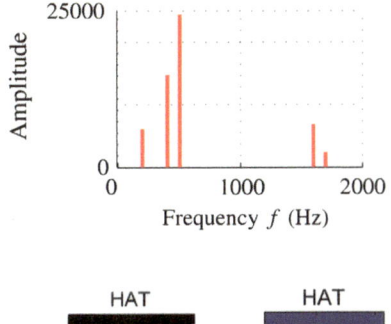

Fig. 5.15 The spectrogram of the word "hat" in gray level and colour. Frequency is on the y-axis, and time in milliseconds is on the x-axis. From [3]. Used with permission

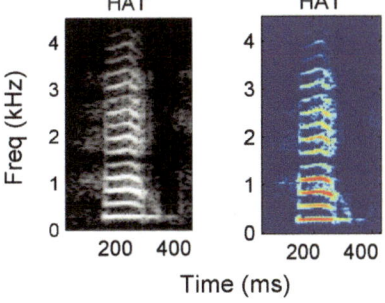

Fig. 5.16 The spectrogram of a C major scale. Each note is played for 0.2 s. From [1]. Used with permission

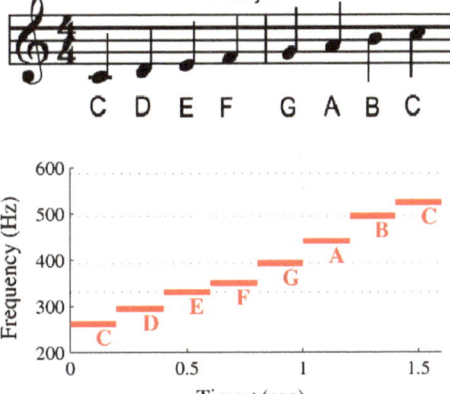

5.4 Dealing with Noise

5.4.1 Digital Filters

For many reasons, a digital sound recording is a mix of wanted and unwanted signals. All these unwanted signals that contaminate the useful signal fall in the category *noise*. A *filter*, in general, is a system designed to maximize the useful signal, while removing the noise. Filters can be *analog*, implemented in hardware

Fig. 5.17 The principle of
digital filtering for
one-dimensional signals

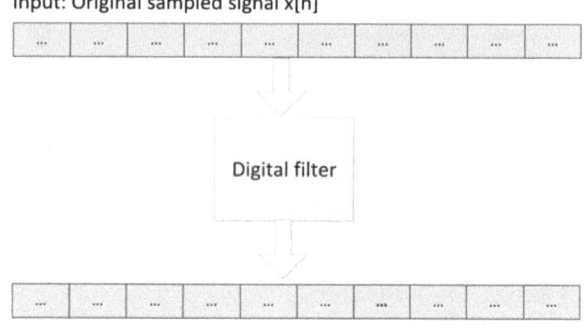

Input: Original sampled signal x[n]

Digital filter

Output: filtered signal y[n]

using electronic components, such as capacitors and resistors, or *digital*, implemented in software running on a digital processor. This processor can be an ordinary microprocessor or a specialized chip, called DSP (digital signal processor).

The principle of a *digital filter* is illustrated in Fig. 5.17. A digital filter can be seen as a black box that accepts at its input a digitized signal, denoted by a vector $x[n]$, and alters it, eventually producing at its output a new, filtered, "clean" signal, denoted by a vector $y[n]$.

Filters come in two flavors: *finite impulse response* (*FIR*) and *infinite impulse response* (*IIR*), or recursive filters. In FIR filters, each output sample is the sum of a finite number of weighted input samples. In IIR filters, each output value is calculated by involving, besides input values, also previously computed values of output signal. Because the output is fed back to be combined with the input, these systems are examples of feedback systems. In this section, we will present a few ideas commonly used for filtering one-dimensional digital signals, such as sound, acceleration, temperature, and bio-signals.

5.4.2 Filtering in Time Domain

Have you ever repeatedly measured the temperature in a room using a digital thermometer? If you did, you probably noticed that even if nothing has changed during recordings, each time you read a value, you got a slightly different result. This is the effect of *random* or white noise, manifested by small fluctuations in the measured signal values. A very simple way to eliminate this random noise is to *average* a few consecutive measurements in time domain. This is the principle of a *moving (or running) average* filter. The approach works surprisingly well, based on the assumption that if we measure many times the same quantity, the useful signal will tend to accumulate, whereas the noise, being random, will tend to cancel itself.

The moving average filter calculates each point in the output signal, $y[i]$, by averaging M consecutive input samples, according to the formula:

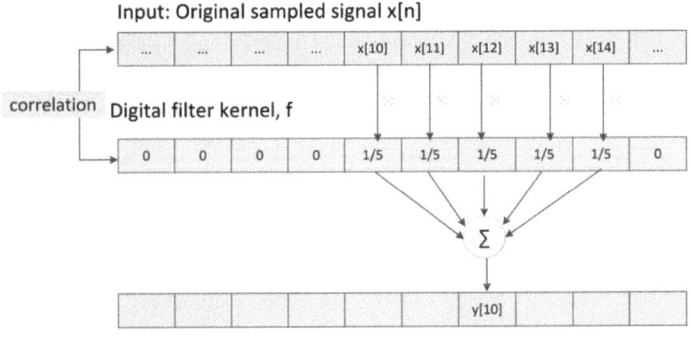

Fig. 5.18 The principle of a moving average filter for $M = 5$

$$y[i] = \frac{1}{M} \sum_{j=0}^{M-1} x[i+j] \qquad (5.9)$$

Figure 5.18 illustrates the principle of the moving average filter for $M = 5$.

For example, in a 5-point moving average filter ($M = 5$), sample #10 in the output vector will be calculated as follows:

$$y[10] = \frac{1}{5} (x[10] + x[11] + x[12] + x[13] + x[14]) \qquad (5.10)$$

The moving average filter is an example of FIR filter. The output vector is calculated as the convolution between the input sampled vector $x[n]$ and a kernel filter vector $f[n]$, with the same length as x, filled with zeros, except for M positions starting from index i. Can you see the similarity with image filtering, explained in Chap. 4?

The parameter in this method is M, the number of measurements in the average, called *history length*. The level of noise reduction is equal to the square root of this number [5]. For example, a 100-point moving average filter reduces the noise by a factor of 10. Intuition would say that the higher the M, the better the filtering effect. However, as M increases, the noise becomes lower, but the signal starts to get deformed. This means that when selecting the history length M, a compromise must be found that takes into consideration the frequency of the signal, the application needs, the memory capacity, the computation time, etc.

5.4.3 Filtering in Frequency Domain

The previously discussed moving average filter is the best solution in removing random, unpredictable noise. However, in some cases, with a little bit of luck, we do have a priori information about the noise. For example, when we record a speech signal in a kitchen, and the microphone is located very close to a fridge, we can expect that the "ubiquitous" noise called power hum will contaminate our recording. Our a priori knowledge about this power hum, or *power line interference* (*PIL*), is that its frequency is 50 Hz in Europe and Asia and 60 Hz in North America. Another example is the fetal electrocardiography (ECG) recording of the heart activity of a baby still swimming in its mother's womb. The a priori knowledge here is that the baby heart activity signal is buried in all kinds of noise, such as line power interference, but also muscle contraction and respiration noise and, of course, the mother's ECG [4]. The adult heartbeat frequency is ca 70 beats per minute, meaning 1.25 Hz.

This knowledge about noise allows us to do more than just averaging. Because we know exactly which frequencies have to be eliminated, it is wiser to filter the signal in the frequency domain. A *frequency-selective filter* behaves like a gate-keeper, allowing only selected frequencies, while blocking the rest. It works as follows.

First, the input signal in time domain is transformed into the frequency domain, by using the fast Fourier transform (FFT). A filter's frequency-selective behavior is specified by its *frequency response*, a function that can be visualized in a plot, with frequency on *x*-axis and amplitudes on *y*-axis. Figure 5.19 shows some examples of frequency response plots. In these graphs, we can distinguish the following characteristics of a filter: the *passband* that refers to those frequencies that are passed, the *stopband* that specifies those frequencies that are blocked, and the *transition band*, that lays in between. The division between the passband and transition band is called the *cutoff frequency*.

Second, the input signal's frequency spectrum is multiplied by the filter's frequency response function, having as result that some frequencies will be eliminated. Note that convolution in time domain corresponds to multiplication in frequency domain. Figure 5.19 illustrates the behavior of four types of commonly used filters: The *low-pass* filter that suppresses the high frequencies of the input, while leaving the rest unchanged; the *band-pass* filter that lets only a range of frequencies

Fig. 5.19 Frequency responses for four common frequency-selective filters. Adapted from [5]

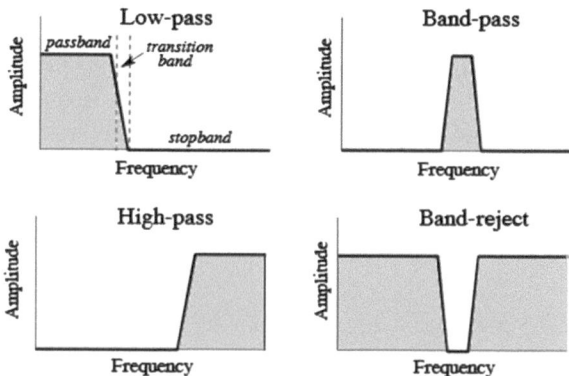

unchanged, while eliminating the extreme low and extreme high frequencies; the *high-pass filter* that lets only high frequencies through; and finally, the *band-reject* filter that blocks a range of frequencies and lets the rest to pass unchanged. A *notch* filter is essentially a very narrow band-reject filter that attenuates several singular frequencies while preserving the rest.

Finally, the resulted spectrum is transformed back into the time domain, using an operation similar to FFT, called *inverse Fast fourier transform (IFFT)*. This time, the new output signal is cleaner, and the noise is filtered.

Can you already say which type of filter can eliminate the 50/60 Hz power line interference? An idea is to use a very narrow band-reject notch filter, with a stopband centered at 50 Hz, of say [48.5–51.5 Hz]. Figure 5.20 illustrates filtering the power line interference in an ECG signal using such an approach [6]. This is, however, not always an ideal solution. The notch filter approach suffers from "throwing the baby out with the bathwater" effect, because it might happen that also a useful ECG component of around 50 Hz will also get eliminated.

As you can see, noise canceling in frequency domain is not easy. Although many types of filters exist, their mathematics is rather complex. Therefore, we will not get

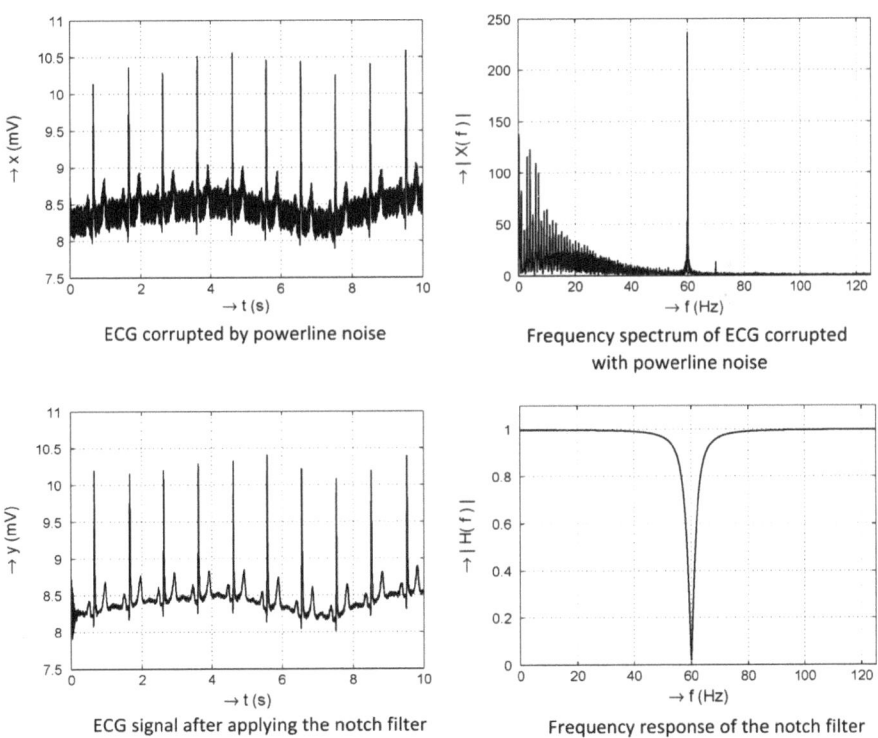

Fig. 5.20 An electrocardiogram (ECG) bio-signal corrupted by the 60 Hz power line interference noise (*top* to the *left*) and the result of its filtering in frequency domain, using a 60 Hz notch filter (*bottom left*). From [7]. Used with permission

into the details of frequency-selective filter design. This is also not necessary, as nowadays built-in functions exist in all digital signal processing (DSP) packages, including MATLAB. All these functions need to know is the type of filter and its frequency response. Only one line of code is needed to apply the filter and obtain a "clean" signal. When you need to filter in frequency domain, you should use all the a priori knowledge you can get about the noise and try to apply different types of frequency-selective filters, to see which one performs the best.

5.5   Conclusions

- Information can be coded in the frequency of a one-dimensional signal.
- Normally, a one-dimensional signal does not have one single frequency, but a spectrum of frequencies. Information about this frequency composition can be gained by using a mathematical technique, called Fourier analysis.
- Fourier analysis can decompose any signal in a sum of sinusoidal signals, having different frequencies and amplitudes. The amplitudes are called Fourier coefficients and can be calculated using the Fourier transform. FFT is a fast algorithm to realize this in practice. The results of a Fourier analysis are plotted in a frequency spectrum plot.
- If the frequency spectrum varies in time, like in the case of human speech, the signal must be processed in time chunks, called windows or frames. If during these windows, the signal can be considered quasi-periodic, then FFT can be again applied. The results can be plotted in a spectrogram.
- Digital filtering of noise in sound recordings can be done by averaging in time domain, or by frequency-selective filtering in frequency domain.

5.6   Exercises

1. What is a frequency spectrum plot and how can we obtain it?
2. Draw a sketch of the frequency spectrum for:

   a. A sinusoidal signal with the frequency of 20 Hz.
   b. A sum of a sine wave of 20 Hz and a sine wave of 60 Hz, the first with a three times larger amplitude.

3. What is FFT? Sketch the FFT algorithm as a black box and identify its inputs and outputs.
4. FFT is applied on a digital signal with 1000 samples using a sampling frequency $F_s = 8000$ Hz. Describe the vector returned by FFT. What is its length? How many elements can we really use? What is the role of the first element? the last element? How large is the frequency step between two sequential elements?

5. What does windowing mean and why do we need it?
6. A 20 kHz speech wave represented with 16-bit samples is windowed with frames of 20 ms. The frame overlapping period is 50% of the frame size. How many bytes (chunks of 8 bits) are needed to store a 10-s-long speech wave?
7. If a sound waveform is sampled with $F_s = 8000$ Hz and we perform FFT for $N = 1000$ samples, how many FFT coefficients do we have to plot in order to clearly visualize the range [0–800 Hz] in the frequency spectrum plot?
8. What is a spectrogram? How can we plot it? Sketch a spectrogram of a 0.1-s-long 100 Hz periodic signal.
9. Explain how moving average filter works. Compute the output $y[n]$ of a 3-point moving average filter for the following input $x[n]$:

n	$n < 0$	0	1	2	3	4	5	6	7
$x[n]$	0	2	4	6	4	2	0	0	0

10. Sketch the frequency response graphs for the most common types of frequency-selective filters.

References

1. McClellan, J., Schafer, R.W., Yoder, M.A.: *Signal Processing First* (2003)
2. Theodoridis, S., Koutroumbas, K.: *Pattern Recognition* (2008)
3. Schnupp, J., Nelken, I., King, A.J.: *Auditory Neuroscience*. MIT Press (2010)
4. Maartens, S.M.M., et al.: A robust fetal ECG detection method for abdominal recordings. Physiol. Meas. **28**(4), 373 (2007)
5. Smith, S.W.: *The Scientist and Engineer's Guide to Digital Signal Processing* (1997). Available from: http://www.dspguide.com
6. Ondracek, O., Pucik, J., Cocherova, E.: Filters for ECG digital signal processing, in Trends in Biomedical Engineering. University of Zilina, Slovak Republic (2005)
7. Kasteren, T.L., et al.: An activity monitoring system for elderly care using generative and discriminative models. Personal Ubiquitous Comput. **14**(6), 489–498 (2010)

Chapter 6
Classification

> *For a few moments, Henry allowed his mind to dwell upon the marvelous things he would be able to do if he could read cards from the back. He would win every single time at canasta, and bridge and poker. [...] But could he do it? Could he actually train himself to do this thing?*
> Roald Dahl, The Wonderful Story of Henry Sugar

When set off for this journey, we promised to reveal the mysteries of pervasive computing systems that infer their context through pattern recognition, be it self-driving cars, voice-controlled wheelchairs, or smart homes. By now you should understand a lot about these systems; how they sense signals from environment, how they decipher simple information from these signals, and how they send control commands to affect back the environment. However, extracting a sensible context still remains a mystery; even the most accurate sound frequency spectrum cannot tell much about which words have been uttered, or by whom; and even the clearest image of the street scenery will not make a car understand that the approaching obstacle *is* a pedestrian. In case you start worrying about all this reading being in vain, please do not lose heart. We are almost there, yet we owe you one more story; this time, about pattern recognition, the last missing piece in the puzzle. Actually, all the previous chapters were preparation for this "big push."

Recognition of patterns in data happens mostly through *classification*, a process of organizing things into groups or *classes*. Pattern recognition answers questions, such as "Was the spoken command *Right*, *Left*, or *Stop*?" or "Is the detected obstacle in this image *a pedestrian,* or some *other object*?". While for us, humans, pattern recognition is a trivial, ubiquitous task, computers find it extremely difficult. Machine learning algorithms are needed to empower computers with pattern recognition skills. Be aware that there is no single silver bullet algorithm that can solve all classification problems. The challenge is to find—for each particular case—the most realistic and acceptable solution. This is why this substantial chapter will expose you to various ideas of how to approach classification in general, and image and sound recognition in particular.

© Springer International Publishing AG 2017
N. Silvis-Cividjian, *Pervasive Computing*, Undergraduate Topics
in Computer Science, DOI 10.1007/978-3-319-51655-4_6

6.1 The Classification Problem

The data sensed in Chap. 2 has worked its way through the pervasive computing system; it had been already digitized, filtered, and is now waiting to be classified. Pattern recognition and classification, in particular, is something we do on daily basis before taking a decision—before we chose a menu, a school, a partner, or a route in a new city. Take a look at the picture in Fig. 6.1.

Even a child could easily say that we are looking at some old steam locomotives. This is because the human brain recognizes the *pattern* of a steam engine in these objects—seen probably many times before, labeled as such, and imprinted somewhere in memory. A pattern is some kind of regularity in data, described by a set of features. Perhaps the most characteristic feature of a steam locomotive is that it has a chimney. Based on these features, the child knows how to *classify* the objects he is seeing, into two classes: steam engines and something else, different from steam engines. Computers, however, are more naïve and inexperienced and cannot perform this task as easily as we, humans, do. Software must tell them what to do. This chapter is an attempt to teach computers how to classify.

Mathematically, the classification problem can be stated as follows. Given we have N disjoint *classes*, and a certain test object, a classification system has to decide which of these N classes this new object belongs to. Let us illustrate this problem

Fig. 6.1 View from a railway museum

with an example [1]. Suppose that we want to design a system that can classify the five currently used New Zealand (NZ) coins (see Fig. 6.2). When the classification system receives a coin as input, it should identify the class it belongs to.

Let us try to atomize the operations we, as humans, perform, in order to recognize a certain coin. First, we identify the classes playing a role in this case. We come up with five classes: 10c, 20c, 50c, $1, and $2. The next step is to select some measurable quantities, called *features*, that can help us to reliably distinguish between two different coin classes. This property, which a feature can have or not, is called *discriminatory power*. We know that the coins are round and are made of different metals. Their parameters are summarized in Fig. 6.3.

Choosing only the color, given by the Composition column in Fig. 6.3 as a feature, will help to distinguish between 10c and 20c coins, but not between 20c and 50c coins. We say that this feature does not have sufficient discriminatory power. The solution is to add new features, keeping in mind that we need to achieve a compromise: not too many features, because this means higher computational needs (the "curse of dimensionality"), and not too few, because then we cannot correctly distinguish between all the coins. We will show that adding the diameter as a second feature allows us to successfully solve the coin classification problem.

The set of all features form the *feature vector* that can be represented graphically in a scattered plot, called *feature space*, as shown in Fig. 6.4. If the classes create clusters (regions distinct from each other), in this feature space, that are situated far from each other, then one can be sure that the right features have been selected. If the classes are close to each other, or even overlap, then the selected features are useless. In Fig. 6.4, we see that the classes can be separated quite well, meaning that color and diameter are the right features for this particular classification problem.

| | 10c | 20c | 50c | $1 | $2 |

Fig. 6.2 The NZ coins that have to be classified. From [2]

Fig. 6.3 Some information about the NZ coins. From [2]

Value	Technical Parameters			
	Diameter	Thickness	Mass	Composition
10c	20.50 mm	1.58 mm	3.30 g	Copper-plated steel
20c	21.75 mm	1.56 mm	4.00 g	Nickel-plated steel
50c	24.75 mm	1.70 mm	5.00 g	
$1	23.00 mm	2.74 mm	8 g	Aluminium bronze
$2	26.50 mm	2.70 mm	10 g	

Fig. 6.4 The five coin classes, plotted in the 2D feature space created by their color and diameter

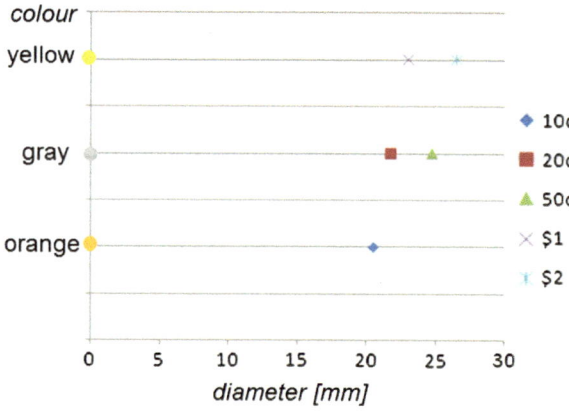

Fig. 6.5 The block diagram of a classifier

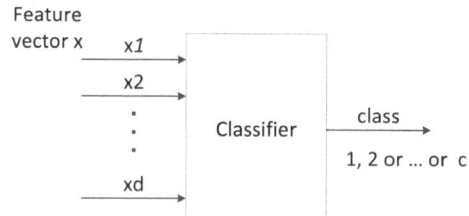

In the more general case, the input in a classifier is a feature vector, with d features, x_i, where $i = 1, 2, \ldots, d$. Each feature vector identifies uniquely a single pattern (class). The classifier has to decide to which class a newcomer belongs to, based on its feature vector, as shown in Fig. 6.5. Basically, the classifier's role is to divide the feature space into regions that correspond to each class. We have no guarantee that the decision is always correct. If the decision is not correct, then we say that a *misclassification* occurred.

The simplest classifier that can be imagined is the *rule-based* classifier. This type of classifier works based on a set of simple conditional if-then rules, to separate between classes. For our coin example, the rules could be as follows:

> IF (colour is Copper) and (diameter is 20.50 mm) THEN class is 10c
> IF (colour is Nickel) and (diameter is 21.75 mm) THEN class is 20c
> and so on…

This approach will work fine for two or three features, but if the number of features grows, then a rule-based classifier is no longer efficient. Other classifiers have to be investigated, and a suitable domain where we can search for solutions is the machine learning domain.

Machine learning is the science of making computers modify and adapt their actions so that the actions become more accurate. The accuracy is measured by how well the chosen actions reflect the correct ones. Learning is defined as getting better at some task through practice. Machine learning algorithms implement different types of learning, such as supervised, unsupervised, reinforced, and evolutionary.

Supervised classification relies on having a set of examples (feature vectors) whose true class is known. The outputs, called *targets*, are also known. It is like having a teacher to train us by showing examples. These examples are called *training patterns* (training feature vectors). Based on this training set, the algorithm generalizes to respond correctly to all possible inputs. Template matching, decision trees, neural networks, and naïve Bayes are some commonly used supervised classifiers that will be discussed later in this chapter.

By contrast, *unsupervised* classification does not rely on possession of examples from a known class. The system does not have a teacher with correct answers. Instead, it tries to identify similarities between the inputs, so that inputs that have something in common are categorized together. Clustering techniques are examples of unsupervised classification.

In conclusion, a pervasive computing system that uses classification to determine its context consists of the following components: a sensing module, a preprocessing mechanism, a feature extraction mechanism, a classifier, and if the classifier uses supervised learning, a set of already classified examples (training set). Finally, an evaluation of the classification must take place. Therefore, the steps necessary to build a supervised learning classification system are:

- Sense data from the environment.
- Preprocess sensor data.
- Explore data. Define the classes.
- Identify possible attributes (features) which will allow discrimination between classes. They should be compact and have discriminatory power.
- Process data to extract these features.
- Design a classifier and train it. For each training example, provide at least one feature vector.
- Evaluate the classifier. The classifier should be assessed to see how well it can generalize to new examples.

The basic stages in designing a classification system are shown in Fig. 6.6. Although a lot of steps can be performed automatically, human experts are still essential to specify which classes we have to consider, which features to use and to train the classifier for supervised classification.

Fig. 6.6 The basic stages involved in the design of a classification system

6.2 Typical Features for Image Classification

Image recognition is widely used in pervasive computing systems; for example, in autonomous cars, to recognize traffic lights or pedestrians on the road; in forensic applications to recognize people's faces; in smart homes to recognize user's mood and emotions; in medical imaging systems, to recognize and localize certain organs and tumors; in *optical character recognition (OCR)* systems (Fig. 6.7), for automatic license plate recognition or text-to-speech assistants for blind people; and in banks, for signature verification and identification of customers.

In this section, we will describe some typical features, commonly used for image pattern recognition. It is good to say from the beginning that we cannot prescribe a perfect, universal set of features. The idea is to show you different approaches, with their advantages and disadvantages.

6.2.1 Single-Parameter Shape Descriptors

In some cases, one can be lucky and be able to fairly discriminate between objects in an image, only based on their geometric shape characteristics, such as perimeter, area, form factor, roundness ratio, and Euler number. For example, for a convex shape, the *form factor* is defined as follows:

$$f = \frac{4\pi A}{P^2} \tag{6.1}$$

where A is the shape's area and P is its perimeter. This feature works well if one has to distinguish between round and elongated objects, such as coins, apples, buttons versus needles, drills, pens, cucumbers, because a circular object happens to have a form factor close to one, whereas any non-circular object has a smaller form factor.

Fig. 6.7 An OCR system

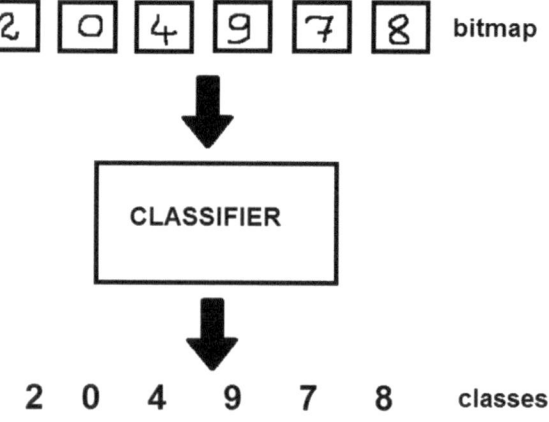

Another useful shape feature is the *Euler number*, defined as the total number of objects in the image, minus the total number of holes. A negative Euler number indicates that the number of holes is greater than the number of objects. For example, for an image containing only the character "0", the Euler number is 0, whereas for an image containing only the character "1", the Euler number is 1. This means that the Euler number alone can be used to distinguish between some digits, but not all of them. In many cases, two of such shape features are needed. For example, if we have a key, some small and large coins, and a screw, as shown in Fig. 6.8, then one can separate them pretty well by selecting two features: their form factor and their relative area. The five objects cluster nicely in four different regions in the feature space, meaning that the choice of these two features is adequate.

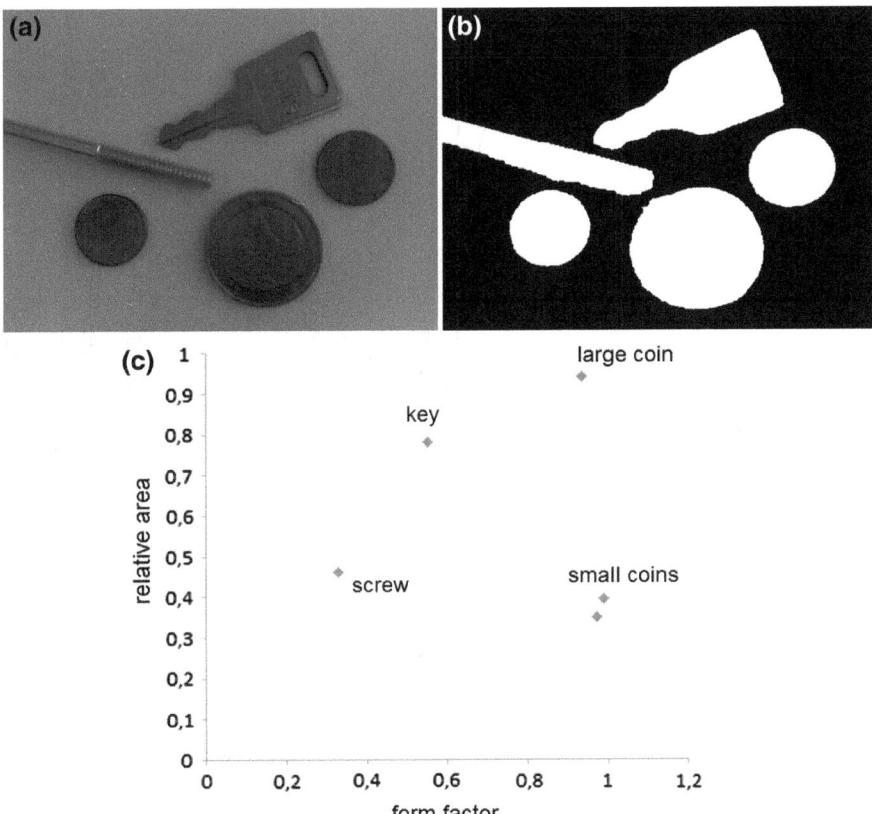

Fig. 6.8 a *To the left*, the original RGB image showing large and small coins, a key, and a screw. **b** *To the right*, the same image, converted to a binary format and processed so that the BLOBS can be clearly identified. **c** The objects from Fig. 6.8a plotted in their 2D features space. One can distinguish four classes (key, screw, large coin, and small coin)

6.2.2 Statistical Image Moments

In other situations, single geometric descriptors as described earlier are not sufficient to obtain a good classification. In this case, *statistical moments* might help. The concept of statistical moments comes from probability theory, where they describe the shape of a probability density function that in its turn describes the distribution of a random variable x. Examples of statistical moments are the 0th moment, which describes the area under the curve (AUC); the 2nd central moment, called *variance*, which shows how spread out the curve is; the 3rd central moment, or *skewness*, which is the tendency of the curve to shoot further on one side of the mean than the other, a measure of the degree of asymmetry of a distribution. If the left tail is more pronounced than the right tail, then the function is said to have a negative skewness. If the reverse is true, it has positive skewness. If the two are equal, it has zero skewness. The 4th central moment is called *kurtosis* and is defined as the degree of peakedness of a distribution.

In image processing, the image intensity function $I(x, y)$ can be viewed as a probability density function of two variables, defined as the likelihood of a particular intensity of a pixel at location (x, y). Therefore, statistical moments can be calculated for an image as well. In the case of a binary image with one object of interest, or BLOB denoted by C in Fig. 6.9, the image intensity can only take two values 0 and 1, given by:

$$I(i,j) = \begin{cases} 1 & (i,j) \in C \\ 0 & \text{otherwise} \end{cases} \tag{6.2}$$

where 1 means black (the BLOB), and 0 means white (the background).

For a binary image, an *image statistical (or geometric) moment M_{pq}* of order $p + q$, is defined as follows:

$$M_{pq} = \sum_i \sum_j i^p j^q, \quad (i,j) \in C \tag{6.3}$$

These moments directly describe the shape of the BLOB. For example, for the binary image with only one BLOB shown in Fig. 6.9, the 0th moment, M_{00}, gives the area of that BLOB, equal to the total number of pixels. The center of mass, or centroid of a physical object, is defined as the location on the object where you

Fig. 6.9 An image with only one object BLOB of interest, denoted with C

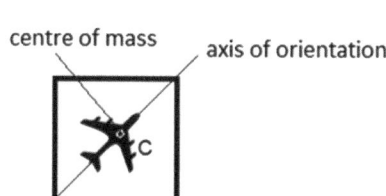

centre of mass

axis of orientation

should place your finger to balance the object. For a binary image, the coordinates $\{x, y\}$ of its center of mass are given by M_{10}/M_{00}, and M_{01}/M_{00}, respectively, where M_{10} and M_{01} are two first-order moments of the object. The second-order moments give the axes of orientation, etc.

Any of these geometric moments can be used as features for BLOBs classification, as long as they can distinguish well between different classes of objects.

However, geometric moments have the disadvantage that they work fine only when the training patterns and the newcomer are of same size and orientation, which is unfortunately not always the case. For example, the input in a handwritten OCR could be letters written by different people, with different sizes and orientation. In this case, other, better features are needed for character classification.

Luckily, these better solutions exist. The *seven invariant moments of Hu*, firstly introduced to the pattern recognition community in 1962, can be used to describe an object shape, regardless of its scaling, translation, or rotation [3]. For example, the first two invariant moments of Hu, denoted by ϕ_1 and ϕ_2, are defined by

$$\begin{aligned} \phi_1 &= \eta_{20} + \eta_{02} \\ \phi_2 &= (\eta_{20} - \eta_{02})^2 + 4\eta_{11}^2 \end{aligned} \tag{6.4}$$

where η_{pq} are the normalized central moments:

$$\eta_{pq} = \frac{M_{pq}}{M_{00}^\beta} \quad \text{where } \beta = \frac{p+q}{2} + 1 \text{ and } p+q \geq 2$$

Note: You do not have to understand or remember these formulas. We only want to show that such formulas exist.

We can see in Fig. 6.10 that even when a symbol is rotated, scaled, or translated, its seven Hu invariant moments barely change. Therefore, these moments are very suitable features for character recognition, for the complex cases when size, positioning and orientation may vary. Third-party MATLAB(R) libraries are available that calculate the invariant moments of Hu.

6.2.3   Zoning

Zoning, illustrated in Fig. 6.11, offers a simple alternative to extract features from the binary image containing an object of interest, for example, a character. Zoning works as follows: the rectangle circumscribing the character is divided into several, overlapping, or non-overlapping, regions, and the densities of black points within these regions are computed. This means to subdivide the character image into several equal quadrants (2, 4, 8, etc.) or bins and count the black pixels in each quadrant. These numbers create the feature vector.

Fig. 6.10 A Byzantine symbol scaled, translated, mirrored, and rotated, and its seven Hu invariant moments. From [3]. Used with permission

Moments	0°	Scaled	180°	15°	Mirror	90°
ϕ_1	93.13	91.76	93.13	94.28	93.13	93.13
ϕ_2	58.13	56.60	58.13	58.59	58.13	58.13
ϕ_3	26.70	25.06	26.70	27.00	26.70	26.70
ϕ_4	15.92	14.78	15.92	15.83	15.92	15.92
ϕ_5	3.24	2.80	3.24	3.22	3.24	3.24
ϕ_6	10.70	9.71	10.70	10.57	10.70	10.70
ϕ_7	0.53	0.46	0.53	0.56	−0.53	0.53

Fig. 6.11 Illustration for image feature extraction by zoning. Projection histograms of the character "*a*" on *x*- and *y*-directions

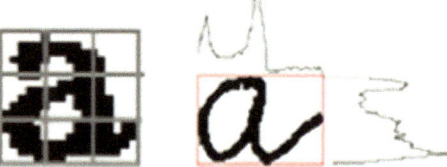

Higher-order statistical moments can be also calculated for each direction. In this case, they are called *projection moments*, extracted from the *projection histograms*. Projection histograms count the number of black pixels in each column and row of a binary image. Some examples are as follows: the variance of the image along the *x* and *y* coordinates (second moment), or higher-order moments, like the skewness and kurtosis, separated on *x*- and *y*-directions. These features, although independent to noise and deformation, still depend on rotation.

6.3 Typical Features for Sound Classification

An Automatic Speech Recognition (ASR) module is an inherent component in smartphones, voice-to-text translators in medical world, and live subtitling systems for TV. The goal of an ASR system (Fig. 6.12) is to accurately and efficiently convert a speech signal into a text transcription, independently of the device used to record the speech, the speaker accent, or the acoustic environment in which the speaker is located (quiet office, noisy room, outdoors, etc.). Speech is not the only type of sound that needs to be classified in pervasive computing systems. For example, environmental noise recognition is a less intrusive way to infer user's

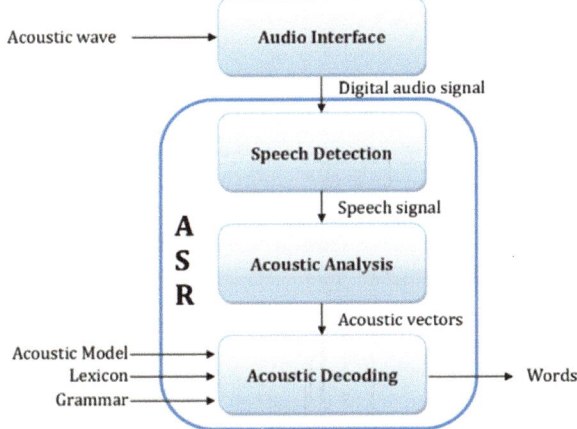

Fig. 6.12 An automatic speech recognition system (ASR). From [4]. Used with permission

daily activities (bathing, cooking, watching TV, vacuum cleaning, or sleeping) or location (indoors and outdoors).

Let us take the example of a speech-controlled wheelchair. The system should recognize and react appropriately to a set of spoken commands, for example ("Go," "Stop," "Left," and "Right"), that together form the ASR's lexicon, or vocabulary. The acoustic model describes the relation between the audio signal and the phonetic units in a language. The grammar models the word sequence in a language. The question now is, what kind of features can be used to distinguish between two spoken commands, such as "Go" and "Stop"? Here, we must also say that there is no one, standard set of features, suitable for all ASR applications.

In any case, it is obvious that by only using the time waveforms shown in Fig. 6.13, it will be hard to distinguish between the two words. This section will present other, more advanced features, suitable for sound recognition in general, and of speech in particular.

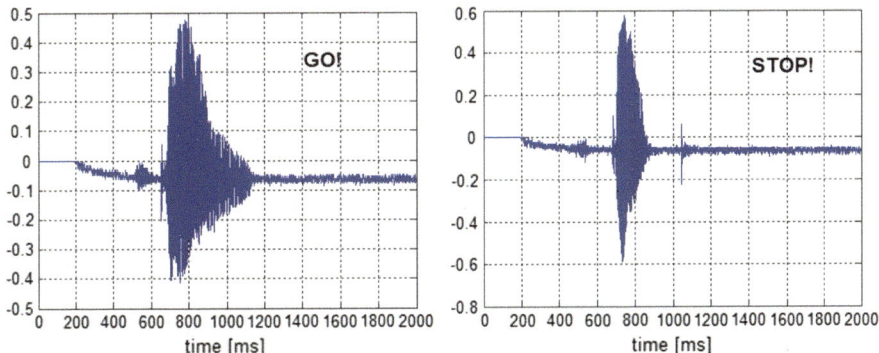

Fig. 6.13 The time waveforms for Go and Stop spoken commands

6.3.1 The Frequency Spectrum

The next best feature we can try to use for sound classification is the frequency spectrum, calculated using the fast Fourier transform (FFT), as already explained in Chap. 5. The feature vector will be the vector containing the FFT coefficients. This simple method works fine in case we want to classify periodic sounds, such as vowels. You can see, for example, in Fig. 6.14 the frequency spectra of two vowels.

It is obvious that there are enough differences between the two spectra, making the frequency spectrum a suitable, relatively easy to calculate, candidate for classification feature.

Specific properties of frequency spectra can be used in particular cases. For example, a distinct characteristic of a periodic signal with period T is its *fundamental frequency*, $f_0 = 1/T$. In the case of voiced speech signals, the fundamental frequency is also called *pitch*. For male speakers, this frequency lies in the range of 80–200 Hz, and for women in the range of 150–350 Hz, making the pitch a good feature to distinguish between male and female speakers. However, in the case of some musical instruments, the fundamental frequency might not be present in the frequency spectrum.

Two other spectral features are adequate for vowels classification, namely the frequencies of their first two formants, denoted by F1 and F2. *Formants* are defined as peaks in the frequency spectrum of the vowel signal. Figure 6.15 shows ten English vowels, in the 2D feature space created by their first two formants. This graph makes it obvious that these two features are sufficient for the perceptual identification of vowels.

6.3.2 Spectrograms

Unfortunately, the frequency spectrum does not always perform well as a feature in sound recognition. The problem occurs when the sound, be it speech or noise, is not

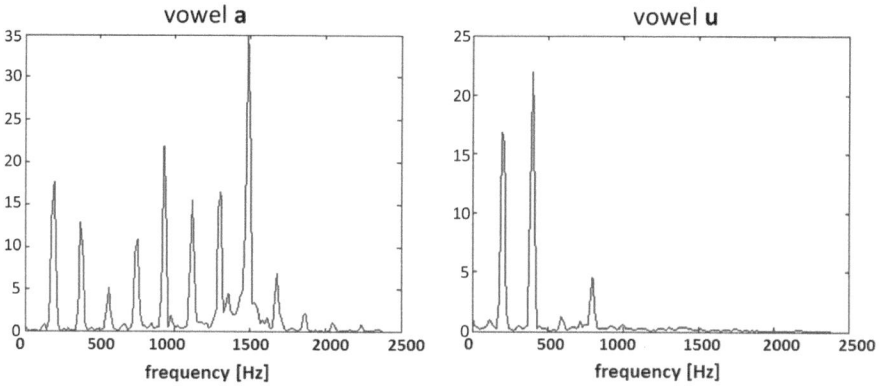

Fig. 6.14 The frequency spectra of the vowel a (as in "father") and u (as in "pool"), respectively

Fig. 6.15 The frequencies of the first two formants F1 and F2 for ten English vowels, spoken by 76 speakers. Adapted from [5]. Used with permission

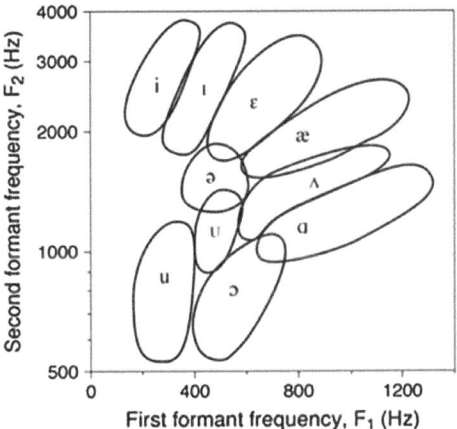

a stationary signal. Human speech, for example, can be decomposed in phonemes such as vowels (/aa/, /i/, /u/), diphthongs (/ay/, /aw/), and consonants (nasal: /m/, stops: /b/, /p/, fricatives: /v/, /s/, whisper, etc.). Each phoneme has a different frequency spectrum. This means that the frequency spectrum of a speech recording varies in time.

A solution in this case is to cut the sound recording into partially overlapping time frames. This operation is called *windowing*, already described in Chap. 5. During these time frames, the sound can be considered *quasi-periodic,* and calculating its FFT makes again sense. If for every time frame, we calculate the short-term frequency spectrum (STFFT), and we plot these next to each other on the time axis, then we will obtain a so-called *spectrogram*, also explained in Chap. 5. Each phoneme will have its own unique pattern in the spectrogram. This can be visualized in Fig. 6.16 that shows spectrograms of different noises and spoken words. From both examples, one can deduce that spectrograms are indeed a suitable feature for audio signals classification.

6.3.3   *Mel-Frequency Cepstral Coefficients (MFCC)*

Although there is evidence that spectrograms provide a good visual representation of audio signals and can be therefore used as feature for classification, we must say that this works well only when all test and training inputs are recorded in the same conditions. In reality, not all persons start speaking at the same moment, the words might be pronounced slightly faster or slower, with accent or without, or with different intensities and pitch. All these variances will result in different spectrograms for, in fact, recordings of the same word.

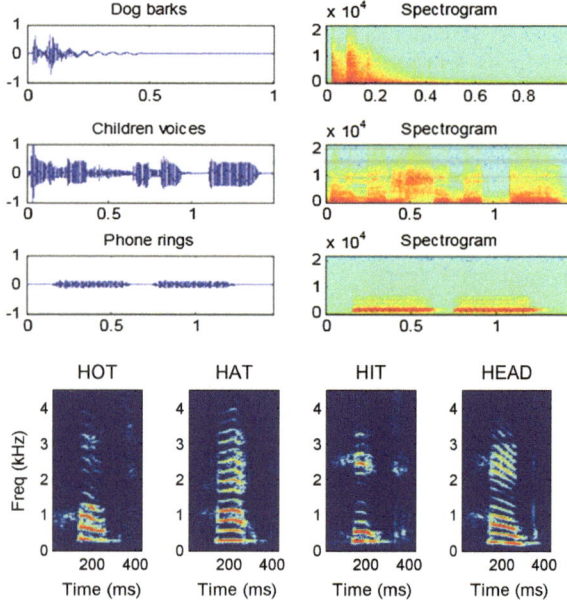

Fig. 6.16 a Audio waveforms and spectrograms for three environmental noises. From [6]. **b** Spectrograms of the words hot, hat, hit, and head. From [7]. All images used with permission

A more stable representation for the different utterances of a word can be obtained by using a special type of acoustic features, called *Mel-frequency cepstral coefficients* (MFCC). The *cepstrum* is a Fourier spectrum of the logarithmic amplitude spectrum of the signal, in fact a spectrum of a spectrum. Just as a spectrum gives information about the frequency components of a signal, a cepstrum gives information about how these frequencies change. MATLAB has in its Signal Processing Toolbox a function that calculates the cepstrum of a unidimensional digital signal. The input in this cepstrum function is a vector containing the sound samples, and the output is also a vector, whose elements are called *cepstral coefficients*.

If one analyzes the first the cepstral coefficients of the uttered words "One" and "Left," shown in Fig. 6.17, one can see that each chart has a different shape, characteristic for that specific word. This is good news, because it means that the first cepstral coefficients, with their good discriminative power, can be used with success as features for audio classification.

The M in MFCC refers to the Mel-frequency, another way to represent sound frequency that more closely resembles how we perceive sounds, such as music and speech.

In practice, for speech recognition, the signal must be divided into windows of ca 20 ms, with an overlap of 50%, and the first 12 or 13 MFCC coefficients form the feature vector. Third-party MATLAB libraries are available that calculate these MFCC coefficients.

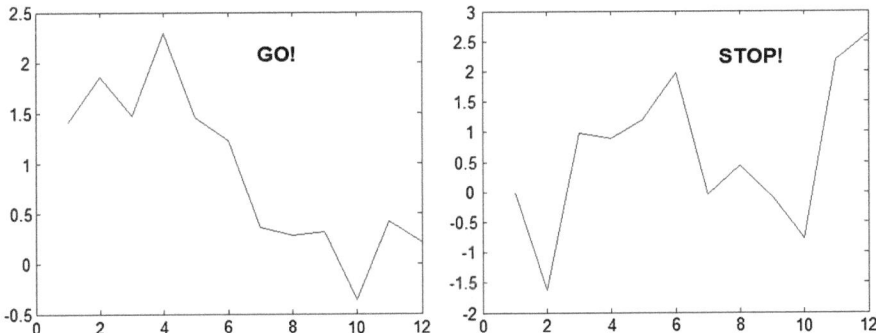

Fig. 6.17 The first 12 Mel cepstral coefficients for the two commands "Go," to the left, and "Stop," *to the right*

6.4 Classification Algorithms

The last two sections presented best practices for features selection in image and sound classification. However, the classification problem is now only half solved. These features that characterize the sensed signal create a feature vector that must be fed as input to a classifier that in its turn will decide which class the signal belongs to. The question that has to be answered now is, which algorithms are there to implement the classifier? We have already shown an example of a simple rule-based classifier, but there are also a lot of other more complex algorithms, usually coming from the AI domain, particularly machine learning that can be used for classification. Some of them are probabilistic, meaning that they use statistics, such as Bayes classifiers, hidden Markov models (HMM), and some of them are not, like neural networks or decision trees. This section will present different options one has when choosing a classification algorithm. Some algorithms perform better than others for a given data set. Therefore, it is always recommended to compare different classification algorithms on the particular data set and choose the best one while weighting the prediction performance versus computational efficiency.

6.4.1 Rule-Based and Decision Tree Classifiers

No doubt you have played, as a child (or parent), the guess-who type of game, called "Who is it?" The goal of this game is to guess the identity of a person selected by our opponent. The strategy is to repeatedly ask a question like "Is it a woman?", "Does the person wear a hat?", or "Are the eyes blue?". Guided by the opponent's (yes/no) answers, we can gradually narrow down the options, until we guess the right person. If we try to build a tree that mimics our reasoning during the guessing process, we will end up with something as shown in Fig. 6.18.

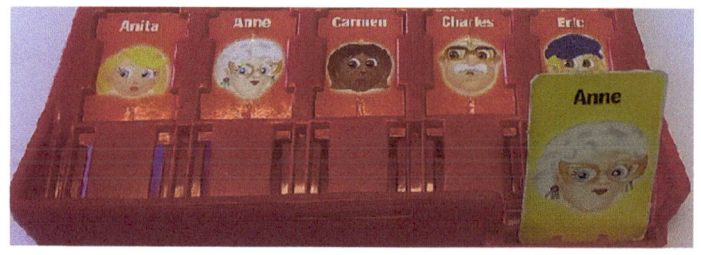

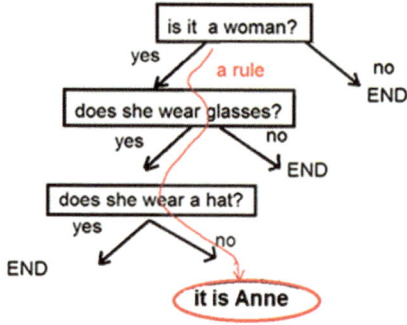

Fig. 6.18 The reasoning flowchart in the "Who is it?" game

A rule-based classifier distinguishes between different classes by using a collection of this kind of "if...then" *decision rules*. The general form for a rule is as follows:

(Condition) → *y*,

where *Condition* is a conjunction of features, and *y* is the class label.

For example, given five classes of animals {Bird, Fish, Mammal, Reptile, Amphibian} and a set of features {Has Fur, Has Feathers, Has Scales, Has Gills}, the following set of decision rules make it possible to classify any animal.

```
Rule 1: (Has Fur = yes) → Mammal
Rule 2: (Has Feathers = yes) → Bird
Rule 3: (Has Scales = yes) AND (Has Gills = yes) → Fish
Rule 4: (Has Scales = yes) AND (Has Gills = no) → Reptile
Rule 5: (Has Fur = no) AND (Has Feathers = no) AND (Has Scales =
        no) → Amphibian
```

The requirements for a good rule-based classifier are as follows: (1) it should have mutually exclusive rules, meaning that no two rules are triggered by the same record and (2) the rules should be exhaustive, meaning that there exists a rule for each combination of attribute values. Together, these properties ensure that every record is covered by exactly one rule.

If we go back to the vowels classification example, based on the position of their first two formants, F1 and F2, in the features space (see Fig. 6.15), one can formulate a possible decision rule.

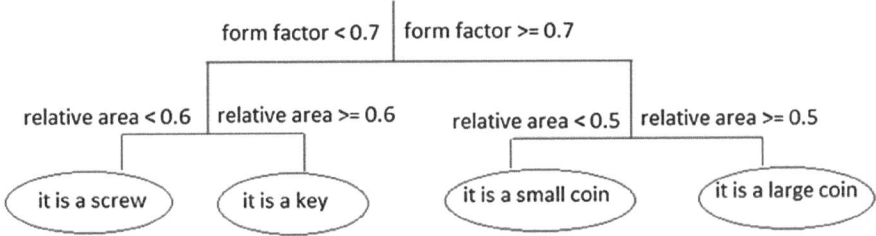

Fig. 6.19 A decision tree for image classification

IF (F1 < 400 Hz) AND (F1 > 180 Hz) AND (F2 < 1200 Hz) AND (F2 > 500 Hz) THEN "it is a u".

However, if we look better at Fig. 6.15, we can also conclude that we will not be able to classify correctly *all* vowels using a rule-based classifier, because some of the clusters overlap, breaking the first requirement for a good rule-based classifier.

In many applications, the decision rules can conveniently be fitted together in a tree structure, called *decision tree*. A decision tree classifier sequentially rejects classes, until it reaches a finally accepted class. When the feature vector arrives, the searching of the class which the newcomer belongs to is achieved via a sequence of decisions starting from the top, along a path of nodes. Each node in the decision tree is usually a binary question, of the form "is feature $x_i < \alpha$?" where α is a threshold value. The terminal nodes or leaves in a decision tree indicate the result of classification. Figure 6.19 shows a decision tree built to classify the objects in Fig. 6.8a by using the form factor and the relative area as features. MATLAB has in its Statistics and Machine Learning Toolbox some built-in functions that implement different flavors of decision tree algorithms for classification.

6.4.2 Template Matching

Template matching is a natural approach to classification. The method assumes that each class is represented by a single reference pattern or *template*. Templates for all classes are stored in a database. Given a new, unknown test pattern, template matching searches the database for the reference pattern that is the most "similar" to the given test pattern. As a result, the class corresponding to that most similar template is the one we are looking for. For example, imagine we all look like the characters in Fig. 6.20 and there is a photograph of each of us, stored in a template database. One day, the police is searching for the identity of a person found guilty of a bank robbery. The only evidence is a photograph of the suspect. If this test input image is of the same size as the templates, then the police can try to find the thief by simply comparing the evidence photograph to all available templates. The template that resembles the most new input will dictate the class to which the

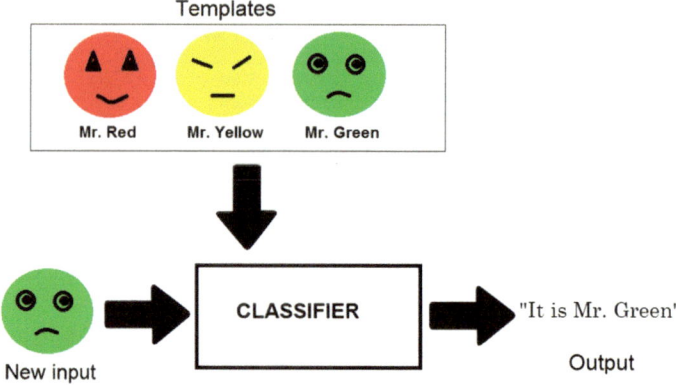

Fig. 6.20 Illustration of the template matching technique

new input belongs, and thus reveals the identity of the suspect, as illustrated in Fig. 6.20.

Of course, all images involved in template matching will need some processing prior to classification and this will result in some binary images. The resemblance between a binary test input and a binary template can be measured in two equivalent ways:

1. Count the number of agreements (black matching black and white matching white) and pick the class that has the highest number of agreements. This is the so-called *maximum correlation* approach. The maximum correlation approach calculates the correlation between the two images (test input and template) and the class with the highest correlation wins. MATLAB has in its Statistics and Machine Learning Toolbox a built-in function that calculates the correlation between two 2D matrices. The highest correlation is equal to one when the images are identical.
2. Count the number of disagreements (black where there should be white, or white where it should be black) and choose the class with the lowest number of disagreements. This is the *minimum error* approach. This approach needs to calculate an error, given by the distance between the two images (input and template). The template which generates the smallest error, "wins".

Template matching can be used, for example, for automatic speech recognition. The system needs a collection of words that it can recognize, called lexicon or *vocabulary*. The speech signal must be first segmented into words, and the task is to classify each word into one of the vocabulary classes. Each word class has its own template, represented by a feature vector or *fingerprint*. This feature vector can contain the sampled sound signal itself, which is a simple, but not very accurate solution, or other more complex features, as already discussed in Sect. 6.3. Each time a new word is presented at the input of the classifier, the similarity between the feature vector of this new input, and of each template fingerprint, is calculated. The word featuring the highest similarity will win.

Fig. 6.21 Template matching for pedestrian detection. From [8]. Used with permission

pedestrians templates

Another application of template matching is in pedestrian recognition from video images in autonomous, smart cars. Templates of pedestrians' images are created from training data and then recognized in street scene video images, as shown in Fig. 6.21.

To conclude, template matching, when appropriate, is a very simple and effective method of classification. However, it is very computationally intensive. Moreover, the method is less simple when the inputs and the templates do not have the same size, or when other distortions of the characters occur, such as translation and rotation. In this case, it can still be used, but with other features for fingerprints, such as the seven invariant Hu moments for images, or Mel-frequency cepstral coefficients for speech, as already explained in Sect. 6.3.

6.4.3 Neural Network (NN) Classifiers

Rule-based and decision tree classifiers are very simple to implement. The problem is that when the number of rules grows, the software implementing such a classifier becomes complex, difficult to debug and difficult to be interpreted by humans. An interesting approach in this case is the neural networks one. We will explain in this section what neural networks are in general, and how they can be used for the classification task, in particular.

A (artificial) *neutral network* (*NN*) is a computer learning system, inspired from biology. The human brain is actually a biological neural network; it is a conglomeration of nerve cells, called *neurons*, which communicate through electrochemical signals and work together, allowing us to think and learn. A biological neuron has some inputs, called *dendrites*, that can receive electrical signals from other neurons; it has a cell body, called *soma*, and one output, called *axon*, which connects to other neurons (see Fig. 6.22). The connections between dendrites and soma are called *synapses* and can amplify or attenuate incoming signals.

Fig. 6.22 The structure of a biological neuron. From [9]

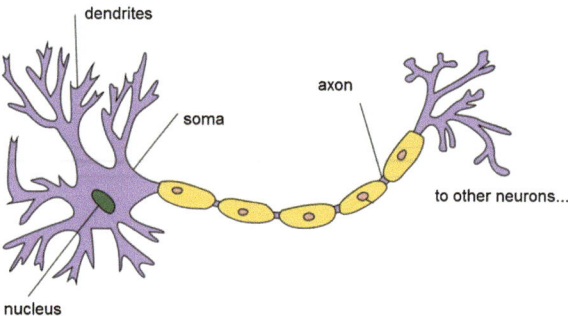

Fig. 6.23 The mathematical model of an artificial neuron

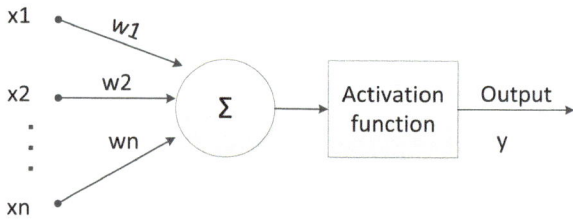

The neuron "fires" and generates an electrical signal spike at its output, if the sum of all signals in the soma exceeds a certain value, and it does nothing if the total stimulation is low.

An artificial *neuron* [1] is a mathematical model, inspired by the functioning of a biological neuron, proposed by McCulloch and Pitts in 1943 (see Fig. 6.23).

In analogy with biological neurons, the artificial neuron has several *inputs* x_1, x_2, ... x_n, and each input has a fixed *weight,* denoted by wi. The weights describe how "important" each input is. They mimic the strength of the synaptic connection between biological neurons. The weights can be positive (excitatory), or negative (inhibitory). The input values, multiplied by their weights, are summed in the *summation* block and fed to an *activation function* block. The neuron's *output* y is finally calculated as follows:

$$y = \sum_{j=1}^{n} x_j w_j \qquad (6.5)$$

If this sum exceeds a certain threshold θ, then the neuron will "fire," meaning that the output y will be 1. Otherwise, the neuron will be switched "off" and the output y will be 0. This type of activation function is called a *threshold* function.

An interesting fact for us is that the neuron's output is always binary (0 or 1), meaning that this simple neuron can classify any set of its inputs into two different classes. However, this classification lacks flexibility, because the weights and the threshold have fixed values. This means that a simple neuron cannot *learn* to classify. An improvement can be achieved if we connect more neurons in a structure, called *neural network*, and we thus get the possibility to adjust the weights.

The simplest neural network is a single-layer one, with one layer of inputs, and one layer of outputs, called a (single-layer) *perceptron*. The input layer just passes the signals on, and the output layer consists of McCulloch and Pitts neurons, which actually perform the calculations. The activation function for a perceptron is also a threshold activation function. Figure 6.24 shows a perceptron, with three inputs and one output neuron. To understand how a perceptron works, think of a manager in a company who has to take a decision. The manager listens to several opinions, which are combined together, and eventually takes a yes/no decision, based on these opinions. Each opinion at the input is weighted, where the weights denote how important each input is, according to the manager. A high weight will give a strong input that has a lot of influence on the output decision, whereas a low weight will only influence it slightly. Note that a large number of small positively weighted inputs may be overwhelmed by a single strong negative input.

The advantage of such a neural network, when compared with a simple neuron, is that it *can learn*. The perceptron in Fig. 6.24 can learn, for example, how to classify. Let us explain how its task is to read a vector with three features, presented at its inputs (x_1, x_2, x_3), and come up with the class which they belong to, codified with 1 or 0. Obviously, our perceptron can discriminate only between two classes, because it has only one output neuron. But in general, a perceptron with more output neurons will be able to label more classes.

As the perceptron does not have any a priori knowledge, the initial values for the weights w_1, w_2, w_3 are first assigned randomly. Learning is done by adjusting these weight coefficients, during *training*. A *training set* contains examples of inputs (the features x_1, x_2, x_3) and the corresponding correct output (the class $c = 0$ or 1). For our manager example, a training set example could be as follows: inputs (Opinion1 = 1, Opinion2 = 1, Opinion3 = 0), and output (decision = 1 (YES)). For each pair (inputs, output) from the training set, the perceptron will start a learning process, described as follows:

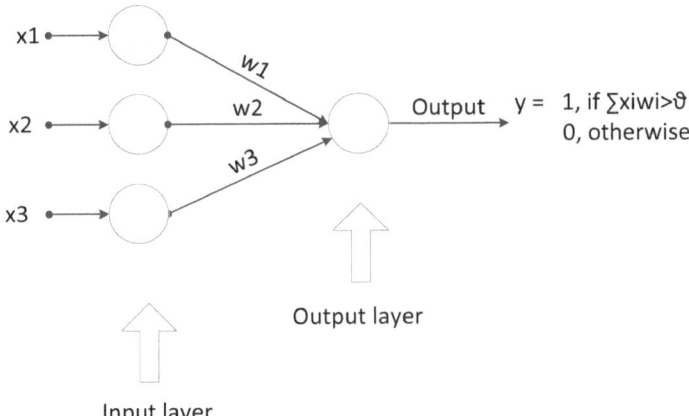

Fig. 6.24 A perceptron with three inputs and one output

1. Read the input features vector (x_1, x_2, x_3).
2. Start an iterative process of adjusting the weights.

   a. The output y is calculated using formula (6.5).
   b. The output y is compared to the desired output.
   c. If they are equal, which is probably not the case in the first iteration step, then the process of learning stops.
   d. Otherwise, the weights are adjusted to reduce the error, and go to step 2a.

The same adjustment steps will be repeated for the second training pair (inputs, output), until the whole training set has been exhausted. By each training step, the network will become better in classification; its produced output will be closer and closer to the right answer. At a certain moment, the perceptron has learnt enough. Its weights are set to perfect values, and they do not have to change anymore. This is a very important moment. Now the perceptron is ready to classify. For all examples from the training set, it will come out with the right class, and if we are lucky, it will also be able to *generalize*, meaning that even if presented with an input that is new, not from the training set, it will produce the good output.

Normally, ANNs are more complex than the perceptron described above. They always have one input layer and one output layer, but these two layers can be internally connected by more than one *hidden layers* of neurons.

The *multilayer perceptron* (*MLP*) has the same structure as a single-layer perceptron, but features one or more intermediate hidden layers. Figure 6.25 shows a MLP with an input layer made of three neurons, one hidden layer with two neurons, and one output layer with three neuron. The hidden layer is "hidden," not because we cannot see it, but because it has no direct connection to the outside world, contrary to the input and output layers. The activation function can be a threshold function, but can also take other forms.

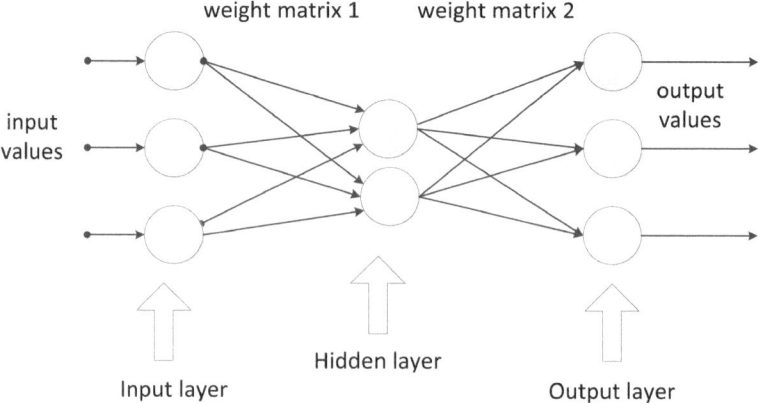

Fig. 6.25 A multilayer perceptron with one hidden layer with two neurons, three input neurons and three output neurons

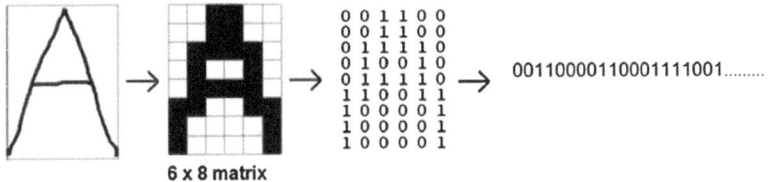

Fig. 6.26 Transformation of the handwritten character into a feature vector

The training of an MLP works in the same way as for a perceptron. Once a neural network has been sufficiently trained, then it is ready to work as a classifier. The inputs are the feature vector of the newcomer. The neural network becomes a black box we can ask to decide which class this input, given its feature vector, belongs to.

In case you are now enthusiastic about this type of classifier, let us try to use a neural network for handwritten character recognition. The written character has to be first scanned and transformed in a binary image, represented, for example, by a 6×8 matrix, using zoning (see Fig. 6.26).

We transform this matrix into a feature vector with $6 \times 8 = 48$ elements, where each pixel is a feature, that can be 0 (white) or 1 (black). The input in our NN will be this vector, containing 48 elements. Therefore, our NN will need an input layer, consisting of 48 neurons. We will use for simplicity only one hidden layer. If we want to classify all the letters in the Latin alphabet, then we will need an output layer with 26 neurons, one for each letter, as illustrated in Fig. 6.27.

A less ambitious solution would be to use only two output neurons and classify only between "A" and "B" characters. In this case, we can make a convention that the output will be (1 0) if it is an "A", and (0 1) if it is a "B". MATLAB turns again to be very helpful, as it has a Neural Networks Toolbox that implements the NN classification algorithm. The only thing we have to do is to specify the neural network topology and train it, by providing enough test data of handwritten letters, together with their correct labels. After training, the neural network will be able to classify any other, never seen before, handwritten character that fits in a matrix of 6×8.

We can anticipate a little and worn you that sooner or later you will discover that people write awful letters, of different sizes and orientation. Therefore, even to classify between "A" and "B" will turn out to be difficult. But do not give up hope, try to use more sophisticated features, such as the seven invariant moments of Hu, and experience their advantages. What we try to make you understand is the trade-off between high classification accuracy on the one hand, and the necessary amount of work and skills, on the other hand.

6.4.4 Probabilistic Classifiers

The goal in this book is to create smart systems that sense, understand, and improve the world. We must admit that up to now, we were looking at this world through

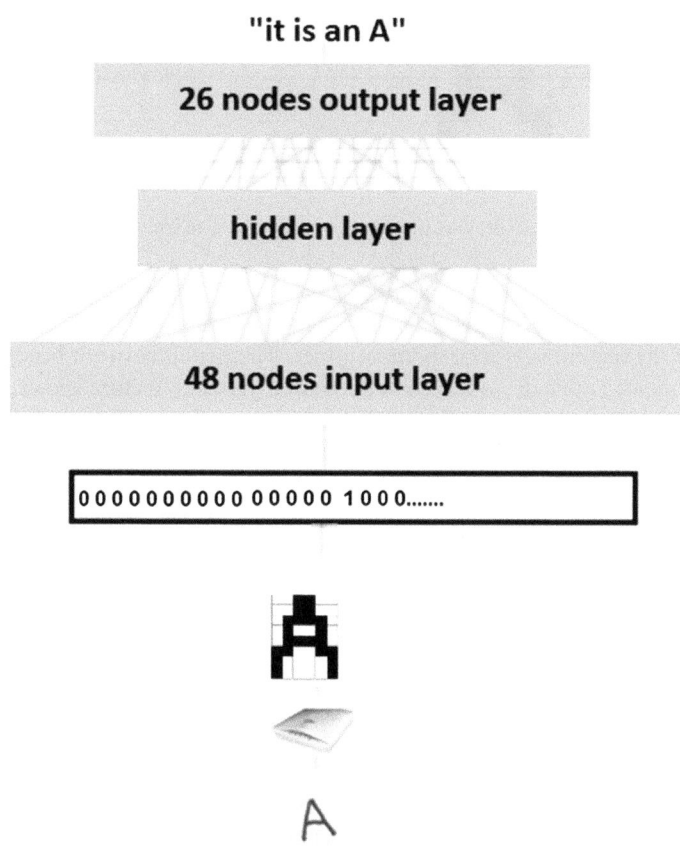

Fig. 6.27 A neural network classifier for all handwritten letters from the Latin alphabet. Adapted from [10]. Used with permission

pink glasses. In reality, we cannot be sure of anything, as the world is full of uncertainties; and these uncertainties can result in a wrong classification, and consequently a wrong decision taken by the, in this case, "not so smart" system. This might happen because, for example, the processed sensor data is not the actual data, but only an older, approximated version of the entity being monitored. Moreover, the sensors are often subject to errors such as systematic errors, caused by imperfect measurement methods and instrumentation, but also unpredictable, random errors, called noise. Worse, the measured data might be not complete, because some sensors broke and ceased to transmit data. Data is, in conclusion, noisy, inconsistent, and sometimes even incomplete. For all these reasons, a system can never be sure that "the temperature in room T4.06 is exactly 20 °C." It is safer to say that "the room temperature is in the interval [19 °C–21 °C] with a probability of 0.8." As a result, a classifier cannot 100% guarantee that "it is warm in the room T406," and not cold. This is *probabilistic language*, which offers a more realistic description of the world we intend to improve with our smart systems.

Our brain is very skillful in dealing noisy and incomplete data, but computers unfortunately do not. A solution for dealing with uncertainty in automatic classification is to use probabilistic models. These are algorithms that improve themselves through experience, for example, naïve Bayes classifiers and Hidden Markov Models (HMM). All these models use a very important theorem, known as the *Bayes rule*. The Bayes rule states that

$$P(B|A) = \frac{P(A|B) \times P(B)}{P(A)} \tag{6.6}$$

where A and B are random events, and $P(A|B)$ is the *conditional probability*, meaning the probability that "event A is true, given that B is true." For example, if A is the event "I have flu" and B is the event "I have headache," then $P(A|B)$ is the probability that I have flu, if I already know that I have a headache. In contrast, $P(A)$ is called the *unconditional* or *prior probability* that A is true.

Basically, the Bayesian approach provides a mathematical rule, explaining how our existing beliefs, denoted by $P(B)$, should change in light of new evidence, denoted by A. Usually, the probabilities $P(A|B)$, $P(B)$, and $P(A)$ in (6.6) are known. $P(B|A)$ is not known and can be calculated by using this Bayes rule. Take this nice illustrative example, from an article in The Economist [11], telling the story of a precocious newborn, observing the sunset and wondering whether the Sun will rise next day or not. We denote with B the event "*the sun will rise tomorrow.*" The evidence is the event "*the sun rises today,*" denoted by A. Each morning when the Sun rises (event A), the boy puts a red marble in a bag. If the Sun does not rise, he puts a black one. The number of red marbles is his belief that the Sun will rise again, knowing that today it did, denoted with $P(B|A)$. Let us see how this belief evolves, from the unconditional probability $P(B)$ before the experiment, toward the current belief, $P(B|A)$. Before the experiment starts, the chances are equal: the boy had one red and one black marble in the bag. This is the *prior probability* that the Sun will rise again tomorrow, $P(B)$, which is initially equal to 0.5. Next day, the Sun rises and so, he puts a red marble in the bag. The probability that the Sun will rise again, given by the number of red marbles in the bag, is rising from 1/2 to 2/3. This is the *posterior probability* after new evidence, $P(B|A)$. Next day, this will raise to 3/4, and so on. Gradually, the initial belief $P(B)$ will be growing, and the current belief $P(B|A)$ eventually will become a near certainty, equal to one.

Let us take another example, of diagnosing dyslexia with a test, and see how Bayes rule can be applied here. Let the events be as follows: A = "*dyslexia test turned out to be positive*" and B = "*you have dyslexia.*" We know $P(A|B)$, the probability that the test is positive, knowing that you have dyslexia. But we do not know the $P(B|A)$. This can be calculated using the Bayes rule.

Before the test, our belief (the prior unconditional probability) $P(dys)$ that we are dyslectic is 1%, taken from a medical book, for example. But if we take a test that is 95% accurate, and this test turns out to be positive, then our belief that we are dyslectic, given by the posterior conditional probability $P(dys|test\ positive)$, increases to 16%. Below follows the proof.

$P(\text{dys} = \text{true}) = 0.01(1\%)$

$P(\text{test} = \text{positive}|\text{dys} = \text{true}) = 0.95$

$$P(\text{dys} = \text{true}|\text{test} = \text{positive}) = \frac{P(\text{test} = \text{Positive}|\text{dys} = \text{true}) \times P(\text{dys} = \text{true})}{P(\text{test} = \text{positive})}$$

$P(\text{test} = \text{positive})$

$= P(\text{test} = \text{positive}|\text{dys} = \text{true}) \times P(\text{dys} = \text{true})$

$\quad + P(\text{test} = \text{positive}|\text{dys} = \text{false}) \times P(\text{dys} = \text{false}) = 0.95 \times 0.01 + 0.05 \times 0.99$

$P(\text{dys} = \text{true}|\text{test} = \text{positive})$

$$= \frac{0.95 \times 0.01}{0.95 \times 0.01 + 0.05 \times 0.99} = \frac{0.0095}{0.0095 + 0.0495} = \frac{0.0095}{0.059} = 0.161\,(16.1\%)$$

Bayesian classifiers in general try to infer the conditional probability that a newcomer belongs to a certain class, given its features vector. For example, they can calculate the probability that "it is a bird," knowing that "it is yellow and it can fly."

Let us focus on the classification task with only two classes. Let ω_1 and ω_2 be the two classes, to which our patterns may belong. The feature vector of the object that has to be classified is denoted by x. We assume that the prior probabilities that the object belongs to a class ω_1 or ω_2, $P(\omega_1)$ and $P(\omega_2)$, respectively, and the prior probability $P(x)$ are known. The other statistical quantities assumed to be known are the class-conditional probabilities $P(x|\omega_1)$ and $P(x|\omega_2)$, describing the probabilities that the object from class ω_1 or ω_2, respectively, has the features vector x. All this information can be learned from training data, by observing and recording the modeled process for a period of time. What we actually want to know are the conditional probabilities $P(\omega_1|x)$ and $P(\omega_2|x)$ that the test object belongs to each class, knowing that the feature vector is x. And here, the Bayes rule can help, as shown below:

$$P(\omega_1|x) = \frac{P(x|\omega_1)P(\omega_1)}{P(x)} \quad P(\omega_2 x) = \frac{P(x|\omega_2)P(\omega_2)}{P(x)} \tag{6.7}$$

A *naïve Bayes classifier* calculates both probabilities and then applies the following classification rule:

If $P(\omega_1|x) > P(\omega_2|x)$, then the test input is classified to class ω_1
If $P(\omega_2|x) > P(\omega_1|x)$, then the test input is classified to class ω_2.

In case of equality, the input object can be assigned to either of the two classes.

The naïve Bayes classifier is called *naïve* because it assumes that the features x_i are mutually independent and that all attributes that influence a classification decision are observable and represented, which is not always the case. By independence [12], we mean probabilistic independence, that is, A is independent of B, given C whenever $P(A|B \text{ and } C) = P(A|C)$, for all events A, B, C with $P(C) > 0$. One problem that arises when the features are not independent is that the classifier can end up "double counting" the effect of highly correlated features, pushing the classifier closer to a given class than is justified. Think, for example, what happens if a certain word occurs twice in a vocabulary of a speech recognizer. In this case, that word gets double the weight of other words, and this double counting biases the classifier's verdict. Despite all this, the naïve Bayes classifier performs amazingly well in a lot of situations.

Let us go back to the example used when we explained template matching. As you probably suspected, things are not as simple as we presented them there. Fortunately, we do not all look like Mr. Red, Mr. Yellow, and Mr. Green, so the police needs other, more sophisticated techniques to find the identity of suspect persons. These are called face recognition techniques. Face recognition from images, a very widely used task in pervasive computing, can be done based on a set of facial geometric features. For example, a set that proved to have good discriminative power, contains: eyebrows thickness and vertical position, nose vertical position and width, mouth vertical position, width and height of upper and lower lips, the shape of the chin, face width at nose position and halfway between nose and eyes [13]. The naïve Bayes classifier illustrated in Fig. 6.28 uses these features to predict which class the owner of these features, the most likely, belongs to. In other words, the classifier reveals the identity of a person by analyzing geometric facial features on its photograph. The success of this method depends on the training data, which must contain a rich collection of photographs of different persons, linked to their identity.

Naïve Bayes classifiers assume that there is no relation between various classes. For example, in a system that recognizes animals based on their features, there is no relation between the class Reptile and the class Mammal. In other words, having a feature vector x from a class ω_1, the next feature vector could belong to any other class. This is the so-called *context-independent* classification. However, this is not always the case. In speech recognition, for example, the word uttered at a certain moment does depend on what has been said previously. For example, after the word "the" there is a very low probability that the next word will be again "the" or a verb, and a high probability that it will be an English noun. In this type of classification systems, *time* does play a crucial role.

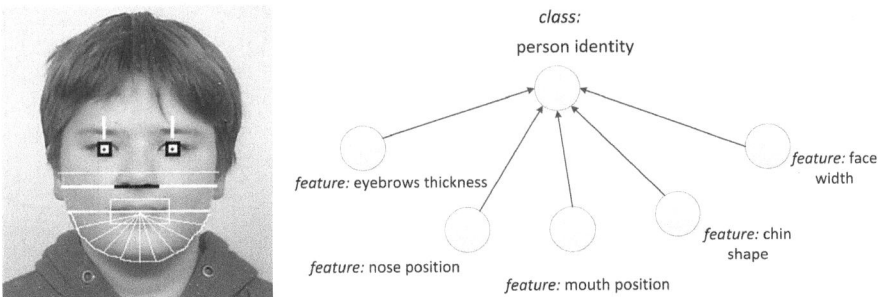

Fig. 6.28 Geometric features (in *white*) for face recognition, *to the left*. Adapted from [13] with permission from the author. A naïve Bayes classifier for face recognition, *to the right*

This brings us to the Hidden Markov Model (HMM) classifier, a graphical, Bayesian probabilistic reasoning algorithm, suitable for modeling dynamic systems, such as speech recognition, location, and activity recognition systems [14–16].

In a HMM model, a system is at the moment t in state $x(t)$, but at the next clock tick, it jumps into the state $x(t + 1)$ that can be the same state, or another one. Typically, in a Markov process a state depends only on its previous state, and not on older states. Obviously, a system that has to classify an animal will not profit much from this type of classifier, but a system that has to recognize the daily activities of a person in a smart home will certainly do.

What makes HMM special is that it can classify states that are not visible. Instead, one sees some *observations* that depend on the system's state. We say that each *hidden* state *emits* an observation at each time tick, as a result of a jump into another state (see Fig. 6.29). Given these observations, the HMM helps to deduce the system's state. This is very often the case in pervasive computing systems, right? For example, in the case of a system that monitors diabetic patients, we do not know exactly the blood sugar level, which is a hidden state, but we can *measure* this level with a sensor, and this is the observation we can access. Or, we do not know that a user is preparing a meal. What we can "see" is that the sensor in the kitchen door fired, that the person touched the RFID sensor attached to a knife, that the fridge door has been opened, that the gas sensor detected some flow, etc. In this case, these sensor readings are the observations that can be measured, and the hidden state is the current user's activity.

Suppose we want to use an HMM to infer the activity performed by a person in a smart kitchen, by analyzing the object he/she touched [17]. In order to build the HMM, one must first identify the hidden states and the observations involved. In this case, the possible states could be the following: Have soup, Cut steak, Pick food, and Drink water. The observations are given by the object that is currently used: Spoon, Knife, Fork, and Glass.

Fig. 6.29 The principle of the hidden Markov model. Adapted from [17]. Used with permission

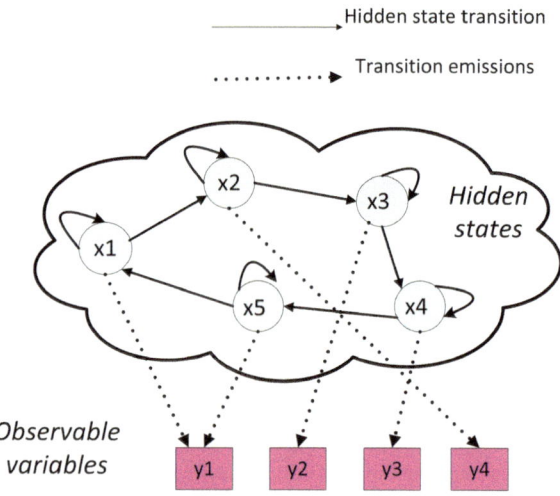

The result of this first step is illustrated in the first illustration in Fig. 6.30a. Notice that the transitions between states are drawn using a solid line, whereas the observation emission events are drawn with dotted lines. Probably you have already noticed that there are more transitions possible between the states hidden behind the curtains. We deliberately omitted them in this first attempt. We added them in the second drawing, though, shown at the bottom of Fig. 6.30a.

Fig. 6.30 a Building an HMM classifier—step 1. Adapted from [17] with permission. **b** Building an HMM classifier—step 2. HMM annotated with probabilities. Adapted from [17] with permission

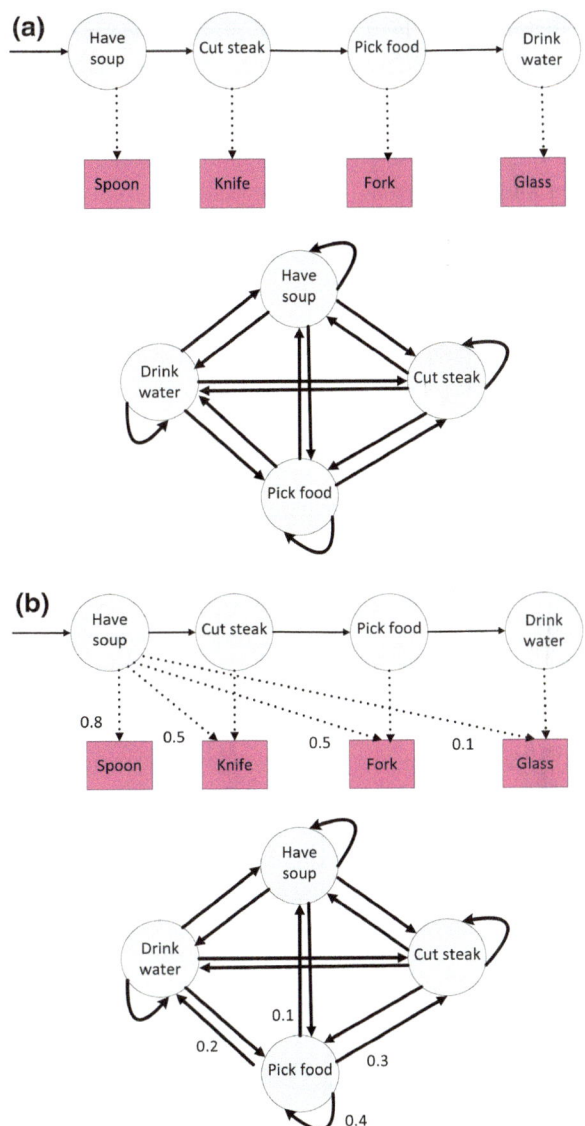

The next step is to calculate the probabilities attached to all transition and emission events. Three kinds of probabilities need to be calculated. First is the *prior probability* $P(x)$ that the person is in a certain state x. Second is the *transition probability*, $P(x_j|x_i)$, giving the probability that the next state will be the state x_j, given that now the state is x_i, for example, the probability that the person will drink some water in the next moment, knowing that right now he is picking some food. Furthermore, we have to calculate the *observation emission probability*, defined as the conditional probability $P(y_i|x_i)$, to see the observation y_i, given that the person is in state x_i, for example, the probability that the person uses a fork, given that he is picking some food. All these probabilities have to be determined from experience and/or during a training phase. Training a HMM needs long days of observations. Based on this data, the probabilities in HMM can be computed. Figure 6.30b shows the HMM in an advanced design stage, already annotated with some of these probabilities. As soon as all these probabilities have been estimated, the HMM graph is sufficiently trained and ready to classify. Given a new observation vector, y, saying, for example, that a knife and a fork are currently being used, the Bayes rule can be used to infer the four conditional probabilities that the user is performing activity x_i, $P(x_i|y)$. The state x_i, with the highest conditional probability, will win.

6.4.5   Classification Performance Measurement

Previous sections presented some examples of classification algorithms. We cannot end this chapter without showing how to quantify their performance. The most used criterion to evaluate a classifier is its *predictive accuracy*, given by the number of new unseen instances, that is correctly classified. This accuracy cannot be calculated, but can be evaluated through an experiment. For example, the so-called *train-and-test* experiment divides the data set in two parts, one destinated for training and the other one for testing [18], as shown in Fig. 6.31. Usually, 70% of the data set is used for training, and 30% for testing.

For example, if an OCR tested for 100 letters "A" recognized them as "A" in 85 cases, then one can claim that the classification accuracy was 85%.

But we can also evaluate the performance of a classifier in a more refined way. In general, if we have a simple 2-class classification problem, with a class A and a class (not A), and we classification error have a test data set with positive (A) and negative *classification accuracy* (not A) instances, then the classification test results will fall in one of these four categories:

- *True positive* (*TP*)—a positive instance is correctly classified, as being from class A.
- *True negative* (*TN*)—a negative instance is correctly rejected, as not being from class A.

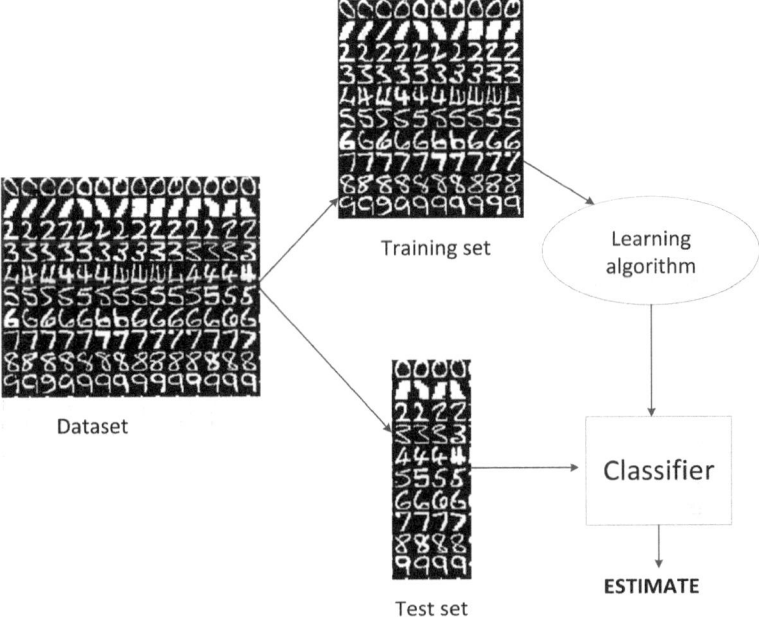

Fig. 6.31 The train-and-test strategy. The data set image is retrieved from: http://www.cs.nyu. edu/~roweis/data.html

- *False positive (FP)*—a negative instance A is misclassified, as being in class A.
- *False negative (FN)*—a positive instance was wrongly rejected, as not being from A.

In these four labels, "positive" means that an instance has been accepted as being from class A. "Negative" means that an instance has been rejected, as not being from class A. "True" means that the result corresponds with the reality. "False" means that the decision taken by the classifier was wrong. For example, in the case of automatic pedestrian detection, a false negative is the most dangerous outcome, corresponding to the situation when the system fails to recognize real pedestrians on the road. Obviously, the number of positive instances in the data set is $P = TP + FN$ and the number of negative instances is $N = FP + TN$.

A *confusion matrix* is an instrument useful for summarizing the results of a classification test; it tells all about successful and less successful classifications and helps to evaluate a certain classification approach. A complete confusion matrix should show all four experimental results, given by *TP, TN, FP,* and *TN*, as shown in Table 6.1. In this example, the data set contained 1000 instances, from which

Table 6.1 An example of a confusion matrix

		Recognized as		
		+	−	Total instances
Actual class	+	**TP** 800	**FN** 100	**P** 900
	−	**FP** 5	**TN** 95	**N** 100

900 were positive and 100 negative. From the positive instances, 800 have been classified correctly and 100 have been misclassified. From the negative instances, 95 were correctly classified as negative and 5 not.

Some confusion matrices show only information on how frequently instances of class A were correctly classified as class A, or misclassified as another class. Look at the confusion matrix in Fig. 6.32 and try to decipher the story it tells. For example, the first row says that a "walking" activity was correctly recognized as "walking" in 942 cases. However, it was misclassified as "walking/carry" in 46 cases, as "standing still" in two cases, and so on. Can you already envision the confusion matrix for a perfect classifier? The confusion matrix for a perfect classifier should have non-zero values only on its diagonal.

Summarizing, the commonly used performance metrics for the evaluation of a classifier applied to a data set are as follows:

- *Accuracy*, $a = (TP + TN)/(P + N)$, defined as the proportion of instances that were correctly classified.
- *True-positive rate*, $TPR = TP/P$, also called *detection rate* or *hit rate*, defined as the proportion of positive instances that are correctly classified as positive.
- *False-positive rate*, $FPR = FP/N$, or *false alarm rate*, defined as the proportion of negative instances that are erroneously classified as positive.
- *Error rate*, $er = 1 - a = (FP + FN)/(P + N)$, defined as the proportion of instances that are incorrectly classified.

Another way to present the results of a classifier's performance measurement and especially to compare several classifiers is the *receiver operating*

a	b	c	d	e	f	g	h	i	j	k	l	m	n	o	p	q	r	s	t	< classified as
942	46	0	0	2	0	0	0	8	3	8	1	4	2	7	0	3	8	8	8	a = walking
83	1183	9	0	3	2	0	0	8	1	3	8	14	1	16	0	8	53	38	11	b = walking/carry
0	9	762	11	0	1	17	3	0	0	0	0	0	0	1	0	0	0	0	0	c = sitting relaxed
0	0	10	893	9	1	0	1	0	1	0	0	0	0	1	0	0	0	0	0	d = computer work
0	0	0	7	774	11	0	0	6	1	2	2	0	4	0	2	0	0	0	0	e = standing still
0	2	1	0	12	712	9	1	0	0	2	1	10	1	18	0	26	1	4	3	f = eating/drinking
0	0	42	21	0	1	320	28	0	0	0	0	0	0	0	0	0	0	0	1	g = watching TV
0	0	23	1	1	6	16	961	9	0	2	0	0	1	0	1	2	0	2	22	h = reading
14	12	0	0	1	1	0	17	491	10	1	1	1	1	0	1	3	4	1	i = running
0	1	0	0	5	0	0	0	8	830	10	0	1	0	3	0	2	1	0	1	j = bicycling
9	3	2	16	30	22	45	9	3	35	309	37	26	21	99	1	38	12	3	26	k = stretching
4	10	0	0	6	5	2	7	0	6	23	500	13	2	9	3	6	5	3	2	l = strength train
1	7	0	0	5	10	0	0	0	0	3	9	403	11	10	1	26	1	6	4	m = scrubbing
1	0	0	0	0	3	1	0	0	2	0	1	9	885	11	0	1	0	2	2	n = vacuuming
1	1	0	0	1	6	0	0	0	1	4	1	4	7	822	8	4	0	1	3	o = folding laundry
0	0	4	9	0	2	1	7	0	0	0	0	1	0	10	791	8	0	0	0	p = lying down
1	2	0	0	3	32	0	0	0	1	5	0	18	7	10	9	637	10	2	10	q = brushing teeth
7	14	0	0	1	1	0	0	0	3	2	1	1	0	2	0	12	351	10	5	r = climbing stairs
84	70	0	7	20	60	0	0	8	40	33	11	24	34	40	0	0	59	502	160	s = riding elevator
5	2	0	0	5	6	0	1	0	1	0	3	3	1	0	0	3	7	16	127	t = riding escalator

Fig. 6.32 Confusion matrix for a system that recognizes physical activity. From [19]. Used with permission

Fig. 6.33 An ROC graph showing the evaluation results of three classifiers: A, B, and C

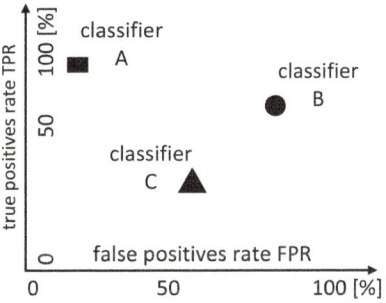

characteristics (*ROC*) graph. ROC has its name from signal processing theory, where it has been used to illustrate the trade-off between hit rates and false alarm rates over a noisy communication channel. An ROC graph shows the classifiers' performance in two dimensions, with the false-positive rate, FPR, on the *x*-axis, and the true-positive rate, TPR, on the *y*-axis. Each classifier is represented by one point on the graph, as shown in Fig. 6.33. High-quality classifiers should cluster in the top left-hand corner of this graph. For example, we can say that classifier A performed better than classifiers B and C on the same data set. However, one cannot say anything about which one is better, B and C. Classifier B has a higher true-positive rate, but it also has a higher false-positive rate, and we do not know what is better; this depends only on the relative importance the user gives to both metrics [18].

Some classifiers lend themselves to tuning, making reasonable to think about series of classifiers. During tuning, we assign one point in the ROC graph for each value of some variable in the classification algorithm, known as a parameter. If we join all these points for a certain classifier, then we obtain a so-called *ROC curve*. The performance of different types of classifiers using different parameters can be compared by analyzing their ROC curves, as illustrated in Fig. 6.34. A single run of the classifier produces a single point on the ROC curve and the closer to the top left-hand corner it is the better. The best classifier has the largest AUC.

Fig. 6.34 ROC curves for a system for texture-based classification of pedestrians. From [20]. Used with permission

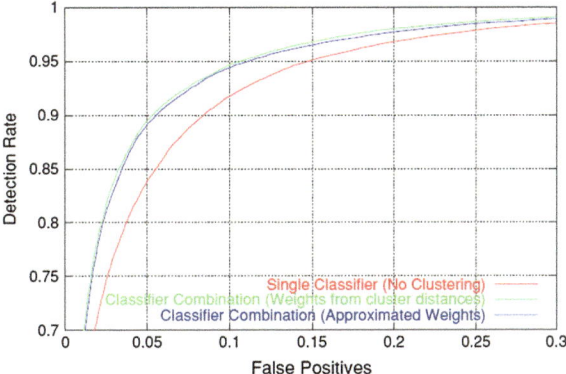

6.5 Conclusions

- Classification is the most complex operation that data must undergo in a smart system. Through the pervasive computing system.
- The basic activities involved in the design of a classification system are the following: sensing, preprocessing of raw sensed data, feature selection and extraction, classifier design, and finally the classification evaluation. Sensing and preprocessing have been treated in the previous chapters. In this chapter, we showed the best practices for extracting features, and choosing a classifier, with a focus on image and speech recognition.
- Good features are measurable quantities that are compact and have good discriminatory power. There is no one standard set of features, good for all classification problems. This chapter presented some typical commonly used features. For image processing, these are: single-shape descriptors and image statistical moments. For speech recognition, these are the frequency spectrum, spectrograms and the Mel-Frequency cepstral coefficients (MFCC).
- The classifier has the role to decide, given an object characterized by a feature vector at its input, the class which this object belongs to. There is no standard, best, classification algorithm. Its complexity depends on the application, the number of features in the features vector, the required accuracy, the programmer's skills, the available computational power, etc. The simplest classifier is the rule-based classifier. More sophisticated classifiers belong to the machine learning domain.
- The classifier can improve its quality by supervised or unsupervised learning. Supervised learning requires a set of training examples. Supervised classification has two phases: the training and the recognition. We presented a few supervised learning classifiers: template matching, neural networks, naïve Bayes classifiers, and HMM.
- The performance of a classifier can be estimated with a train-and-test experiment. The results are presented in a confusion matrix, or in an ROC graph.

6.6 Exercises

1. Explain the classification problem. Give an example.
2. What characterizes a "good" feature for classification? Give an example.
3. What typical features can be used for image recognition?
4. What typical features can be used for speech recognition?
5. What does learning mean? Explain how supervised learning works.
6. Enumerate the components of a classification system.
7. Enumerate the steps in the design of a classification system.
8. Draw a decision tree for a few vowels classification, using a chart with the frequencies of the first two formants F1 and F2.

9. How does template matching work? What are the advantages and disadvantages of this method?
10. What is an artificial neuron? How does it work?
11. Can a single artificial neuron classify? How? What are the limitations?
12. What is a perceptron? Can a perceptron classify? How?
13. What is a neural network?
14. Why is completely automatic supervised learning not yet possible?
15. What are probabilistic models and why are they necessary?
16. Define the terms prior probability and conditional probability. Give an example for each.
17. Write down the Bayes rule and explain its essence.
18. What is a naïve Bayes classifier? How does it work? Why is it called naïve?
19. What is a HMM? How does it work as a classifier? Draw a diagram of an HMM for activity recognition in an elderly home.
20. What is confusion matrix? Give an example.
21. What is an ROC graph?

References

1. Marsland, S.: Machine Learning—An Algorithmic Perspective. CRC Press, Boca Raton (2009)
2. New Zealand Dollar (2016) Available from: https://en.wikipedia.org/wiki/New_Zealand_dollar
3. Theodoridis, S., Koutroumbas, K.: Pattern Recognition Academic Press (2008)
4. Dutoit, T., Couvreur, L., Bourland, H.: How does a dictation machine recognize speech? In: Applied Signal Processing. Springer, Berlin (2009)
5. Peterson, G.E., Barney, H.L.: Control methods used in a study of the vowels. J. Acoustical Soc. Am. **24**(2), 175–184 (1952)
6. Sameh, S., Lachiri, Z.: Multiclass support vector machines for environmental sounds classification in visual domain based on log-Gabor filters. Int. J. Speech Technol. **16**(2), 203–213 (2013)
7. Schnupp, J., Nelken, I., King, A.J.: Auditory Neuroscience. MIT Press, Cambridge (2010)
8. Gavrila, D.M.: Pedestrian Detection from a Moving Vehicle. In: Vernon, D. (ed.) Computer Vision—ECCV 2000: 6th European Conference on Computer Vision Dublin, Ireland, June 26–July 1, 2000 Proceedings, Part II, pp. 37–49. Springer, Berlin (2000)
9. The Structure of a Neuron: Available from: https://en.wikipedia.org/wiki/Soma_%28biology%29
10. Faaborg, A.: Using Neural Networks to Create an Adaptive Character Recognition System. Cornell University, Itaca (2002)
11. The Economist: In praise of bayes. In: The Economist (2000)
12. Friedman, N., Geiger, D., Goldszmidt, M.: Bayesian network classifiers. Mach. Learn. **29**, 131–163 (1997)
13. Brunelli, R., Poggio, T.: Face recognition: features versus templates. IEEE Trans. Pattern Anal. Mach. Intell. **15**(10), 1042–1052 (1993)
14. Gales, M., Young, S.: The application of hidden Markov models in speech recognition. Found. Trends Signal Process. **1**(3), 195–304 (2007)

15. Lee, S., Lee, K.C., Cho, H.: A dynamic bayesian network approach to location prediction in ubiquitous computing environments. In: Papasratorn, B., et al. (eds.) Advances in Information Technology: Proceedings of 4th International Conference, IAIT 2010, Bangkok, Thailand, November 4–5, 2010, pp. 73–82. Springer, Berlin (2010)
16. Kasteren, T.L., et al.: An activity monitoring system for elderly care using generative and discriminative models. Personal Ubiquitous Comput. **14**(6), 489–498 (2010)
17. Helal, Sumi, Kim, Eunju, Cook, Diane: Human activity recognition and pattern discovery. IEEE Pervasive Comput. **9**, 48–53 (2010)
18. Bramer, M.: Principles of Data Mining Undergraduate Topics in Computer Science edition. Springer, Berlin (2007)
19. Bao, L., Intille, S.S.: Activity recognition from user-annotated acceleration data. In: Ferscha, A., Mattern, F. (eds.) Pervasive Computing: Proceedings of Second International Conference, PERVASIVE 2004, Linz/Vienna, Austria, April 21–23, 2004, pp. 1–17. Springer, Berlin (2004)
20. Gavrila, D.M., Munder, S.: Multi-cue pedestrian detection and tracking from a moving vehicle. Int. J. Comput. Vision **73**(1), 41–59 (2007)

Chapter 7
Systems Engineering

Build a system that even a fool can use, and only a fool will use it.
A Murphy Law

Previous chapters explained how pervasive computing systems work. As we are secretly hoping you would also like to build such a system, the story would not be complete without an attempt to show you how this is done in real life. We enter now the field of *systems engineering*, an interdisciplinary, team-based approach that means to enable the realization of successful systems. In a pervasive computing system, software and hardware are working together, in order to enable the desired functionality. For example, a smart car is a system of interconnected sensors (gyroscopes, odometers, cameras, and LIDARs), actuators (displays, speakers, brakes, and motors) and software agents (map matching, shortest-path planning, traffic light recognition, pedestrians recognition, and automatic cruise control) that work together with other systems (GPS, traffic control systems, and digital map databases), with the purpose of a safe navigation of its passengers to their destination. In many pervasive computing systems, the physical devices, and even some of the software toolboxes, are ready-made. Therefore, the main challenge consists of developing the complete software application and integrating it with the existing hardware. This is why the main focus in this chapter will be on software. Software is nowadays the product of a team of software engineers. The first thing this software team does is, not as you might think, directly jump into programming. The team first writes down what the product should do, who and how will use it, how much time it will take to build it, what is its architecture, how it will be tested, what can go wrong, etc. This disciplined, engineering-like approach of "making" software, called *software engineering*, is proved to increase the project success and is benefic when it comes to maintainability and accident analysis. Software engineering is thus a part of system engineering, concerned with all aspects of software production, from system specification to maintenance. This chapter highlights the best practices in system engineering in general, and in software development process, in particular.

© Springer International Publishing AG 2017
N. Silvis-Cividjian, *Pervasive Computing*, Undergraduate Topics
in Computer Science, DOI 10.1007/978-3-319-51655-4_7

7.1 Systems and Software Development Models

A *system*, in general, is a combination of interacting elements, organized to achieve
one or more stated purposes. In a pervasive computing system, software and
hardware components work together to improve the quality of life. The making of
these systems is a synchronized effort between technical, management, and marketing teams within a company. Management activities typically include the following: planning, managing risk, monitoring performance, and improving the
process. Marketing activities are concerned about the product profitability and sale
ability. Technical activities, in which we are particularly interested in this chapter,
can be summarized in a *systems engineering V diagram*, shown in Fig. 7.1. On the
left hand side of this V diagram, the system definition progresses from a general
view of the user, through a decomposition of functionality, toward a specific design.
Based on this design, the hardware and software are implemented, at the bottom of
the "V". On the right hand side of the diagram, the components of the system are
gradually integrated, and the result of integration is tested, to measure how well it
meets the user's needs. The complete system is then released and put in operation.
During operation, the system undergoes periodic maintenance.

Software development follows the same steps as in systems engineering (specification, design, implementation, testing, and maintenance). Different software
development models exist nowadays, where these phases occur in different order, or
time length. For example, in the oldest and most widely used *waterfall model*, the
phases follow each other on the time line, as shown in Fig. 7.2. A software project
developed using a waterfall approach may take a few months and even years until
completion.

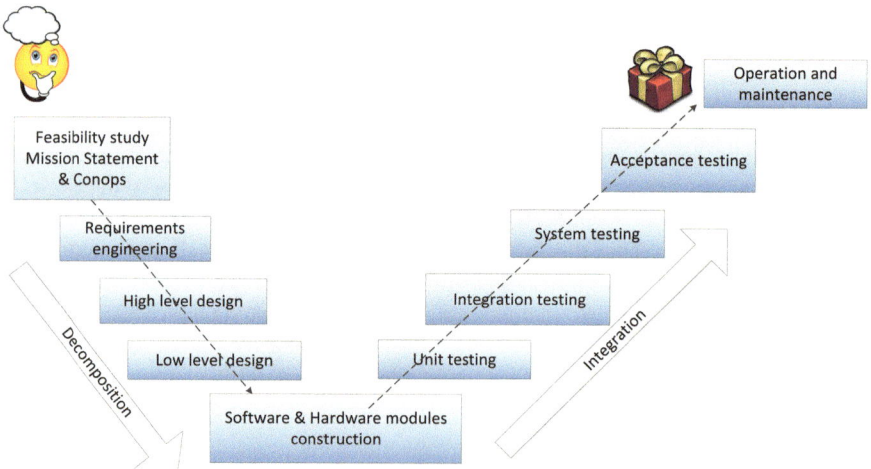

Fig. 7.1 The systems engineering V diagram

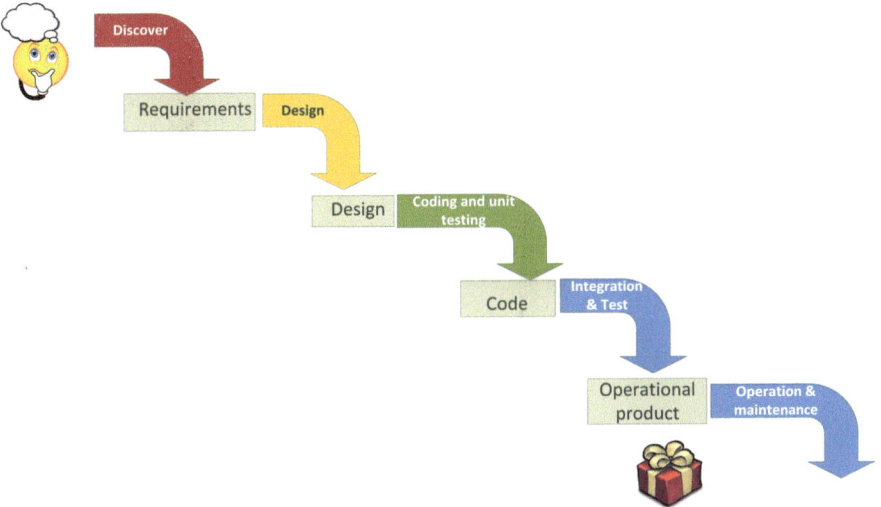

Fig. 7.2 The waterfall software development model

A more modern software development model, called *Agile*, proposes an incremental and iterative approach to software development, exposing more often the intermediate product to user feedback, and evolving it through several versions. Development happens in *sprints* of 2–3 weeks, where each sprint is a sequence of the same phases: requirements, design, implementation, and testing (see Fig. 7.3). Agile methods only define very minimalistic requirements beforehand and work out the more advanced ones on the way. Planning happens only for each sprint, and not for the whole development process.

A rather unusual, yet interesting software development model related to Agile, is the *test-driven development* (*TDD*) [1]. This approach features the same phases, but in a different order in time (see Fig. 7.4). In TDD, first the tests for a small functionality are written, which will of course immediately fail, because there is no corresponding code yet. Next, some code is written, just enough to pass these tests. After that, new tests are added, followed again by coding, and the iteration continues, until all the functionality has been implemented.

At the moment, there is no one generally accepted model good for all software development projects. Each model has its advantages and shortcomings. The waterfall model is stable and well documented, but it requires the requirements to be frozen before the design and implementation can start, which makes it difficult to respond to changing customer requirements. Moreover, any errors and omissions in the requirements risk to be found late, during testing or even later, during operation and maintenance and therefore will cost a lot.

In contrast, in an Agile model, working software is delivered very often, and requirements can be changed on the fly. Testing happens in each sprint, and therefore, the cost of accommodating changes needs and correcting errors is

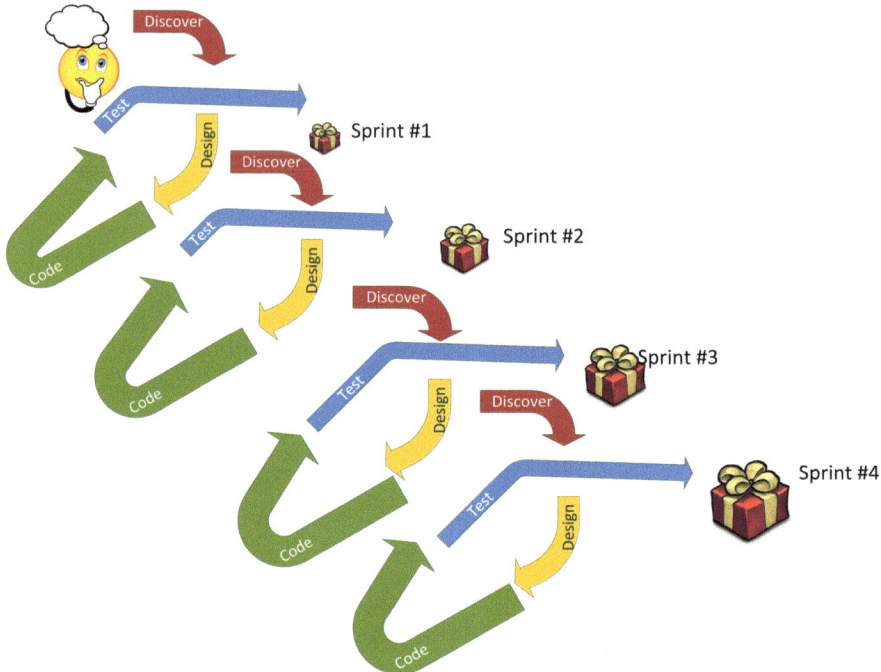

Fig. 7.3 The Agile software development process

Fig. 7.4 The principle of test-driven development (TDD)

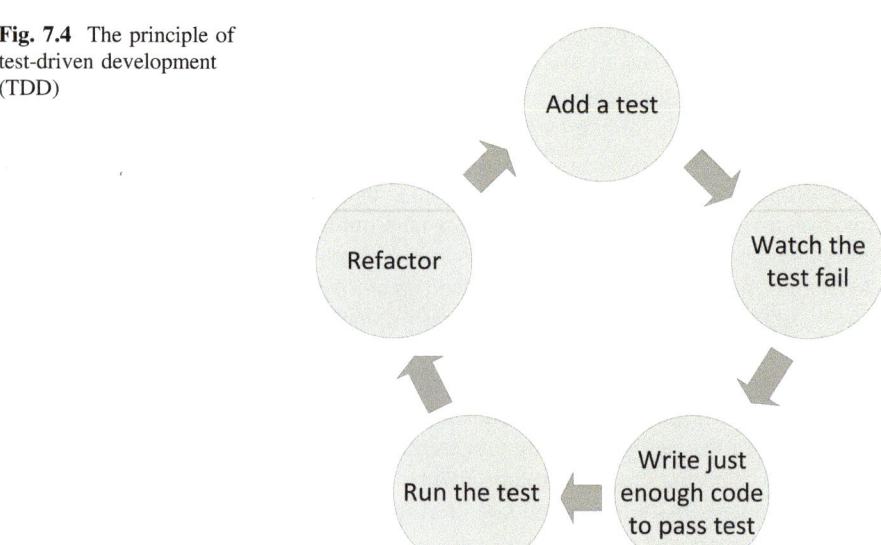

reduced. Moreover, it is easier to get customer feedback, because the customer can actually see the product any time during its development. The disadvantage of the Agile approach is that there is no long-term plan for developing and testing the product, and the documentation is not extensively maintained. In TDD, the advantage is that there is always a set of tests ready, and also a not complete, yet working code. In practice, legacy systems and safety-critical systems are mainly developed using waterfall model, but even there, attempts are being made to shift toward more Agile practices.

In the next sections, we will walk through the system engineering V diagram and investigate all the stages involved in the development of a new system.

7.2   Getting Started

Nowadays, pervasive computing systems are too complex to be built by one person. A team of engineers is therefore needed, working in a *project* framework. A *project* is defined as a temporary enterprise with constrained resources, composed of various coordinated activities, with well-defined start and stop dates, undertaken to create a unique system. Every project starts when there is a problem to be solved, and at least one idea on how to solve it.

Let us take the following example from the medical domain, diabetes in particular. Diabetes mellitus or Type 1 diabetes is an incurable disease, characterized by abnormally high blood sugar levels. It affects, according the World Health Organization, more than 175 million people around the world.

Living with diabetes presents a major challenge. In medical terms, the blood sugar level is called blood glucose concentration (BCG). Ideally, a person in fastening state should have a BGC level in the range [4–5.5] mmol/L. A too low (hypoglycemia) or a too high value (hyperglycemia) for a long period of time can damage the health, causing heart attack, stroke, and eyes or kidneys failure.

The pancreas is an organ in the human body that regulates the BGC level and keeps it in a normal range, through the following process. After physical exercise or fastening, the blood glucose decreases. The pancreas produces then a hormone called *glucagon*, which stimulates the liver to make new glucose in the blood. On the other hand, after a carbohydrate-rich meal, a peak of BGC takes place, like shown in Fig. 7.5. What the pancreas does in this case is producing *insulin*, another hormone that decomposes the sugar into other substances. As a result, the BGC level falls back into a normal range.

This is the way blood sugar gets regulated in a healthy person. The *problem* of diabetic patients is that their pancreas fails to properly produce the hormones necessary for blood sugar regulation. An easy solution in case of low BCG levels is to consume some glucose-rich food or drink. Unfortunately, there is no simple solution in case the BGC level reaches a too high value. In this case, the pancreas has to be helped with an artificial supply of insulin.

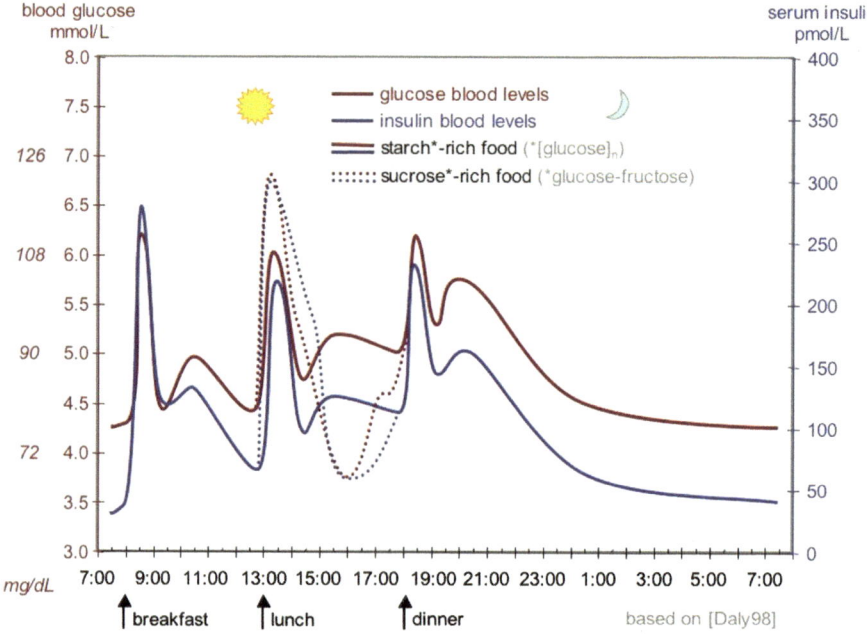

Fig. 7.5 The fluctuations of blood glucose and insulin in a healthy person after taking a meal. From [2]. Used with permission from the author

This happens currently with an injection shot of insulin, administrated by the patient himself, two or more times a day, after each meal, and before the night sleep. The insulin dose of each shot depends on the current BGC level, as measured by the patient after each meal, corrected with the caloric value of the meal, according to a complicated formula. These injections, administrated with a syringe or pen, are a great inconvenience, because they limit the diabetes patients' activities and restrict their movements. Moreover, due to large day-to-day fluctuation in blood sugar levels in a person with Type 1 diabetes, the injected insulin dose does not very accurately reflect the demands of the pancreas.

At this moment, semiautomatic, wearable devices exist,[1] like the one shown in Fig. 7.6. In this device, a sensor measures the blood sugar from a sample supplied by the user. The BCG value is then wirelessly sent to the insulin pump controller. The controller reads this BGC value, an insulin log, and the number of carbohydrates the patient is going to eat, and calculates the appropriate dose of insulin, called bolus. However, in these devices, the user is the one who decides when to inject this insulin, and with which rate. The controller is just an advisor, which only suggests the appropriate insulin dose and pump rate, performs the subcutaneous insulin administration, and issues alarms and notifications, as well as diabetes

---

[1]https://www.medtronic-diabetes.co.uk/minimed-system/minimed-640g-insulin-pump.

Fig. 7.6 A Medtronic 640
semiautomatic insulin pump.
Published with permission
from Medtronic

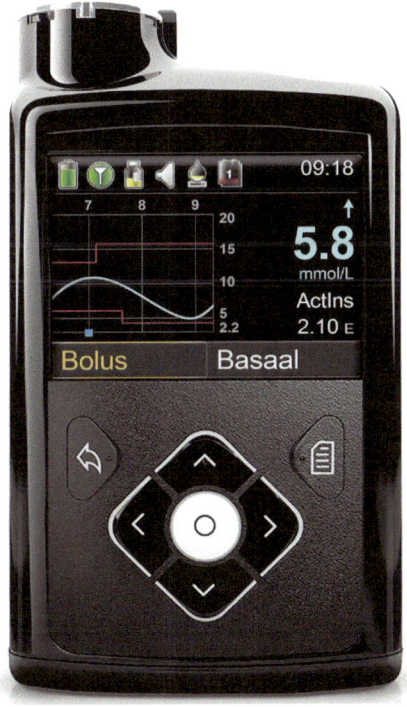

therapy advice. Modern versions also cease the insulin delivery if the patient does
not react at the hyperglycemia alarm.

We could improve this situation, by building a fully automatic wearable device,
where the blood glucose is continuously monitored, and the right dose of insulin is
calculated and administrated subcutaneously, without user's intervention. In other
words, the idea is to build a seamless, pervasive computing system that mimics in
real time the glucose regulating function of a pancreas in case of hyperglycemia.
Such device is called a *closed-loop automatic insulin pump*.

Does this concept ring a bell? Can you already envision a block diagram with a
feedback loop, linking a blood glucose sensor, an infusion pump and a software
controller? If yes, we feel rewarded, because this was in fact our goal: to teach you
how to approach smart systems from an engineering perspective.

The first step when undertaking the development of a new system is a *feasibility
study*. This activity aims to check whether the product *can* be realized, if the user's
needs can be satisfied using current software and hardware technologies, and if the
product can be built within the budget and it is cost-effective. For, our insulin pump
example, one must prove first that a fully automatic solution is technically feasible,
that it will bring a significant improvement to the life of diabetes patients, that
serious risks can be mitigated, the costs are affordable and enough people will buy
it.

Provided that the answers to all these concerns are affirmative, the project will get the green light. The next thing needed is a concise description of what the product is supposed to do. Such a statement is often called a system *mission statement*, or *concept of operations* (*ConOps*). The ConOps is a document that frames the overall system and sets the technical course for the project. Its purpose is to clearly convey a high-level view of the system to be developed that each stakeholder can understand.

A *stakeholder* is anyone with an interest in, or an effect on, the outcome of the product. This includes customers that can be the system's intended *users*, but also the persons who commission the construction of the system, called *clients*, sponsors, all responsible technical persons, managers, regulators (government), society, and environment. For example, for the automatic insulin pump, the stakeholders are its users, i.e., the diabetes patients and their families, the client company that commissions to build this system, the technical staff who will build and maintain the system, the medical doctors who treat the patient, the governmental regulatory organizations, the experts in Internet security and law, and the safety assessors. In a ConOps, the project stakeholders reach a shared understanding of the system to be developed, and how it will be operated and maintained. A good ConOps answers the *who, what, where, when, why, and how* questions about the project, from the viewpoint of each stakeholder. The main questions that have to be answered are as follows [3]:

- What is the problem or opportunity addressed by the system?
- Who are the stakeholders involved with the system?
- What are the elements and the high-level capabilities of the system?
- What is the geographic and physical extent of the system?
- What is the sequence of activities that will be performed?
- How will the system be developed, operated, and maintained?

A product mission statement should be short, descriptive, inspiring, yet not too detailed. One of the most widely cited "good" system mission statement is the one associated with the Starship Enterprise from the original Star Trek TV series [4].

To explore strange new worlds, to seek out new life and new civilizations, to boldly go where no man has gone before.

For the Apollo missions, a good mission statement could be as follows: *Transport a man to the moon and return safely before 1970*. For our automatic closed-loop insulin pump, the mission statement could be as follows: *To automate the delivery of insulin to achieve a near normal glycemic condition for a diabetes patient*.

A ConOps often contains also a *system overview*, typically supported by one or more block diagrams that show the scope, the major elements, and their interrelationships in the system. In these diagrams, the system is graphically described, without getting in too many technical details about the implementation. For

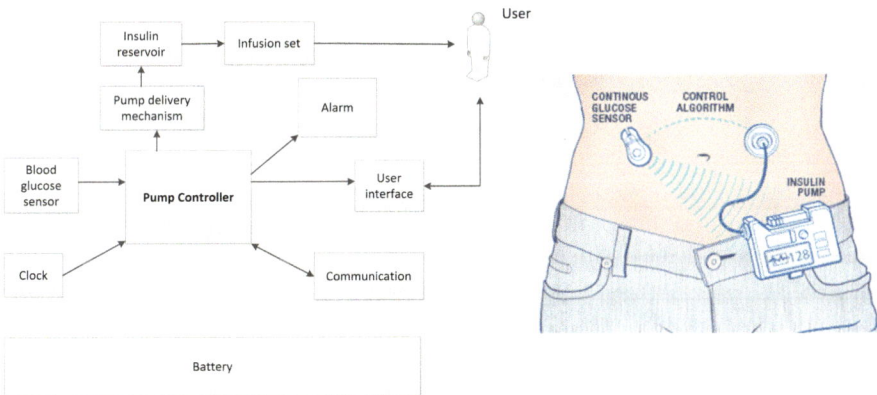

Fig. 7.7 A block diagram of the insulin pump. Adapted from [5] by permission from the author

example, you can see in Fig. 7.7 a possible block diagram of a closed-loop automatic insulin pump. The system consists of the pump itself, a reservoir that stores the insulin, and a disposable infusion set, which is the tubing that connects to the reservoir and which terminates in a cannula or needle, through which the insulin is infused. The needle is inserted under the skin, and the insulin pump itself is worn externally, by the patient. The system should include a glucose sensor, to continuously measure the blood sugar concentration, and a controller to decide when and how much insulin to administrate. The controller sends also the commands to the pump motor to inject insulin.

The system must be not only functional, but also safe. This means that alarms should be raised in abnormal situations, including power failure, empty reservoir, sensor malfunctioning, insulin overdose, and blockage of the insulin tubing. The system can also assist physicians in monitoring patients' glycemic behavior. Therefore, the insulin pumps need mechanisms to transmit and receive data and to be configured via Internet. Time plays an important role in this system, so the system must include a clock as well.

Some *operational scenarios* can also be included in the ConOps, as well. *Scenarios* are real-life examples of how a system can be used, from the perspective of different stakeholders. They can be obtained, for example, by interviewing the stakeholders, or brainstorming in a group of domain experts. Scenarios illustrate major system capabilities and stakeholder interactions, under normal and stressed circumstances. A usage scenario can be just a story, but ideally, it should be more detailed, describing for example, not the normal flow of events but also what can go wrong, revealing possible negative aspects of the product.

7.3   Requirements Engineering

7.3.1   Discovering What the User Wants

A system *requirement* specifies what the system should do and its desirable and essential properties. The sources of the product requirements are its stakeholders. The requirements engineer's role is to understand (*gather, elicit,* or *capture*) these needs and record them (*specify*) in a document, for further communication. This formal and very important document is called *system requirements specification* (*SRS*), an official statement of what is required from the system developers, that serves as a contract between the client and the developer. A project will be successful only if these specified requirements adequately represent the stakeholders' needs and are written so that they will be interpreted correctly by the designers and developers.

Let us investigate the relation between the stakeholders' needs and the product requirements specifications [4]. Ideally, these two sets should be identical. Any system can be imagined as a function that maps inputs to some outputs. Each behavior of the system is then an input/output pair. Obviously, an infinite number of behaviors are possible. We can represent the behavior space of the system with a Venn diagram, as shown in Fig. 7.8.

The red circle, to the left, represents the desired behavior, as understood by the stakeholders. The outside of this circle represents the undesired behavior, together with some desired behavior that the customer has not discovered yet. The requirements engineer produces the specification, represented by the yellow circle, to the right. Being imperfect, this specification not only captures some of the desired behavior (middle orange) but also captures some undesirable behavior (the right, yellow half-moon), called *forbidden functionality*. Also, some of the desired behavior will not be specified at all (red, left half-moon) and is called *missed functionality*.

Fig. 7.8 Desired versus specified system's behavior

Universe of all possible behaviours

Known undesired functionality will take the following form: *The system shall not….*, like: *"The system shall not immediately shut down if main airport power is lost."* This unwanted functionality is also called a *hazard*. A hazard is actually a condition with the potential for causing or contributing to an accident. A failure of the sensor that measures blood glucose is an example of a hazard in the automatic insulin pump. And do not forget the white area in Fig. 7.8, representing the not-known, desired behavior, and the especially dangerous, not-known hazards. Summarizing, the goals of a requirement engineer are as follows: (1) to make the red and yellow circles overlap as much as possible, and (2) try to specify as much as possible the system's behavior, and reduce the white area in the Venn diagram.

Probably only by looking at the Venn diagram in Fig. 7.8, and maybe also from own experience, one can predict that achieving these goals while dealing with a customer can be trouble. The problem is that the requirements in their raw form, as the user wants them, often suffer from some problems, such as follows [4]:

- They do not always make sense,
- They often contradict each other,
- They may be inconsistent,
- They may be incomplete,
- They may vague or wrong, and
- They may interact and may depend on each other.

Therefore, a requirement engineer, besides trying to understand very well the application domain, should be aware that during requirements elicitation: (1) customers do not always know what they want, (2) one should never make assumptions about what customers want, (3) customers can change their minds, and (4) they may have high expectations about what you know and what you will provide. This means that a "good" requirements specifications document should be continuously checked, to ensure the following quality attributes:

- Correctness, meaning that any requirement listed is one that needs to be met.
- Unambiguousness, meaning that each specification can have only one interpretation.
- Completeness, meaning that SRS contains all requirements and all requirements are completely specified.
- Consistency, meaning that no requirement is in conflict with another requirement.
- Testability, meaning that the satisfaction of each requirement can be established using measurement of a fit criterion.
- Traceability, meaning that all requirements are interlinked with their sources, stakeholders, tests, standards, and regulations.

7.3.2 *Specifying the Requirements*

Generally, there are three approaches to represent requirements in a specification document: an informal one that uses natural language; a semiformal one that uses graphical modeling languages, such as UML, SysML, Petri Nets; and a formal one that uses formal languages based on rigorous mathematics, such as B, VDM, Z, and TLA+.

Figure 7.9 shows these notations' prevalence in specifications documents, resulted from a 2014 industry survey [6]. Requirements can strictly adhere to one or another approach, but usually, they contain elements of at least two of these approaches. In this section, we will investigate how to use natural language and graphical models, in order to create requirements specifications.

The most common way to describe requirements is using natural language (English, Dutch, French, etc.), because they are both easy to write and to understand. The problem with pure natural language specifications is that this unstructured prose is potentially ambiguous, and thus prone to misunderstanding.

More structured natural language specifications help to reduce this risk, by limiting the freedom of the writer and forcing him to document all requirements in a standard way. This approach makes use of standards and templates to express requirements. For this purpose, special templates to write requirements are available, such as the IEEE 29148-2011 standard [7], and the Volere templates [8]. Next, we will summarize a few best practices and recommendations on how to write a correct requirement using natural language.

First of all, the generic standard form of a requirement is as follows:

The [noun phrase] shall (not) [verb phrase]

The imperative *shall* is recommended, and, if used, must be used consistently. For example, for a car navigation system, the requirements could be formulated as follows:

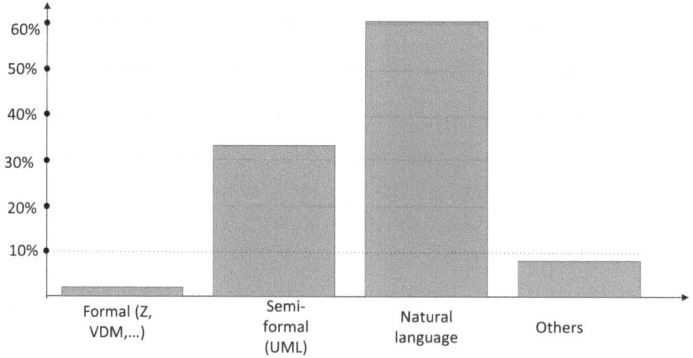

Fig. 7.9 Prevalence of different types of specification languages. Adapted from [6] with permission from the author

REQ 1. The system shall have the capability to determine its current position.
REQ 2. The system shall have the capability to display its current position on a map that can be viewed by the vehicle operator.
REQ 3. The system shall have the capability to accept a trip destination request and plan the optimal route to that destination.
REQ 4. The system shall have the capability to output audio and visual instructions. corresponding to directional maneuvers required to complete the planned route.

Other command words and phrases that are frequently used in a requirements specification include "should," "must," "will," and "responsible for." Some recommend to use *shall* when requirements are mandatory and *should* for optional requirements. However, be aware that misunderstanding can happen, because some developers might understand that this "should" points to a less urgent requirement and will therefore be less motivated to implement it when pressed for time.

Moreover, it is very important, when writing requirements, to use language that can be verified. Therefore, avoid requirements such as follows: *"The system should be completely reliable," "The system should be always fast,"* or *"The product shall be easy to use."* These requirements are unfortunately impossible to check, because one cannot quantify these *easy*, or *fast*, or *completely reliable* attributes. The latter requirement can become measurable or testable, if transformed into the following: *"The product shall be usable by customers with limited experience of using computers."* The Volere templates' specifications ask for this purpose explicitly that each requirement should contain a *rationale* and *a fit criterion* that explains how to test it. For example, the requirement with this description *"The product shall make it easy for a buyer to find his chosen music"* can have the following rationale: *"Music buyers are familiar with internet and are accustomed to convenience and fast response times. They will not tolerate slow searches"* and the following fit criterion: *"90% of music buyers shall be able to locate any piece of music within 6s, using no more than three actions"* [9].

A widely accepted recommendation asks to separate the requirements in functional and non-functional. *Functional* requirements specify *what* the system must do: the behavior of the system, how it interacts with its users and other systems, what capabilities it provides, and what information it consumes and delivers, for example, *"The navigation system shall provide the driver with route information at different levels of detail."* Functional requirements state the *verbs* of the system. They do not address *how* the system should accomplish this *what*. An example of a functional requirement for the automatic insulin pump is as follows: *"The software controller shall compute the necessary insulin dose."* A more specific functional requirement is as follows: *"If the BCG reading is above the recommended level, insulin is delivered, unless the level of blood sugar is falling and the rate of decrease of the blood sugar level is increasing."*

Non-functional requirements, on the other hand, are requirements that are not directly concerned with the specific functions delivered by the system. They define *"how well"* the system must perform its functions. Non-functional requirements describe the system's look and feel, its usability (simplicity of use), performance (response time, accuracy), reliability, safety (freedom of accidents), affordability (cost), maintainability, authorized access policies, privacy, etc. In contrast to functional requirements, non-functional requirements state the *adverbs* of the system. Examples of non-functional requirements are as follows:

> The product shall be attractive to teenagers.
> The thermostat should read the sensor each 10 min.
> The navigation system shall have the capability to determine its current position within 20 m of actual location over 90% of its travel time.
> The system shall recognize a handwritten character with an accuracy of at least 98%.
> The system shall not disclose any personal information about system users apart from their name and library reference number to the library staff who uses the system.

Another non-functional requirement for the automatic insulin pump could be as follows: *"The system should always operate safely"*. As insulin reduces the blood sugar level, an overdose of insulin is life threatening. Therefore, a more detailed safety requirement is needed: *"The operation of the device will never result in a very low sugar level."* A fit criterion for this requirement could be as follows: *"The product shall be certified to comply with the International Electrotechnical Commission (IEC) standard 60601-2-24 for infusion pumps in the US"* [10].

A variety of non-functional requirements imposed by factors outside of your control are called *constraints*. They define "under what conditions" the system must operate. Examples of constraints are as follows: *"the system must be developed in C++,"* or *"The system must be ready until 1 January 2017."*

It is true that sometimes it is difficult to distinguish between functional, non-functional requirements, and constraints. If this is the case, you should not loose time. Their type is not important, but their content is!

User stories

User stories are another way to describe the necessary functionality of the product in natural language. User stories are used by Agile methodologies, as a starting point for initial requirements discovery. A user story describes a new functionality from the perspective of a user. It will describe what the user is able to do. A user story must be small enough to be realized within one sprint. This means that larger stories need to be divided into several stories, with the advantage that they remain manageable. The user story is written in the following form:

As a [role], I want [functionality], so that [reason for or use of the functionality].

For example:

> As a driver, I want to know which parking garage has empty places, so that I can avoid queuing for the wrong one.

User stories are written on story cards, by the product owner, a customer representative who is part of the Agile team. All the user stories are put in a so-called *back log*, a collection of user stories that need to be implemented. After a user story is created, a priority is assigned to it. When starting a new sprint, the developers pick any of the user stories with the highest priority, and start developing code for it.

No doubt that formatted approaches remove some of the problems of natural language specifications. However, it is still difficult to write requirements in an unambiguous way, especially when complicated computations are required. To address this problem, extra information can be added to natural language specifications, by using *graphical models*. These can show how computations proceed, how the system states change, how users interact with the system, and how sequences of actions are performed. Next, we will show a few types of graphical models that can add clarity to the requirements written in natural language.

Maybe it is good to explain first what a model is. A *model* represents the reality simplified for a given purpose. Examples are physical models, like the scale-model of a train, and more abstract models, like an architectural plan for a new building. Obviously, models are simpler and cheaper than the reality, but cannot represent all the characteristic aspects of a system. The Unified Modeling Language (UML) is currently the de facto modeling notation for specifying the structural and behavioral requirements of software-intensive systems [11, 12]. Next we will illustrate three types of UML behavioral models: use cases, state transition diagrams, and activity diagrams.

Use cases

A *use case* depicts the interactions between the system and the environment around the system, in particular human users and other systems. Use cases describe scenarios of operation of the system from the designer's, as opposed to customer's, perspective. Use cases are graphically represented in UML using a *use case diagram*. In Fig. 7.8, you can see a simple use case diagram for a ticket vending machine. A use case diagram shows the functionality of the system, without restricting the sequentialization of those functionalities. In a use case diagram, the box labeled with the name of the system, represents the system's *boundary*. The stick figures represent *actors* that designate external entities that interact with the system. The internal ellipses are the *use cases*. They represent each activity of use, for each of the actors. Each use case is a task that an actor can perform with the help of the system, such as Purchase Ticket.

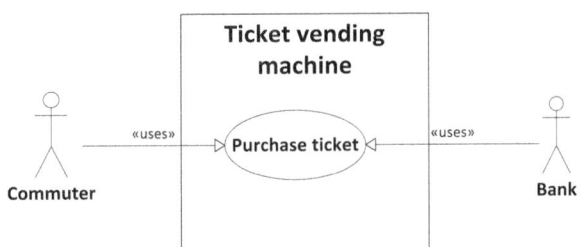

Fig. 7.10 A simple UML use case diagram for a ticket vending machine

Note that in a use case diagram, an actor can be human (a person), as well as not human, such as another system that interfaces with the system, or an input device (a computer, a database, a sensor, etc.). In Fig. 7.10, the bank system is also an actor, because it is needed for the payment transaction.

Figure 7.11 shows a UML use case diagram for a smart car. Each use case represents a goal of a stakeholder, called *primary actor*. Other actors that participate in the use case are called *secondary actors*. For example, in Fig. 7.11 the primary actor is the driver, and secondary actors are the GPS, the camera and ranging sensors, the road network maps database, etc. Note that the use case's name is always a verb phrase, such as `Purchase Ticket`, `Detect Collision`, or `Drive Vehicle`.

In order to capture and specify requirements using use cases, we need to perform the following two steps [13].

1. Identify the actors, by answering to the following questions:

    - Who are the system's primary users?
    - Who requires system support for daily tasks?
    - Who are the system's secondary users?
    - What hardware does the system handle?

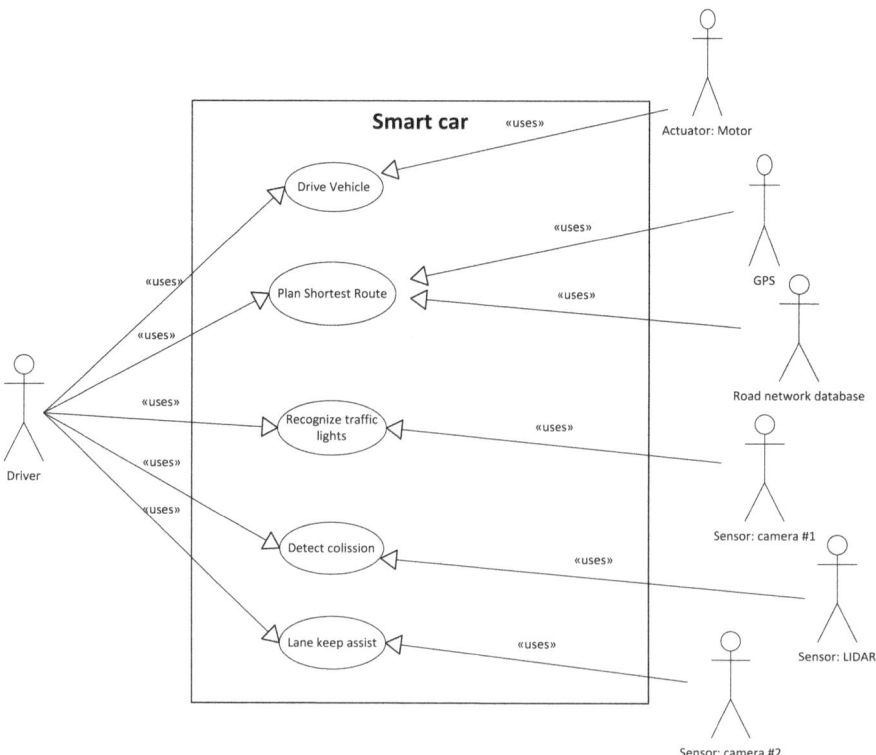

Fig. 7.11 A UML use case diagram for a smart vehicle system

- Which other (if any) systems interact with the system in question?
- Which other entities (human or otherwise) might have an interest in the system's output?

2. For each actor, you have to find out:

- What they need from the system: that is, what use cases there are which have value for them and
- Any other interactions they expect to have with the system, that is, which use cases they might take part in for someone else's benefit.

Although very simple and intuitive, a simple use case can hide quite a complex behavior with a variety of outcomes. Therefore, a textual *use case specification* needs to be created for each use case. This will narrate the sequence of events on how the system and its actors collaborate to achieve the use case goal. A use case specification contains sequences of events. The primary actor initiates an interaction with the system, to accomplish some goal. The system responds, protecting the interests of all other stakeholders. Different sequences of behaviors, called use case *scenarios*, occur, depending on the request and the conditions surrounding the request. The ones describing the flow of events when everything goes fine are called *main flow of events*, or "*sunny day*" scenarios. All alternative flows of events are called *exceptions*, or "*rainy day*" scenarios. A use case specification, should gather all these possible scenarios.

A use case specification should contain the following information:

- Name,
- A short description,
- Precondition: prerequisites for successful execution,
- Postcondition: system state after successful execution,
- System state in case of error,
- Actors,
- Trigger: events that initiate the use case,
- Standard scenario: individual steps to be taken,
- Alternative flow of events: deviation from the standard scenario.

For example, Fig. 7.12 shows a use case specification for the `Plan shortest route` use case for our smart car.

State diagrams

State (transition) diagrams are graphical models suitable for defining the dynamic, temporal behavior of a system. They detail all the states, in which the system can be found, and the transitions between these states, triggered by certain events. A state diagram is a graph, with states as nodes, and state transitions as edges. You can see, for example, in Fig. 7.13, a state diagram that describes the temporal behavior of a lecture hall. The system can be in one of two states: `free` or `occupied`. When the lecture starts in the lecture hall, the lecture hall jumps from the state `free` to the state `occupied`. This change of state is called *transition*, and the start of the

Name:	Plan_shortest_route
Short description:	The way the driver gets instructions for the shortest route
Precondition:	An authorized user is in the car and logged in the navigation system.
Postcondition:	The driver gets a overview map on which the shortest way to the destination is indicated.
Error situation:	The destination does not exist in the map
System state in the event of error:	The driver gets no route.
Actors:	Driver, GPS, road network database
Trigger:	Driver needs to plan the shortest route to a specific destination.
Standard process:	(1) System asks for a destination (2) Driver inputs a destination (3) Driver asks for the shortest route (4) System calculates the route (5) System shows the best route on a overview map
Alternative process:	(3') System cannot find the destination in its database (4') System notifies the driver that an error occurred and asks again for a destination

Fig. 7.12 A UML use case specification for the use case `Plan_shortest_route` in a smart car

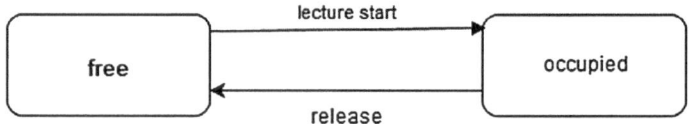

Fig. 7.13 A simple state diagram for a lecture hall. From [13]. Used with permission

lecture is called *event* or *trigger*. Once the lecture has finished, and the hall has been released again, its state reverts to `free`.

If a transition is not self explanatory, the transition line can be annotated with extra information, such as the *event* that triggers the state change, the *action* that follows the transition and a *guard*, which is a condition that only when true, will fire the transition. The annotation has this general form:

event (parameters)[guard]/action

Let us draw a state diagram for a simple robotic vehicle, equipped with two optosensors labeled with R (right) and L (left), that follows a black line. This vehicle mimics the lane departure functionality in a smart car. The controller needed to perform this task has been discussed in Chap. 3. We start by drawing the states in which the system can be found: `idle`, `drive straight forward`, `turn left`, `turn right`, and `stop`. Different events, dictated by the sensors

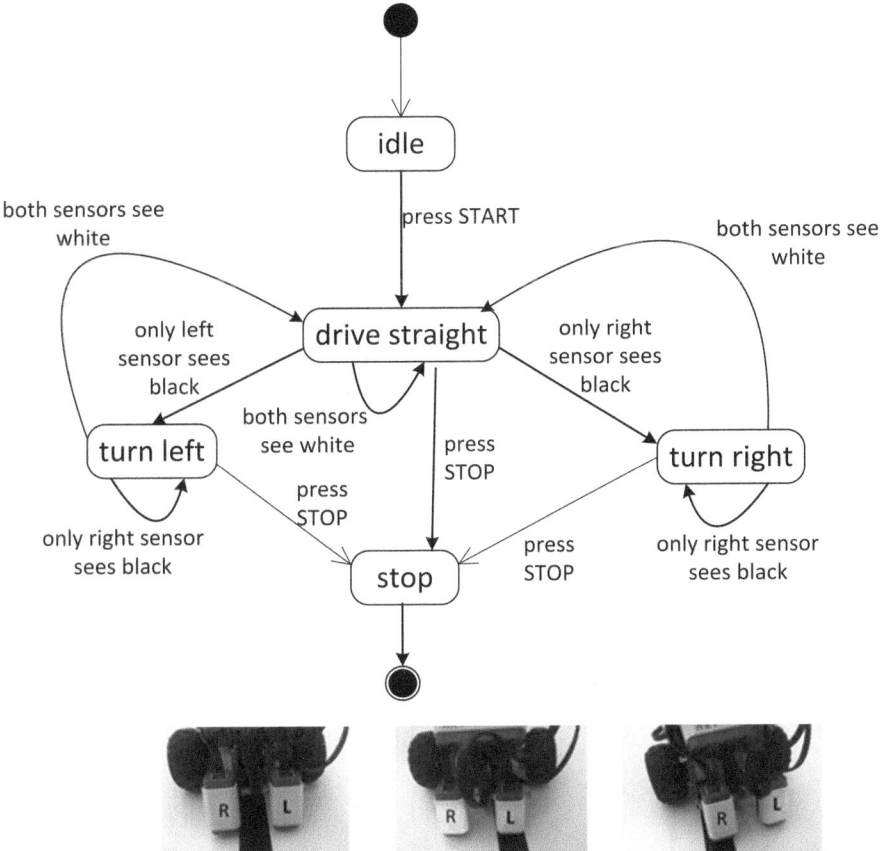

Fig. 7.14 A UML state diagram for a robotic vehicle that follows a *black line*

readings, will trigger transitions between these states. The resulted state diagram is shown in Fig. 7.14. You probably already noticed that this diagram is not yet complete. For example, the behavior in case both sensors shown black is not specified. Yes, you are right, but here we only want to show how to start to draw such a state diagram. Obviously, the state diagram will grow, as we add more behavior details and functionality.

Activity diagrams

Activity models are another modeling instrument that *visualizes the workflow of a use case*. These models are appropriate when the system's behavior changes not as a result of an event, but due to the end of an action, or activity. An *activity diagram* is a collection of nodes and arcs that starts with an initial node and ends with a final node. The nodes are the actions or activities. Activities are things that happen and cannot be broken further in smaller operations. When an activity node completes its execution, the flow of control passes immediately to the next activity node. For example, the UML activity diagram in Fig. 7.15 is modeling a university system and tells the story of a student who needs to register for a course. If the registration is successful, the student can attend the course. After completing the course, the student is allowed to write an examination.

In Fig. 7.15, `Register`, `Attend_course`, and `Write_exam` are activities. The flow is specified by arrows, to show the path of control. The diagram is very simple. However, the diagram can grow, for example, if we want to model the (unfortunate) situation, where the student did not pass the examination and has to attend the re-sit. Therefore, our activity diagram will get two extra merge and decision blocks, like illustrated in Fig. 7.16.

If the course at this university consists of two components, lectures, and practical works, and both must be attended in order to write an examination, the activity diagram can be again detailed, this time by adding a parallelization (fork) and a synchronization (join) node, like illustrated in Fig. 7.17.

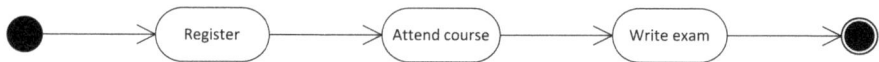

Fig. 7.15 A simple UML activity diagram. Adapted from [13]. Used with permission

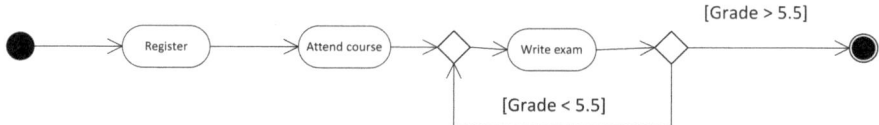

Fig. 7.16 The same activity diagram, extended with decision and merge blocks. Adapted from [13]. Used with permission

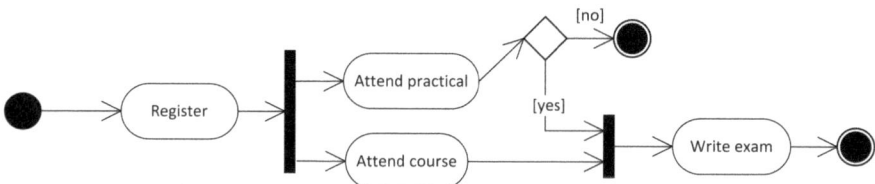

Fig. 7.17 The same activity diagram, extended with fork and join blocks

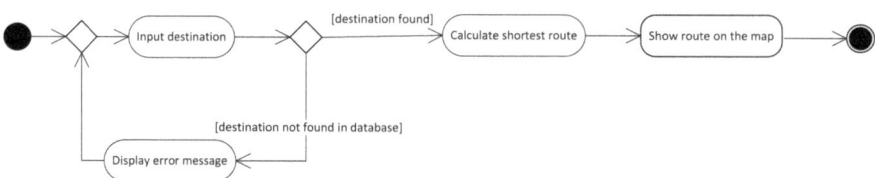

Fig. 7.18 The UML activity diagram for the route planner in a car navigation system

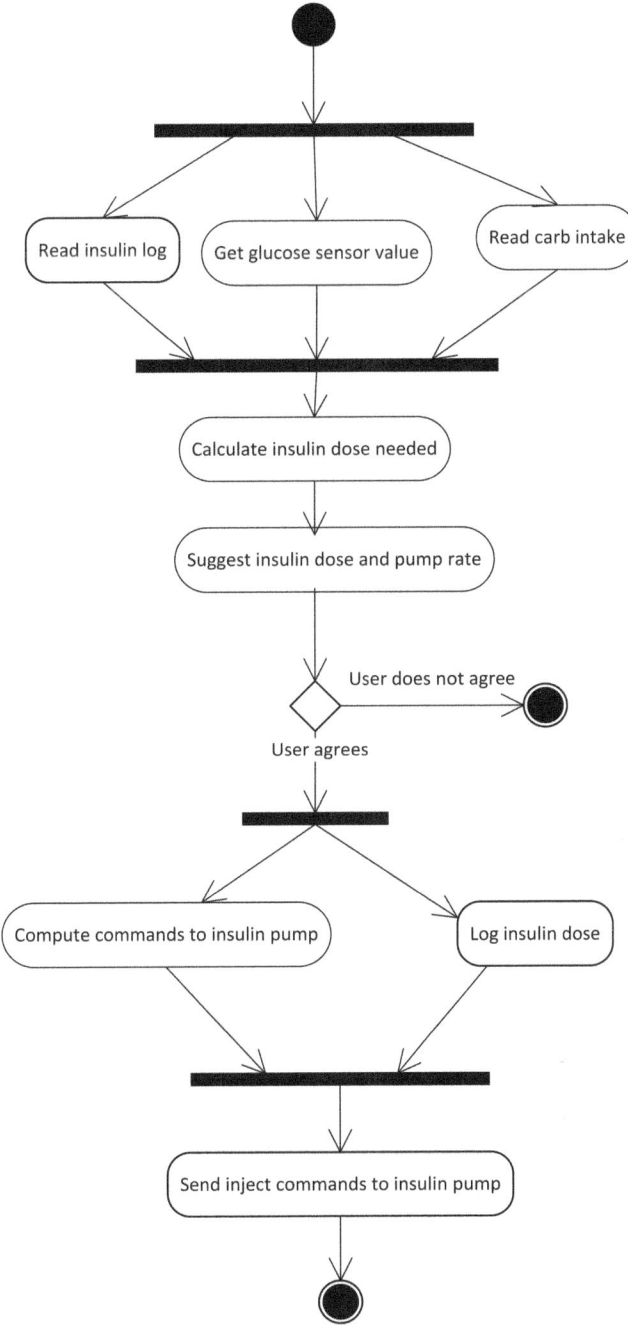

Fig. 7.19 An activity diagram for the insulin administration function of a semiautomatic insulin pump

As examples, Figs. 7.18 and 7.19 illustrate two activity diagrams that describe the behavior of two real-life smart systems: the navigation system in a smart car and the insulin administration function in a semiautomatic insulin pump.

7.4 System Design

At this stage, the engineering team should be in possession of a good, verified requirements document, or SRS. The requirements in this SRS specify *what* the system should do, but not *how* it should be implemented. The previous steps in the "V" model have all focused primarily on defining the problem to be solved. The *system design* step is the first step where one focuses on the solution. This is an important transitional step that links the system requirements with system implementation.

High-level design, also known as *architectural* design, is a process of defining an overall structure of the product with all the hardware and software components and their interfaces. Figure 7.7 shows in fact a high-level design of the automatic insulin pump. Figure 7.20 shows an example of high-level design for a smart vehicle.

The *low-level design* specifies in detail the software, hardware, and communications components, defining how the components will be developed to meet the system requirements. The software design specifications are described in enough detail that the software team can program the individual software modules. The hardware design specifications are detailed enough that the hardware components can be fabricated or purchased. For example, in this phase, we can make a choice

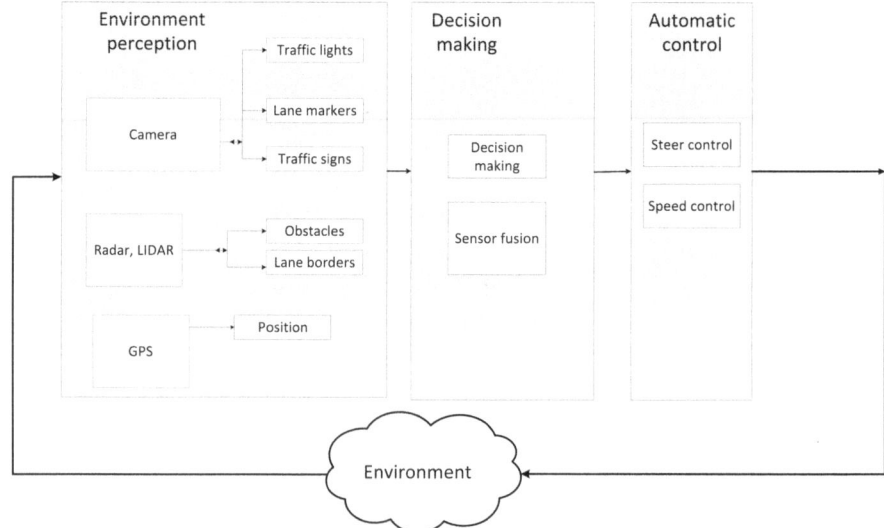

Fig. 7.20 High-level architecture of a smart vehicle

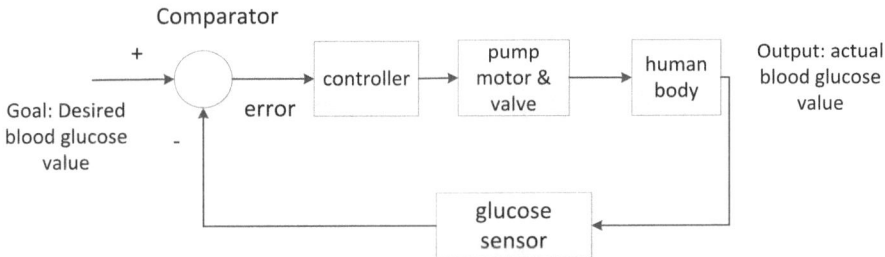

Fig. 7.21 Low-level design of the control algorithm for a closed-loop automatic insulin pump

for the control algorithm for the automatic insulin pump. The controlled variable is the blood glucose concentration (BGC) level, and the control principle can use a reactive, feedback loop. The block diagram in Fig. 7.21 illustrates this control principle. Figure 1.6 showed in fact a low-level design of the traffic light recognition process in an autonomous vehicle.

During the design phase, all the important choices are being made, concerning sensors, actuators, control algorithms, machine learning algorithms, user interfaces etc. In fact, all previous chapters presented different design solutions. Any design is the result of the trade-offs between the available budget, time, skills of the developers, system's criticality, and so on.

7.5 Testing

7.5.1 Why Do We Need Testing?

We reached the stage where all hardware and software components are designed, built, and integrated in a system. This does not mean, however, that the product can be immediately launched on the market. Probably you can remember from Chap. 1 that, according to Mark Weiser, the "most profound technologies are those that disappear" and "technology should be embedded seamlessly into the everyday life" [14]. The goal of pervasive computing is to make technology so familiar to humans, so part of their daily life, that it is not in the focus of daily attention anymore. However, such a close, natural, and invisible interaction between technology and users can be achieved only when the user *trusts* and *accepts* this technology. But when is a system "good enough" to earn and keep the user's trust? What is the best way to persuade potential users to buy and use our product?

Imagine you are a diabetic patient and you are offered the opportunity to use at no costs the brand new model of a totally autonomous insulin pump. Will you immediately agree on it? Or maybe you will first make some inquiries and seek some evidence that the system always functions as expected? Because we all know that technology that does not function properly is extremely confusing and distressing to everybody, but especially for people with disabilities. Second, would you accept this system, knowing that software manages the insulin administration completely independently, without your intervention, and that an insulin overdose is always fatal? Because as we all know, software does behave weird sometimes.... And wait a minute, who said that the compiler used to program this software is error-proof? Or maybe you have concerns regarding your privacy and security? What if a hacker will use the remote programming capabilities and administrate you a lethal dose of insulin. Moreover, *do* you really *want* to be continuously monitored by this gadget? Who else will know now that you have diabetes? And the list of concerns continues...

The point we want to make here is that not only technical perfection but also user-centered qualities are needed, to guarantee a large acceptance of a pervasive computing system. Here, we mean functionality in the first place (does it behave as expected?), but also safety (freedom of accidents), usability (simplicity of use), relevance (how many people are addressed), performance (accuracy, response time, power consumption), low costs, privacy, and ethical correctness. All these product properties, considered important for gaining trust and acceptance, are called *quality attributes*.

In popular views, system quality attributes can be discussed, felt or judged, but they cannot be measured. In a professional view, however, all these quality attributes can be quantified, assessed, monitored, and improved. Assessment of these quality attributes is done by *quality control* or *testing* and covers the phases on the right hand side of the system engineering V model shown in Fig. 7.1.

The stakeholders' wishes on the product's quality attributes can be found in the system requirements specification (SRS), usually separated in the category Functional requirements (functionality) and non-functional requirements (safety, privacy, usability, performance, etc.). If testing is successful, it means that the product conforms to its requirements, and we say that the product is of a high quality.

You can say, "OK, this is the definition of testing, but why do we need it after all?" Well, the problem is that all modules, in a pervasive computing system, can be error-prone, as they are specified, designed, developed, and used by humans, and humans make errors. A *human error*, also called mistake, is defined as a human action that produces an incorrect result. A fault is a defect in the hardware or an incorrect step, process, or data definition in software. This is also called *bug* or *defect*. A *failure* is the inability of a system or component to perform as required or intended. *An accident* is an unplanned event that results in human death or injury. Everybody knows that failures and accidents happen, despite the good intentions of the product's developers and users. Medical devices fail to operate properly. For example, a 10-year retrospective study of adverse events reported to the FDA showed that 1594 reports related to insulin pumps were documented between 1996 and 2005, including 13 deaths [15]. Scary, isn't it? Moreover, privacy-sensitive data leak, banks lose money, planes crash, space missions get lost and systems are recalled from the market because of poor usability. To summarize, on the one hand, we become more dependent on high-quality software systems, but on the other hand all technologies are liable to failure. In other words, systems' quality cannot be taken for granted. As a result, quality control or testing is highly needed, now more than ever, before a product is launched on the market.

Testing is of paramount importance for a special category of smart systems that have the potential to harm human lives in case of failure, called *safety-critical* or *mission-critical* systems. Medical devices are one example and also nuclear power plants, road signaling systems, fly-by-wire airborne systems, autonomous vehicles belong to this category. The fabrication and testing of these critical systems are regulated by various standards. For example, the regulator in USA for medical devices is the Food and Drug Administration (FDA). FDA classifies medical devices in three classes: Class I, II, and III, based on the health hazard these devices present, where the regulatory control increases from Class I to Class III. For example, Class I indicates that there is a reasonable chance that use of the device will cause serious health problems or death. Automatic closed-loop insulin pumps, like the one we wanted to build in our example, do not exist yet on the market. An existing simple semiautomatic version is classified by FDA as a class II device, which needs more than "general controls" to ensure reasonable safety and effectiveness. All these standards impose certain constraints for safety critical devices design, development, and testing. Regulatory organizations' role is to check the conformance of the system engineering process with these special requirements. No safety-critical device can reach the market without their approval and certification.

In this section, we will explain how to test a system for the following quality attributes: functionality, safety, and ethics. In other words, we will show how one checks whether the system functions as expected, is free of accidents and behaves ethically correct.

7.5.2   Does the System Do What It Is Expected to Do?

Let us start by saying that without a system requirements specification (SRS), no testing is possible. What the system is supposed to do can be found in this SRS document, under the category Functional requirements. Assessing whether the product satisfies all its functional requirements is called *functional testing*. Figure 7.22 illustrates the cost of repairing a defect in different phases of the system engineering life cycle. Although there is no consensus regarding the cost escalation factor that varies between 5:1 and 100:1, there is no doubt that the longer a defect persists, the more expensive it will be to correct [16]. Therefore, testing early in each engineering phase is highly recommended. Unfortunately, this does not happen always in practice. Testing is still an operation that under time and budget pressure tends to take a back seat; testing happens not as extensively as desired, and only at the end of the development cycle, when the system is almost ready, resulting in a poorly tested, and badly documented system. It is up to you to change this situation and learn how to build pervasive computing systems properly, while interweaving developing with continuous testing activities.

Software systems testing involves two types of operations, called *verification and validation* (V&V) that ideally should be integrated in all development phases. *Verification* checks whether we are building the system right, according to the

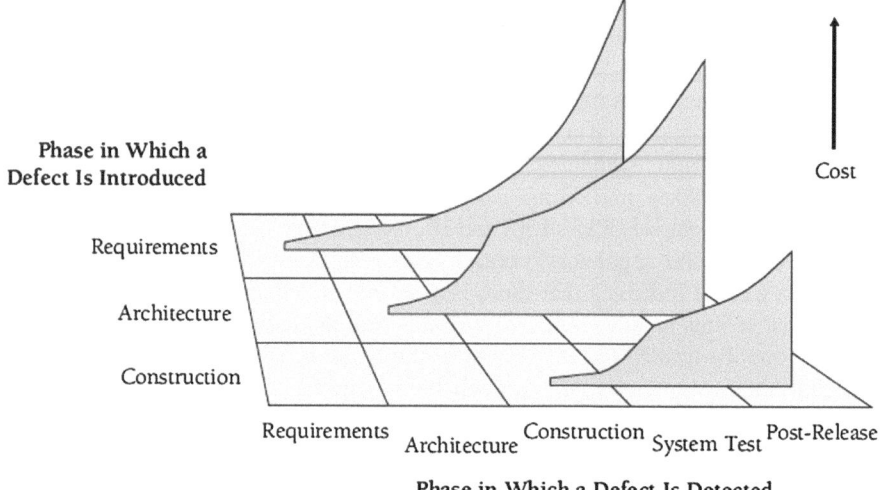

Fig. 7.22 The cost of defects in system's development cycle. From [17]. This figure is from Code Complete by Steve McConnell, © 2004. All Rights Reserved. Used by permission of the author

documents of the previous phase (are the algorithms correct, does the code adhere to the design, etc.). *Validation* checks whether we are building the right system, by asking the user whether the intermediate artifacts still look according to his ideas and expectations. Figure 7.23 shows the V software development model, enriched with V&V annotations. For example, the validation of the requirements document is done by asking the user if he agrees with the SRS, whereas verification of the same document means to check whether the requirements are complete, testable, unambiguous, etc.

In this V model, one identifies the following testing levels. (1) *Unit testing* is verifying each software module, against its detailed low-level design. Let us explain in detail how unit testing works. Each software module can be seen as a black box, with inputs and outputs. Testing can happen *statically* or *dynamically*. A static testing or analysis does not need to execute the code. One or many inspectors or reviewers are reading through the code, trying to find inconsistencies, missing declarations, infinite loops, etc. Dynamic testing, on the other hand, is done by executing the software module for a particular set of inputs. How do we know which inputs to use? This is something that has to be specified in the so-called *test case*. A *test case* is a set of input values, together with the corresponding expected output produced by the tested module. Basically, during testing, the tested module, called *software under test* (*SUT*), is executed with these inputs; the resulted output is observed and compared to the expected output. If these two outputs are identical, then the test case is reported as *passed*. If not, we say that the test case *failed*. A failed test case is a signal that there is a defect in the SUT. Each test case run is documented in the test report and sent back to the developers. The developers will

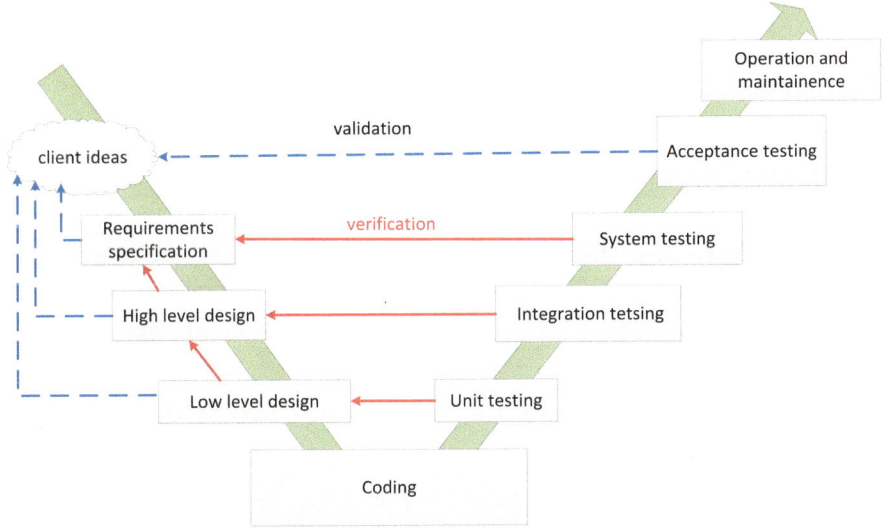

Fig. 7.23 The V model of system development, annotated with verification and validation. Adapted from [18] by permission of the authors

try to debug the code, or change the requirements, or alas, just ignore our testing reported issues, by labeling them as "not really a bug." You can probably understand, after reading this, that the relationship between developers and testers is not always an easy one.

Let us illustrate this dynamic unit testing with an example. Suppose we have to test a software module that calculates the body mass index (BMI). The body mass index (BMI) is a measure of personal body fat, based on the same formula for men as for women

$$\text{BMI} = \frac{\text{weight (kg)}}{\text{height}^2 \, (\text{m})^2} \tag{7.1}$$

The functional requirements for this module were probably stating something like this.

REQ 1: The module shall calculate correctly the BMI given the individual height and weight.
REQ 2: The module shall report an error message in case of invalid arguments.

In Fig. 7.24, we represent the software module as a black box, having two inputs, namely the height (m) and weight (kg), and one output, given by the person's BMI value. Our first test case will test this module for a person of say 1.75 m and 70 kg. Remember that a test case needs inputs as well as an expected output. The inputs for our test case are height = 1.75 and weight = 70. What about the expected output? A trustful source of information is needed, called a test *oracle*,

Fig. 7.24 A block diagram
for the BMI software module

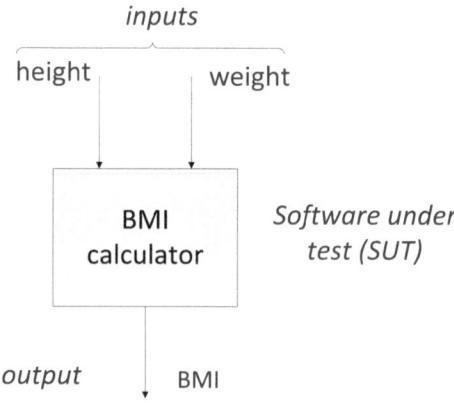

to provide us with the correct expected output. Formula (7.1) can be used, for example, as an oracle. Another oracle can be another BMI calculator, or a book. The expected output can be calculated with formula (7.1) as follows:

$$BMI = 70/(1.75 * 1.75) = 22.86$$

Now we can assemble our first test case and label it with the identifier TC1 as below:

Test case identifier	Input: height (m)	Input: weight (kg)	Expected output (kg/m^2)
TC1	1.75	70	22.86

For sure, one test case will not be enough to thoroughly test this module. Usually, more test cases have to be designed that form together a *test suite*. Of course, we will not be able to test all the possible inputs, but we have to be smart and try to test interesting inputs that cover well the input domain and bring the program in difficulties. For example, we can design another test case, where the height is zero, that should return an error message. In this way, testing covers also the second requirement, REQ 2. We say that this way, our testing achieved 100% requirements coverage.

(2) *Integration testing* is a next level of testing that verifies all the software modules integrated together, against the architectural design. This is a very important testing activity, especially when more development teams had been working on the same software. A notorious failure in integration testing was the Mars Orbiter loss in 1999, when teams from USA and UK "forgot" to agree on the units (imperial and metric) they were going to use for programming a critical spacecraft control operation.

(3) *System testing* is the next testing level, which verifies the whole system against the system requirements specification and users scenarios. If the system is a combination of hardware and software, which is mostly the case in pervasive

computing, system testing might use software simulators to replace the expensive real equipment in early testing phases.

(4) *Acceptance testing* is the last level of testing that validates the system against the wishes of the user. The purpose is to guide a decision whether to release the product or not. After the release of the product, the project is declared "completed." But this does not mean that testing has to stop. Fault and incidents reports are still being collected during the operation and maintenance in the field, in order to learn and improve the development in future projects.

All testing documentation and artifacts created during the project (the test plan, together with all the test cases and the test reports) can be required for audit at any time by the safety regulation agencies, such as FDA, in order to grant the product certification.

As you probably understood by now, software testing is more or less hunting for bugs or defects. Obviously, testing for all possible inputs and combinations of inputs, also called *exhaustive testing*, is practically impossible. The "holy grail" of testing is to select a "smart" set of inputs that will discover the maximum number of defects, in the shortest time. *Testing techniques* are continuously being developed just with this one purpose in mind. Some testing techniques are called *black box* techniques, because they only use information from the requirements document; others belong to the category *white box*, because they use additional information from the internal structure of the module, meaning that also the code is available.

Most testing techniques use the requirements specified in natural language. Other promising techniques, from the model-based testing (MBT) group, use requirements specified in UML or formal languages.

We must disappoint you, by saying (again!) that a perfect, silver bullet testing technique simply does not exist; each type of requirements is suitable for a certain testing technique. Moreover, safety standards that apply for a certain type of device reinforce certain demands on the testing techniques that have to be applied. Other factors that influence the choice of testing techniques are the available time and resources. Next, without aiming to be exhaustive, we will briefly highlight a few test generation techniques.

Scenario testing

Scenario testing is a light-weight testing technique that emulates the actual use of the software from the user's perspective. Basically, a *test scenario* is a motivating and credible story, about someone, trying to accomplish something with the product under test [19]. Test scenarios are extracted from requirements and can be therefore informal, or more rigorous. For example, for the route planner module in a car navigation system, we can imagine the following informal test scenario.

> Bob unlocks his car located in the parking area in front of his house on Johan Huizingalaan, 40 in Amsterdam. He takes a sit in the driver's place, starts the engine and turns on the navigation system. He logs into the system, enters the destination 1081HV, 1081 and asks the system to show the shortest route to this destination. In no more than 2 s, the shortest route appears on the overview map on the screen.

More rigorous test scenarios can be generated from UML use case specifications, if these are available in the SRS. For example, based on the use case specification from Fig. 7.12, we can create one test scenario based on the normal flow of events, when everything goes fine, and one test scenario for the alternative flow, when the user inputs a destination that does not exist in the database. We can go on and have fun in imagining all kinds of diabolic scenarios that force the software module into problems. The more exaggerated and absurd the scenario is, the more powerful and useful it becomes. For example, here is a disaster scenario for the navigation system, adapted from [20].

Sheila is in a hurry to get to the party at her friend's house. She gets in the car and turns on the navigation system. The car's battery is faulty so all the information she has entered into the device has been lost. She has to tell the device again het destination by choosing from a long list of towns and roads. Eventually, she finds the right address and asks for the quickest route. The device take ages to respond, but after a couple of minutes displays an overall view of the route it has found. To Sheila's dismay, the route chosen includes one of the main roads that is being dug up over this weekend, so she cannot use the route. She needs to find another route, so she presses the cancel button and tries again to search for her friend's address through the long list of towns and roads. By this time, she is very late.

Boundary value analysis (BVA)

Boundary value analysis (BVA) is a systematic black box test generation technique, suitable for requirements that restrict a variable to a certain range. This method is based on the heuristics that often programming faults are introduced at the edges of valid intervals. If a variable x is restricted by requirements to a certain interval [xmin, xmax] and the minimum increment of the variable is 1, then the test inputs suggested by BVA are as follows: xmin, xmin + 1, a nominal value in the middle of the interval, xmax − 1 and xmax, as illustrated in Fig. 7.25.

For example, if we test a program that requires an input variable called age, which is an integer in the range between 18 and 55 years, then a possible set of test inputs suggested by BVA is {18, 19, 35, 54 and 55}. The so-called *defensive* testing extends BVA also outside the legal interval to xmin − 1 and xmax + 1. This will add more input values that need to be tested, such as 17 and 56. Let us take another example, that of the insulin pump, where the BCG level must be in the range [4–5.5] mmol/L. This means that there should be a requirement in SRS, saying that if the BCG falls under 4 mmol/L, a hypoglycemia alarm should be raised, and likewise, as soon as BCG exceeds 5.5 mmol/L, another hyperglycemia alarm should be raised. BVA will suggest in this case to test the pump for the following BGC measured values: {2.0, 3.9, 4, 4.1} and {5.0, 5.4, 5.5, 5.6}.

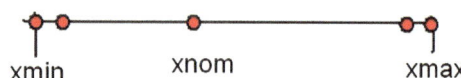

Fig. 7.25 Test inputs suggested by BVA, for a variable restricted to the interval [xmin, xmax]

Equivalence partitioning (EP)

Equivalence partitioning (EP) is another black box test generation technique. This method tries to reduce the huge number of test inputs by dividing the input domain in equivalence classes. Two inputs belong to the same class, if there are reasons to believe that they are processed in the same way by the software. Of course one cannot know this for sure, because the code is not accessible (black box!), but at least we can make a guess based on our programing experience. You can see that programming experience makes you a better tester. After the equivalence classes have been created, the set of test inputs is formed by taking one representative from each equivalence class. As a result, we end up with as many test cases as classes.

For example, suppose that we have to test using EP a virtual family doctor software module that implements the following recommendations for paracetamol administration,

- For adults and children older than 12 years: 500 mg,
- For children aged 8–12 years: 375 mg,
- For children aged 4–8 years: 250 mg, and
- For children aged 2–4 years: 120 mg.

The input variable for this module is the patient's age, whereas the output is the recommended quantity of paracetamol. We can partition the input domain in four valid equivalence classes, as follows:

- EC1: age = 2 up to 4 years,
- EC2: age = 4–8 years,
- EC3: age = 8–12 years, and
- EC4: age >12 and adults.

From each class, we chose one representative, to serve as input in a test case and we eventually obtain four test cases shown below.

Test case identifier	Input: age [years]	Expected output: paracetamol dose [mg]
TC1	3	120
TC2	5	250
TC3	10	275
TC4	15	500

If there is time and money available, one might consider also some invalid classes, such as age <2, age is not a number, and age input missing, or to combine BVA with EP.

In our next example, we use EP to test a software module that processes the destination input in a car navigation system. Suppose that the destination postal code consists of two fields: a four-digit group followed by a two-letter group, for example, 1081HV. Each of the two input domains can be divided in equivalence classes. For the four-digit group, we can think of the following equivalence classes: a valid one—labeled as EC1; an invalid one—labeled EC2—for empty strings;

another invalid class-EC3—for strings containing non-digits; and another invalid class-EC4—for inputs with less than four digits. We will end up with the following set of test inputs: {2222," ", B@#$, 106}.

7.5.3   Is the System Safe?

Safety is defined as the freedom of accidents. For most software products (word editors, tax calculators, and games), this quality attribute does not mean much. However, when the system is safety critical, meaning that it has the potential to kill people, testing needs special care, regulated by standards. If this testing fails, the product cannot be launched on the mission, or sold on the market. All this depends on the guys who have to certify that the system is safe. They belong normally to an independent certified organization, and one thing is certain: they are not interested in how good the system works in *normal* conditions. The goal of safety assessors is to see that the system is safe in *degraded* conditions. This means that even if a hazard happens, the system will know what to do and will always end up in a so-called *fail-safe* condition, with no harm for humans life. For example, in case the injected insulin dose for any reason gets too high, leading to a life threatening low blood glucose level, the pump must issue an alarm and immediately stop the insulin administration. For a high-speed train, a fail-safe state would be to turn off all engines and bring the train to a stop. But what about an airplane? A fail-safe state is different in this case, namely to keep on flying by any means. The result of a safety assessment is an independent safety audit report, a vital part needed to achieve certification.

Testing for safety is based on the product's safety requirements that belong to the non-functional requirements group in a SRS. In order to formulate safety requirements, one has to know first what can go wrong. We can then design a system where nothing will go wrong, or more realistically, to instruct the system what to do in case something will go wrong. Hazards in a system can be of many origins, such as operational, electrical, mechanical, environmental, hardware, software, biological, and chemical. A list of possible hazards or unsafe situations in a system is the result of a *hazard analysis*.

A hazard analysis starts with (1) an identification of all known and foreseeable hazardous situations, together with their possible root causes. To explain this first step, let us consider this very Dutch example of a bicycle. An accident could be a collision in traffic, followed by the cyclist being injured. The hazards that could contribute to this unpleasant event are numerous: black-iced slippery road, the cyclist failing to pay attention, the driver not obeying a traffic light, or the bicycle headlight failing to work in the dark. For this later hazard, let us identify the root causes, based on the block diagram illustrated in Fig. 7.26.

Normally, when the switch is activated, the headlight should be lit. If this does not happen, we are dealing with a hazard, and one cause could be a failure of the battery supply; or maybe the battery is good, but the switch is defective; or maybe they are both working fine, but the cable is broken; or they are all OK, but the bulb is loose in

Fig. 7.26 A block diagram
of the bicycle illumination
system

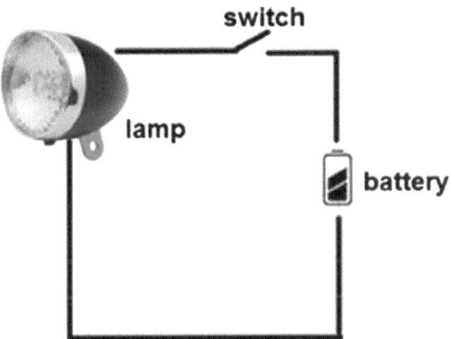

the socket, and so on. For example, in the case of an insulin pump, a hazard could be
under-infusion, when the patient gets a dose that is lower than prescribed. The
primary causes of this hazard could be an empty reservoir, but also some insulin path
obstruction, created by kinked tubes or air in the line. Hazard analysis in system
engineering always needs input from users and domain experts and can be performed
through brainstorm sessions, or by using well-defined hazard analysis technique,
such as failure mode and effects analysis (FMEA), fault tree analysis (FTA), or
Systems-Theoretic Accident Model and Processes (STAMP) [3, 21].

Second, (2) the risk of each identified hazard has to be estimated. The *risk* is
calculated as the product between the *probability* that the hazard will happen, and
its *severity*, or impact. Third, (3) risk evaluation is conducted, to decide whether the
calculated risk of each hazard is acceptable, based on predefined acceptability
criteria. The accepted levels are usually probabilities, specified in the regulating
standards. The outcomes of this risk evaluation can be assessed as follows: intolerable, as low as reasonably possible (ALARP), or acceptable. Ideally, all hazards'
risks should be reduced to zero. In a realistic situation, the goal is to reduce
(mitigate) the risks to an accepted level, through risk control measures, and changes
in design. In Table 7.1, you can see an example of risk estimation for three hazards
in an automatic insulin pump. The most dramatic hazard, with a risk estimated as
intolerable, is over-infusion, when a too high insulin dose is administrated.

Fourth, (4) if a risk is decided to be unacceptable, control measures must be
taken to eliminate it or to mitigate it to an acceptable level. This is done by
formulating an appropriate safety requirement. For example, for the hazard *Insulin
overdose*, the following safety requirement can be articulated and added to the SRS:

SR1. *The system shall not deliver a single dose of insulin that is greater than a
specified maximum dose for a system user.*

If one of the root causes of this hazard is found to be the malfunctioning of the
glucose sensor, then another safety requirement can be formulated, as follows:
SR2. *The system shall include self-testing software that will test the blood glucose
sensor system.*

For another hazard, that of *Insulin underdose*, describing the situation when the
patient receives a lower dose that prescribed, one possible cause could be a delivery

Table 7.1 Risk estimation for a few hazards in the automatic insulin pump

Hazard	Hazard category	Hazard probability	Hazard severity	Estimated risk	Acceptability
Insulin overdose	Therapeutic	Medium	High	high	Intolerable
Insulin underdose	Therapeutic	Medium	Low	Low	Acceptable
User infection	Chemical/biological	Medium	Medium	Medium	ALARP

Adapted from [5, 22]

path obstruction caused by some air in the delivery line or kinked tubes. For this particular cause, an appropriate safety requirement is as follows [23]:

SR3. An air-in-line alarm shall be triggered if air bubbles larger than 200 μL are detected.

Eventually, (5) manufacturers and regulators will have to check during safety testing activities whether the product satisfies all safety requirements. Safety requirements add new test scenarios and test cases to the test plan. For example, for an insulin pump, a test scenario could be the following: "Switch on the insulin pump and let it function for a while, then disconnect the glucose sensor, and observe the pump behavior." If no sensor malfunctioning alarm is raised, then the safety test case failed and the system is not safe yet.

After the product has been released, (6) its safety must be continuously managed. During the operation and maintenance of the system, incidents in the field must be documented and reported back to the developers and safety regulating agencies.

7.5.4   Does the Product Behave Ethically?

Imagine that we built a pervasive computing system that according to its testers is safe and it functions as expected. Does this make it a perfect product? Remember that pervasive computing systems work with people and for people and therefore inevitably have an important impact on the society. The repercussions of such extensive integration of computer technology into our everyday lives are difficult to predict. Engineers, as other professionals, must adhere to a certain codes of conduct, and nobody doubts that their intention is to build systems that always perform "good" actions. But how do we know whether an action is "good" or not? For example, is it good to use machines as replacement for human companions for elderly Alzheimer's patients? Won't the patients get emotionally attached to the robots, and get distressed when the robots are discarded or withdrawn? These types of questions belong to the field of ethics.

Ethics, also called morality, is a branch of philosophy that helps us figure out what actions are right and wrong. Ethics offers normative theories, always involving an "ought"—it is about the way the world ought to be. But what about machine world? Do the same principles hold also for the computer systems we are building? Shall we treat them as humans? What if the systems will not only wish to help and coach, but also act in our place? Even more dramatic questions are not unthinkable. Think about the well-known tunnel problem [24]. You are driving as a passenger in an autonomous smart car. The car detects that there is a child on the road and tries to avoid the collision, by turning to the right. But by doing this, it will definitely kill you, as it crashes with 100 km/h into a tunnel wall. This is an example of an ethical dilemma and a difficult choice for the car control system, right? To kill the child or to kill you? One can argue that not the car controller has the most difficult task, because it just executes what its program says. As a matter of fact, the difficult decision is for the poor engineer, who has to program the controller in one way or another.

Answers to ethical questions are not easy to give. One natural way to create systems that behave ethically is to program them to obey our laws or follow our codes of ethics. Which ethical theories are there? A few moral theories have been developed since antiquity.

According to *Deontological* ethical theory, the consequences of actions do not matter, because we cannot control the future. The theory is based on duties, obligations, and rights, and answers the question: what are the rules to follow in order to be morally right? You can see here an analogy with our legal system. If one obeys the rules, one is moral. Asimov's laws of robotics, mentioned for the first time in the short novel "Runaround" in 1942, are one of the first known deontological proposals to embed ethical concepts in a robot controller [25]. These three laws are as follows:

- **Law 1**: A robot may not injure a human being or, through inaction, allow a human being to come to harm.
- **Law 2**: A robot must obey orders it receives from human beings, except when such orders conflict with the first law.
- **Law 3**: A robot must protect its own existence as long as such protection does not conflict with the first or second law.

Later, Asimov added a law which he named "*Law Zero*," since it has a higher importance than laws 1 through 3. This law states the following:

- **Law 0**: No robot may harm humanity or through inaction, allow humanity to come to harm.

The *Utilitarianism* theory, on the other hand, understands ethics as the science of living a good life, not as being bound by some set of rules. Utilitarians consider that an action is "right," as long as it satisfactorily causes good consequences. In order to know whether something is morally preferable for a utilitarian, we must ask:

"Will it lead to more benefits and less harms than the alternatives?" If the answer is Yes, then this choice is morally preferable. Of course, in many cases it is not clear what constitutes the "greatest good." Some utilitarians consider that what is intrinsically good is pleasure and happiness, while others say that other things are intrinsically good, namely beauty, knowledge, and power [26].

Although both theories have been used to implement ethically sensitive robots, there is still a discussion going on, about which theory is better to use. Even if the problem will be solved in the future, the implementation will not be easy, because robots are not smart enough to understand our laws. Moreover, even if we will succeed to program the robot to understand and obey our ethical rules, in some situations the right thing to do will be to break a rule, for example, for safety reasons.

Another reason of concern is the *use* of pervasive computing systems which also must comply with law and ethics. Think about the controversial use of lethal robots for military purposes that still raise serious, unsolved ethical questions. Another way to build ethical systems is to teach them how to behave ethically in new complex situations. For example, a neural network can be trained to select the most morally acceptable action. In this way, the manufacturer is not responsible anymore for what the robot does. But if the robot starts thinking and behaves morally on its own, then maybe it also needs more rights? New questions will rise, such as is it ethical to arrest a robot? Is it allowed to dismantle a robot and throw it away? The line between right and wrong is very thin, isn't it? See, the discussion can go on like this for a long time. Unfortunately, we do not have time and space to continue the discussion here. What we would like to stress here is that engineers building pervasive computing systems need to have some knowledge of ethics, or at least some thought should be given to the instructions given to the systems they build.

7.6   Project Management

This last section describes some activities necessary to bring a system engineering project to a good end and learn for future projects. These activities are the responsibility of a project manager.

As soon as the requirements for a system are known, the project manager has to set up a *project plan*, to ensure that the product will be finished in time. Although software development methodologies such as Agile are not very keen to use long-term plans, a plan is a useful artifact of any serious system engineering project. A project plan keeps track of the available time and resources. A project plan normally contains the following sections:

1. *Introduction*: A brief description of the objectives of the project, and the constraints that affect it.
2. *Project organization*: The way the development team is organized, the people involved, and their roles in the team.

3. *Risk analysis*: The risks for the project and the measures to mitigate them.
4. *Hardware and software requirements*: The hardware and software necessary to carry out the development.
5. *Work breakdown*: Activities and milestones (stages where progress can be assessed) and deliverables (products that can be delivered to the customer) associated with each activity.
6. *Project schedule*: It shows the dependencies between activities, estimated time required to reach each milestone, and the allocation of people to activities.
7. *Monitoring and reporting mechanisms*: It defines the management reports that should be produced and when, as well as what project monitoring mechanisms will be used.

The role of a project manager is a difficult one. He has to estimate how much time and people the project will take, he has to plan, and to monitor the process in order to make sure that the product will be finished in time. Experience learns that it will never be enough time for everything and yet the business management will urge to release the product. When limited in time, the project manager has to cut in the requirements to implement or in items to test, no matter how nice and well-intended they are. Alas, often releasing a product early and with bugs left in it turns out to be more important for the business, than to launch it late and bug-free. This decision is based on *prioritization*.

The idea of sorting the requirements or test cases into prioritization categories is often referred as *triage*. This term, from the French verb *trier*, meaning to sort, comes from the field of medicine. It was first adopted during the Napoleonic wars, when field hospitals were not capable of treating all soldiers who had been wounded. So the doctors needed to categorize the patients into three groups [9]:

- Those who will live without treatment,
- Those who would not survive, and
- Those who would survive if they were treated.

Due to scarce medical resources, the doctors treated the third group only. The idea of triage can be used in the project work, to prioritize requirements using the following categories:

- Those requirements that are needed,
- Requirements that you would like if possible, and
- Requirements definitely not needed or wanted.

These groups roughly map to the idea of *High, Medium,* and *Low* prioritization categories. There is also the popular *MoSCoW* approach, which stands for **Must** have, **Should** have, **Could** have, and **Won't** have. Prioritization is mainly based on the risks, but also allocated budget, domain-related skills in the building team, etc. Prioritization and unfulfilled dreams are not a bad thing, and everybody knows that they will happen sooner or later during a project. However, it is very important to specify in the project report the reasons that led to a certain prioritization scheme: why certain requirements had priority in implementation, why others were not implemented at all, why some features were not tested, etc.

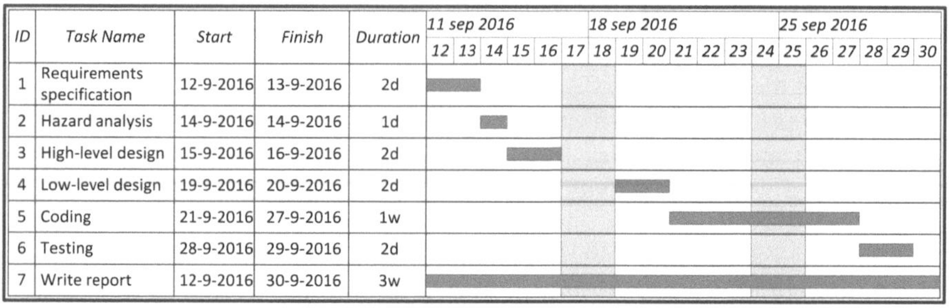

ID	Task Name	Start	Finish	Duration	11 sep 2016						18 sep 2016							25 sep 2016					
					12	13	14	15	16	17	18	19	20	21	22	23	24	25	26	27	28	29	30
1	Requirements specification	12-9-2016	13-9-2016	2d																			
2	Hazard analysis	14-9-2016	14-9-2016	1d																			
3	High-level design	15-9-2016	16-9-2016	2d																			
4	Low-level design	19-9-2016	20-9-2016	2d																			
5	Coding	21-9-2016	27-9-2016	1w																			
6	Testing	28-9-2016	29-9-2016	2d																			
7	Write report	12-9-2016	30-9-2016	3w																			

Fig. 7.27 A Gantt chart showing the main project activities and their scheduling

Project *scheduling* is deciding how the work will be organized as separate and interrelated tasks or activities, and when they will be executed. This is needed both in Agile and plan-driven development, but the former does not need as much details. Tasks should ideally take about one week to finish and no longer than two months. A project activity should contain the following:

- *Duration*: Its estimated duration in real-life time.
- *Effort estimate*: The number of person-days or person-months required.
- *Deadline*: The point in time by which it *must* be completed.
- *Endpoint*: A tangible result of completing the activity (successful tests, a document, review meeting, etc.).

The result is a *project schedule*. One of the simplest and oldest techniques for tracking project progress is the Gantt chart, named after Henry Gantt (1861–1919), an industrial engineer interested in the efficient organization at work. Figure 7.27 shows an example of project schedule, represented as a Gantt chart.

A *postmortem analysis*, sometimes called *lessons learned* or *retrospective*, is an effective tool for discovering the good and the bad of a process, and suggesting remedial actions [9]. People involved in a project should ask the following questions:

- What did we do right?
- What did we do wrong?
- If we had to do it again, what would we do differently?

By looking at honest answers to these questions, the company will get the best chances to improve the process in future projects.

7.7 Putting Things Together

Our journey, started with a simple block diagram of a pervasive computing system, shown again in Fig. 7.28, comes now to an end.

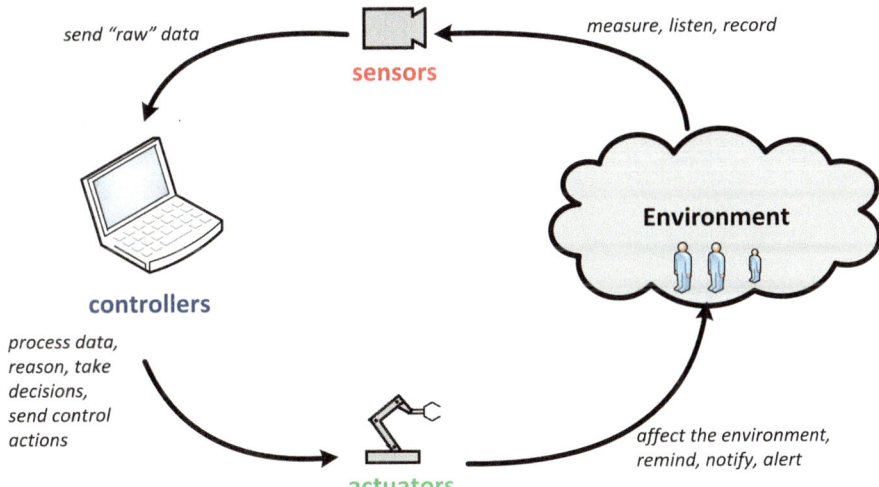

Fig. 7.28 A pervasive computing system

Previous chapters explained in detail what happens to data in each component of this diagram and on the interfaces between them. Finally, this last chapter highlighted the best practices needed in engineering such a system. Let us take one last example to check whether this formula is right.

Imagine we want to build a social robotic companion. The first question is for whom? And why? The good news is that today people can live longer. In 2050, more than 20% of population will be 60 and older compared to only 8% in 1950. The bad news is that we will live longer, but there will not be enough personnel to take care of elderly (us) and we will feel doomed, lonely, and neglected.

A robotic companion could be a solution to this shortage on manpower in caretaking. A mission statement for this pervasive computing system could be as follows: *"To create a friendly, intelligent and helpful companion for all those who feel lonely."* These could be elderly people, but also children with autism, who have difficulties in communication and in making friends. If feasibility is proven, a requirements elicitation and specification process may begin. The requirements have to be set after brainstorming with the users, their caretakers, families, doctors, etc. A possible functional requirement could be as follows: *"The system shall interact with the user* via *speech."* Or *"the system shall recognize the emotional state of the user from touch.* A non-functional requirement should say something about the robot feel and look. Will it take the shape of a box, a fluffy bear, or a humanbeing? Figure 7.29 shows different social robots materialized in different shapes and looks. It is up to *you* to decide the feel and look of this robot. This is a very exciting phase, when you decide the way the robot will look like. This is because everything seems possible and only you will know what is embedded under its skin.

Fig. 7.29 Examples of social robotic companions. *top left* The Scitos G3 Max robot. From [27] © TU Ilmenau, Cognitive Robotics Lab, 2015; *bottom left* The Paro robot, courtesy of Focal BV; *to the right* Alice robot, © Johan F. Hoorn, SELEMCA project

However, in case you are feeling tempted to make it look like a human being, you should be aware of studies that show that people accept a robot as a companion as long as it looks like a robot (see Fig. 7.30). It turns out that the moment a robot looks and acts almost human, a so-called *uncanny valley* appears in our perception [28]. This region of negative emotional response makes us reject it. You see how psychological factors also need to be taken into consideration in this design decision.

Depending on its requirements, the robot will have to recognize the affective (angry, happy, surprised, and frustrated) and mental state of the user (concentrating, agreeing, tired, interested, and unsure), based on many kinds of signals. These can be facial expression, speech, touch, movements, ECG, EEG, etc. The good news is that almost all these signals will fall in one of the categories of one-dimensional or two-dimensional signals, described in Chap. 2. The low-level design will decide what kinds of sensors are needed. Examples are cameras for face and affective recognition, microphones for speech recognition, force sensors for touch recognition, accelerometers for gesture recognition, EEG headsets for brain activity, etc. Preprocessing, discussed in Chaps. 4 and 5, will be first needed, to clean the raw sensed signal. Next, we have to select a suitable algorithm for classification. It can be a simple rule-based one, or maybe you will take the challenge to use a more complex one, like a neural network. Different classification options were presented in Chap. 6. How about control? And actuators? Will the robot be able to speak or will it roar? And

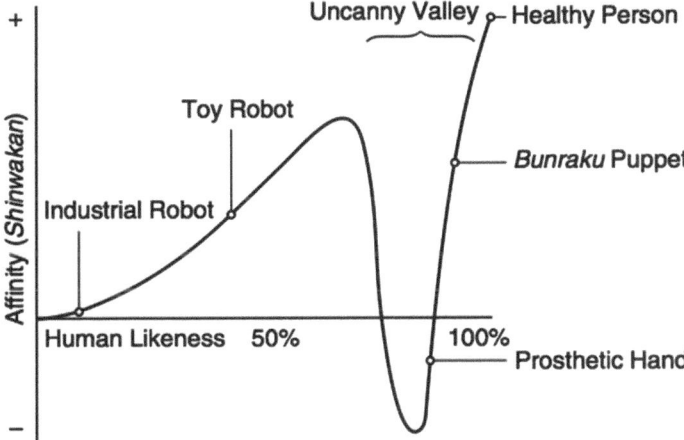

Fig. 7.30 Emotional response of subjects plotted against the human likeness of a robot. From [28]. Used with permission

if it will speak, then in which language? Will it open its eyes, will the eyes follow the speaking person? These aspects have been treated in Chap. 3. Finally, after the system gets assembled and programmed, it will need some testing, to see whether it is safe and really does what it was expected to do. Classifiers need training and testing, and a confusion matrix will show the results. Safety requirements will suggest us which scenarios to build during our testing. Last but not least, some ethical aspects will need to be taken into consideration. Does the elderly user want to have a robotic companion? Moreover, as the robot will be probably expensive and elderly people will get emotionally attached to it—is it ethical to take the robot away from them because the lease contract expired? Or because it needs maintenance? Or a software update? Another ethical question could be as follows: What should the robot do in case the patient refuses to take the suggested medicine? Shall the system insist and force the patient to take it? And then, after a long engineering process, we finally have our social companion, ready to help anyone who feels lonely.

Mission complete? I truly believe that yes. As promised, all these stages of building a smart system were addressed somewhere in this book. In case you have some doubt, try to build a smart system of your own. You will be surprised to see how much you already can. Happy cycling!

7.8 Conclusions

- Nowadays, systems are being built by teams of engineers, working in a project framework.
- A system development process includes technological, marketing, and management activities. The technological process features the following phases: feasibility study, Concept of operations (ConOps), requirements elicitation, design,

device and software building, quality assessment (testing), and operation and maintenance. All stages can be summarized in a system engineering V diagram.

- The role of the requirements engineer is to capture a set of realistic user's wishes. Requirements elicitation is difficult, because users do not always know what they want and they often change their minds. A good requirements specification has the following properties: it is correct, unambiguous, complete, consistent, verifiable, and traceable.
- Specifying requirements is a difficult task and needs good writing skills. Natural language, modeling languages (UML use cases, state diagrams, and activity diagrams), and formal languages can be used to write requirements.
- Testing or quality control checks that the final product adheres to its requirements, either functional—Does the system do what it is supposed to do? or non-functional—Is it safe? Does it behave ethically? etc.
- Exhaustive software testing is in most cases impossible. The "Holy Grail" of functional testing is to select a minimal set of test inputs that will discover the maximum number of defects in the shortest time.
- Safety requirements are non-functional requirements that result from a hazard analysis.
- Besides brilliant technological solutions, a high-quality pervasive computing system requires also non-technological, human-centered challenges to be solved.

7.9 Exercises

1. Draw the system engineering V diagram, and explain shortly all its phases.
2. Formulate a mission statement for an elderly smart home. Who are the stakeholders in this case?
3. Formulate a mission statement for an autonomous driverless car. Who are the stakeholders in this case?
4. What makes a good system requirements specification document?
5. Given this user requirement, "The car user shall be able to stop safely," write a good verifiable system requirement.
6. Draw an UML use case diagram for a social robotic companion.
7. Extend the state diagram for a robotic vehicle equipped with two optosensors, which follows a black line, and stops at a T-junction.
8. Draw a state diagram for a robotic vehicle equipped with an ultrasound sensor that drives until it reaches an obstacle.
9. What is a hazard? Explain how hazard analysis works.
10. Explain the functioning of an automatic closed-loop insulin pump. Draw a block diagram. Draw a low-level design diagram to show how the feedback control works.
11. Define the following terms: software error, fault, and failure. Give an example of each.

12. Define the terms verification and validation and graphically show their place in a software development V model.
13. Define unit testing, integration testing, system testing, and acceptance testing.
14. What is a testing oracle? Give an example.
15. Think about a diabolic test scenario for a university course administration system.
16. Write test cases using boundary value analysis, for a program that gets as input a number consisting of 4 digits and returns the sum of its digits.
17. A human resources department applies the following hire policy: "If the applicant's age is under 15, then don't hire; if the age is between 15 and 20 years, then hire part-time; if the age is between 20 and 65 years, then hire full time; and the applicant is older than 65, then don't hire". Design test cases using equivalence partitioning method to test this program.
18. Think about five ethical questions for a robotic nanny that takes care of small children.

References

1. Beck, K.: Test Driven Development: By Example. Addison Wesley Professional (2002)
2. Suckale, J., Solimena, M.: Pancreas islets in metabolic signaling-focus on the beta-cell. Front. Biosci. **1**(12), 7156–7171 (2008)
3. System Engineering for Intelligent Transportation Systems, U.S.D.o. Transportation, Editor (2007)
4. Laplante, P.A.: Requirements Engineering for Software and Systems. CRC Press (2014)
5. Sommerville, I.: Software Engineering. Pearson (2004)
6. Kassab, M., Neill, C., Laplante, P.A.: State of practice in requirements engineering: contemporary data. Innovations Syst. Softw. Eng. **10**, 235–241 (2014)
7. 29148-2011—ISO/IEC/IEEE International Standard—Systems and software engineering. Available from: https://standards.ieee.org/findstds/standard/29148-2011.html
8. Volere requirements resources. Available from: http://www.volere.co.uk/
9. Robertson, S.: Mastering the Requirements Process. Addison-Wesley Professional (2012)
10. Zhang, Y., et al.: Generic Safety Requirements for Developing Safe Insulin Pump Software. J. Diab. Sci. Technol. **5**(6), 1402–1419 (2011)
11. UML website. Available from: http://www.uml.org/#UML2.0
12. Booch, G., Rumbaugh, J., Jacobson, I.: The Unified Modeling Language User Guide. Addison-Wesley Professional (2005)
13. Seidl, M., et al.: UML@Classroom: An introduction to Object-Oriented Modeling. Undergraduate Topics in Computer Science, ed. Springer. Springer International Publishing (2015)
14. Weiser, M.: The computer for the 21st century. Sci. Am. (Special Issue on Communications, Computers and Networks). September, 94–104 (1991)
15. Heinemann, L., et al.: Insulin pump risks and benefits: a clinical appraisal of pump safety standards, adverse event reporting, and research needs. A Joint Statement of the European Association for the Study of Diabetes and the American Diabetes Association Diabetes Technology Working Group (2015)
16. Boehm, B., Basili, V.R.: Software defect reduction top 10 list. Computer **34**(1), 135–137 (2001)

17. McConnell, S.: Code Complete. Microsoft Press (2004)
18. Pezze, M., Young, M.: Software Testing and Analysis. Wiley (2008)
19. Kaner, C.: The power of 'What If…' and nine ways to fuel your imagination. Softw. Test. Qual. Eng. Mag. **5**(5), 16–22 (2003)
20. Rogers, Y., Sharp, H., Preece, J.: Interaction Design: Beyond Human-Computer Interaction. Wiley (2011)
21. Leveson, N.G.: Engineering a Safer World: Systems Thinking Applied to Safety. MIT press (2011)
22. Zhang, Y., Jones, P.L., Jetley, R.: A hazard analysis for a generic insulin infusion pump. J. Diab. Sci. Technol. **4**(2), 263–283 (2010)
23. Arney, D.E., et al.: Generic Infusion Pump Hazard Analysis and Safety Requirements Version 1.0. University of Pennsylvania Department of Computer and Information Science (2009)
24. Tunnel problem. Available from: https://en.wikipedia.org/wiki/Tunnel_problem
25. Asimov, I.: I, Robot. Doubleday & Company, New York (1950)
26. Tzafestas, S.G.: Roboethics: A Navigating Overview. Intelligent Systems, Control and Automation: Science and Engineering, vol. 79. Springer International Publishing (2016)
27. Gross, H.-M., Müller, St., Schröter, Ch., Volkhardt, M., Scheidig, A., Debes, K., Richter, K., Döring, N.: Robot companion for domestic health assistance: implementation, test and case study under everyday conditions in private apartments. In: IEEE/RSJ International Conference on Intelligent Robots and Systems (IROS). IEEE, Hamburg, Germany (2015)
28. Mori, M.: The Uncanny Valley. IEEE Spectrum (2012)

Appendix A
Getting Started with Signals Using MATLAB

Aim. After completing this tutorial, you will be able to:

- Understand the mathematical description of simple signals,
- Understand the principles of digitization,
- Acquire audio and video signals with a computer.

Method. These experiments have been performed with MATLAB® 2014a, a Microsoft® LifeCam Cinema webcam with an embedded microphone, an A440 tuning fork, and a set of headphones. First, you will get acquainted with MATLAB and the mathematical representation of simple signals. Second, you will use MATLAB to generate and acquire different types of audio and video signals. Finally, you will learn how to perform a simple analysis of the acquired signals. Maybe, you will even discover the gap between simple math and real-life signals.

Experiment 1. **Generate simple signals**

Launch the MATLAB development IDE (see Fig. A.1). Central in the default desktop layout is the Command window, the main area where commands can be entered at the command line. It is indicated by the command prompt ($\gg$).

We start by creating a vector variable, called y, containing the following sequence of numbers: 1, 2, 3, 4, and 5. To do this, type the following command at the MATLAB command prompt:

```
>>y = [1,2,3,4,5]
```

If you press Enter, you will see MATLAB respond with the answer in the Command window:

```
y =
    1 2 3 4 5
>>
```

You will also see that in the Workspace window, a new variable (of type matrix) has been created, called **y**.

© Springer International Publishing AG 2017

N. Silvis-Cividjian, *Pervasive Computing*, Undergraduate Topics in Computer Science, DOI 10.1007/978-3-319-51655-4

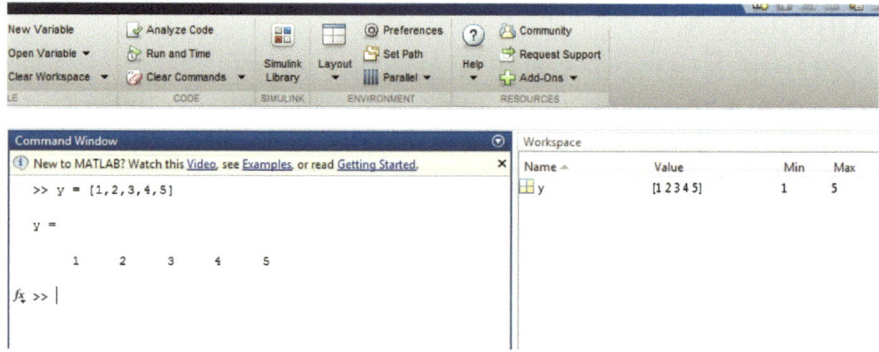

Fig. A.1 A screenshot of the MATLAB desktop layout

If you double-click on the matrix symbol in the Workspace window, another window will open, where you can explicitly see all the elements of the vector.

It is important to know that all numerical variables in MATLAB are *matrices*, a mathematical data type corresponding to a two-dimensional array of numbers. A *vector* is actually just a matrix, but with one of these dimensions equal to 1. In MATLAB, a vector can be a *row* vector, like the one you have just created, or a *column* vector.

If you type the same command, but followed by a semicolon (;), then MATLAB's response will be suppressed. However, you will still be able to see in the Workspace window that the variable *y* has been created.

If the vector elements are regularly spaced, then a more elegant way to create the same vector is by using the colon operator (:).

```
>> y = (1:5)
y =
      1 2 3 4 5
>>
```

You have just created a sequence of numbers from 1 to 5 with a step of 1, which is the default increment. If you want to create a sequence of numbers between 1 and 5 with a step of 2, then you have to write:

```
>>y = (1:2:5)
y =
1 3 5
```

Let us go back to our vector *y*, and fill it with numbers from 10 to 100, with a step of 10 between them.

```
>>y = [10 20 30 40 50 60 70 80 90 100];
```

```
>> y=[10,20,30,40,50,60,70,80,90,100]

y =

    10    20    30    40    50    60    70    80    90    100

>>
```

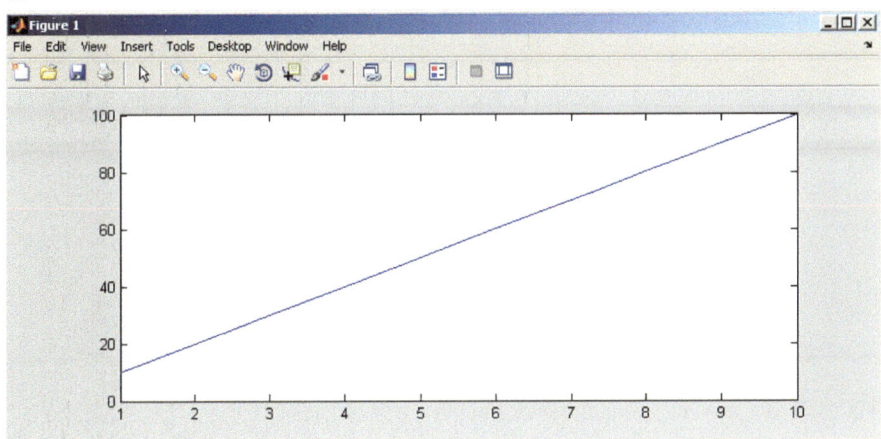

Fig. A.2 A plot of the vector y

Exercise 1 Can you think of another way to generate this vector?

Let us try to visualize its content in a graph. We can do this by using the plot command.

```
>> plot (y);
```

A new window will open, containing a graph, with the 10 points linked together using lines (see Fig. A.2). On the *x*-axis, we see the element's index, from 1 to 10. On the *y*-axis, we see the values of the vector's elements.

You can modify many features of this graph, such as the type and color of the line and the type of markers. For example, by typing this command:

```
>> plot(y,'or');
```

we can make a plot where the points are not linked together with lines, but instead, each element is represented by a red (because of "r") circle (because of "o").

We can also add a grid to the figure to make it easier to see the values, using this command:

```
>> grid on;
```

Figure A.3 shows the results.

This might be a good time to mention that to repeat a command you have already used, you can just double-click on that command in the Command History window.

```
>> plot (y,'or');
>> grid on ;
```

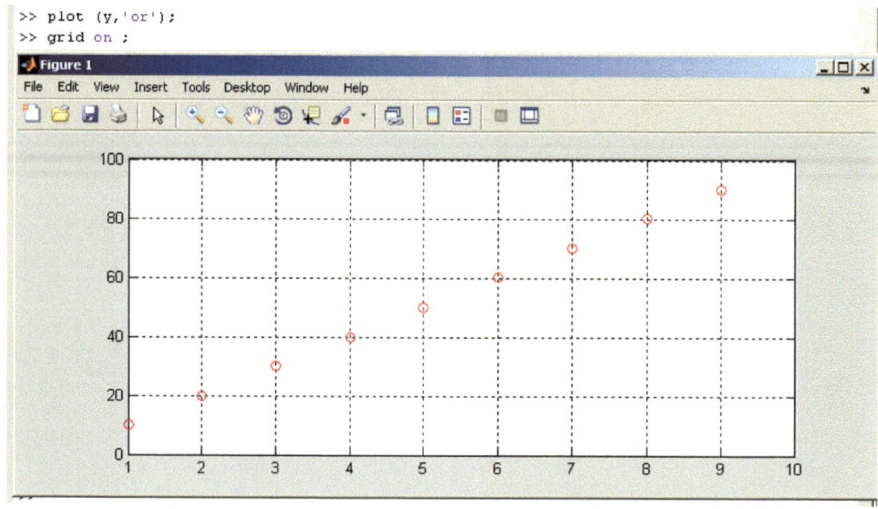

Fig. A.3 The same plot with grid lines and other type of markers

You can also use the <up arrow> at the command prompt to go through this command history, until you find the command you want to repeat.

If you imagine that the elements of the vector y are some samples acquired from a signal, then you can use a MATLAB command specifically intended to plot discrete sequence data, called `stem`. Data is plotted like stems from the x-axis, terminated with circles (see Fig. A.4).

```
>> stem(y);
```

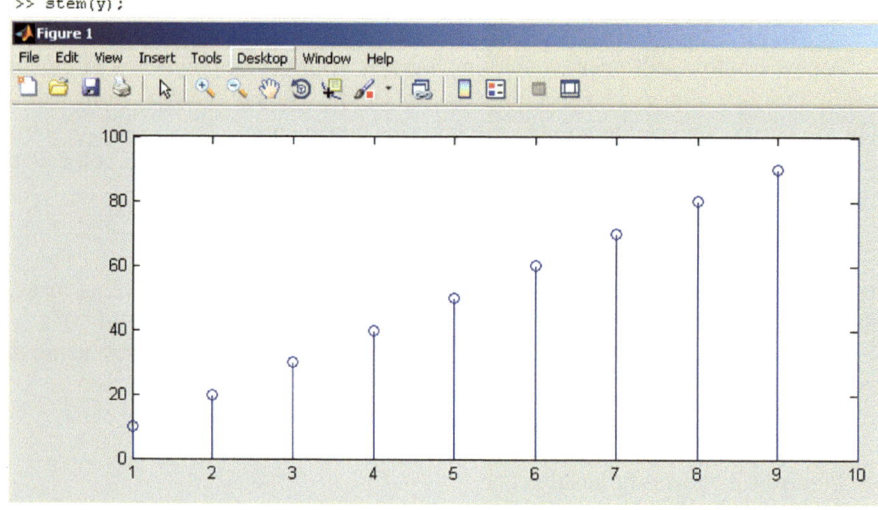

Fig. A.4 The same plot using stems

Exercise 2 Investigate how the MATLAB function rand works. Then, use it to create a vector filled with 10 random numbers, and plot it.

Hint: By typing ≫help xxx, you can find out how any MATLAB function (in this example, xxx) works and how it can be used. Another way to get more information about a MATLAB function is to type the command name at the MATLAB prompt, and then press the F1 key.

In MATLAB, it is very easy to calculate the sum of two vectors; you can just use the + operator. There is one requirement: Both vectors must be of the same length. Let us create a new vector called z, containing 10 elements which are all equal to 5.

```
>> z=[5 5 5 5 5 5 5 5 5 5]

z =

    5    5    5    5    5    5    5    5    5    5
```

Now, we add vector z to vector y. The sum of these two vectors is also a vector, with the same length as y and z, which we will call *sum*:

```
>> sum = y + z

sum =

   15   25   35   45   55   65   75   85   95  105
```

You can see that each element of *sum* is simply the sum of the corresponding elements from y and z.

We can plot all three signals in the same figure by using the command plot (which you have already seen), together with a new command hold on, which will keep all the signals visible on the same graph. In Fig. A.5, the vector y is plotted in red, the vector z in blue, and the resulting sum in green.

```
>> plot (y,'or');
>> hold on;
>> plot (z,'ob');
>> plot(sum,'og');
>> grid on;
>> |
```

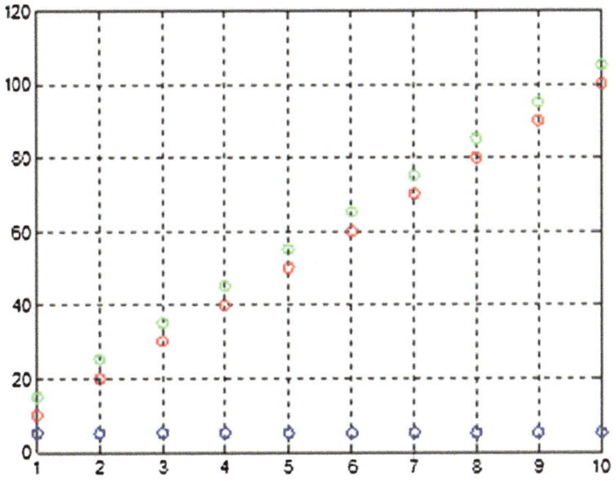

Fig. A.5 The plot of the sum of vector y and vector z

Now, let us create a digital sinusoidal signal and store its samples in a vector and name it *y*. The level of the signal at moment *t* is given by the formula:

$$A \sin(2\pi ft) \quad (*)$$

where *A* is the signal amplitude, *f* is the signal frequency (in Hz), and *t* is the time (in seconds).

Thanks to MATLAB's powerful matrix-oriented features, formula (*) can be applied also to a vector of time moments, *t*[ ]. The result, *y*, will also be a vector, of the same length as *t*.

Let us try to generate a sinusoidal signal with an amplitude of *A* = 1 and a frequency of *f* = 10 Hz, which means that in the span of one second, the signal will oscillate 10 times between −1 and 1.

```
>> A = 1;
>> f = 10;
```

In this case, the period of the signal—meaning the time in which the signal oscillates just once—is *T* = 1/*f* = 0.1 s. The last unknown component in formula (*) is the time vector *t*. We will show next how to generate this time vector.

Suppose that we want to generate a signal corresponding to one cycle of 0.1 s. The signal's time duration is then Td = *T* = 0.1 s. The time vector *t* must contain all the discrete points in time at which the signal will be calculated (sampled).

Let us generate one period of this signal using *N* = 100 samples per period. The first element of the vector *t* is equal to 0 s. The time step, or increment, Δt = Td/*N* = 0.1 s/100 = 0.001 s, because we divided the interval [0..0.1 s] into *N* = 100 subintervals. The last element with the index (*N* + 1) actually belongs to the next period and corresponds to the time moment Td = 0.1 s.

The time vector *t*, starting from 0 s and ending at 0.1 s, has *N* + 1 elements, with a step of 0.001 s between them (see Fig. A.6). This time vector can be generated in MATLAB using the following command:

```
>> t = (0:0.001:0.1);
```

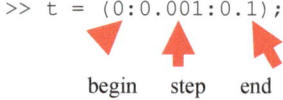

begin   step   end

Fig. A.6 The architecture of the time vector

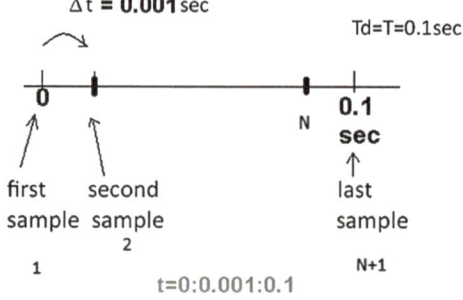

More generally, such a time vector *t* can be generated in MATLAB using the following command:

```
>> t = (0 : Td/N : Td);
```

The sampling frequency, defined as the number of samples taken in a time interval of one second, is fs = $1/\Delta t$ = N/Td = 1000 Hz, meaning 1000 samples per second. This means that given the sampling frequency, we can generate the time vector with this (equivalent) command:

```
>> t = (0 : 1/fs : Td);
```

where fs is the sampling frequency.

Now, we have a well-defined time vector *t*, the last unknown component in the formula (*). We can now generate our sinusoidal signal, by applying the formula (*) and the following MATLAB command:

```
>>y=A*sin(2*pi*f*t);
```

Note that the sin function is applied to the whole vector *t*. The result is *y*, which is also a vector of the same size as *t*—containing in this case 101 consecutive samples of the digital signal.

We can satisfy our curiosity and make sure that we generated the correct sequence, by plotting the vector *y*—containing the samples—against the vector *t*—containing the time. This can be done in MATLAB by using the command plot applied with two parameters:

```
>> plot(t,y);
```

The result can be visualized in Fig. A.7.

Any element of a vector can be accessed by using the name of that vector, followed by the element rank (the index) as a parameter, given between parentheses. Note that in MATLAB, the numbering of the indices starts at 1. For example, we can query the first element of the vector *y*, *y*(1), and we will get its value as answer.

```
>> y(1)

ans =
        0
```

As another example, we can check that around the middle +1 element, which corresponds in our example to sample #51, the signal crossed the *x*-axis and approached zero, which is the expected behavior for a sinusoidal signal.

Fig. A.7 A plot of the generated digital sinusoidal signal

```
>> f=10;
>> A=1;
>> t=0:0.001:0.1;
>> y=A*sin(2*pi*f*t);
>> plot(t,y);
>> grid on;
>> xlabel ('Time t[seconds]');
```

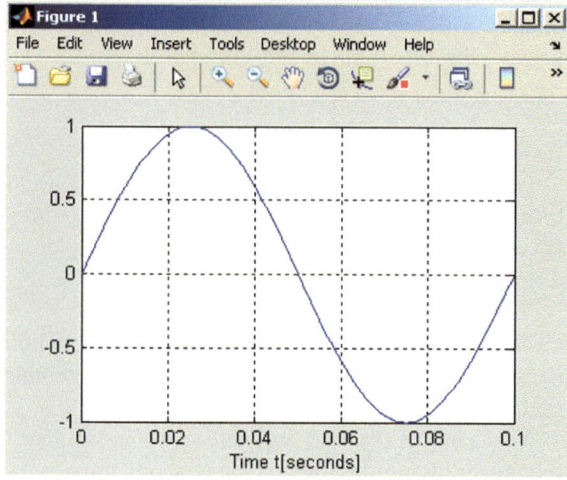

```
>> y(50)
ans =

    0.0628

>> y(51)
ans =

  1.2246e-016

>> y(52)

ans =

   -0.0628
```

Now might be the right moment to write a *script* or an *M-file* instead of typing commands at the MATLAB prompt, because those commands will disappear as soon as you close the MATLAB session. To create an M-file, select New-Script and an Editor window will open. You can then type in the commands you need, and you can start by just copying and pasting them from your Command window. The script is shown in Fig. A.8.

It is highly recommended to use *comments* in a script (by writing text after the symbol % on a line) as much as possible, including a line about what the file

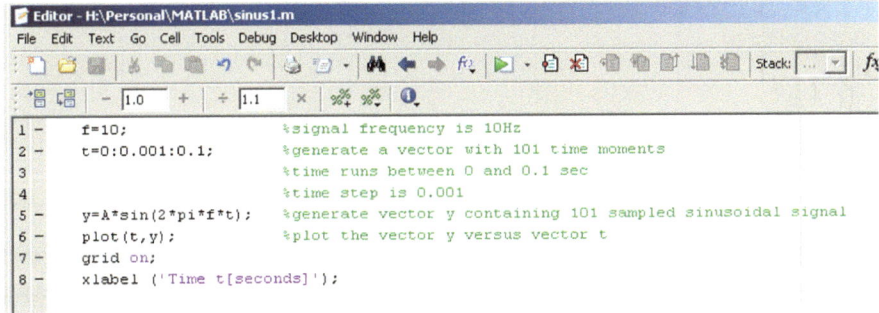

```
1 -   f=10;                    %signal frequency is 10Hz
2 -   t=0:0.001:0.1;           %generate a vector with 101 time moments
3                              %time runs between 0 and 0.1 sec
4                              %time step is 0.001
5 -   y=A*sin(2*pi*f*t);       %generate vector y containing 101 sampled sinusoidal signal
6 -   plot(t,y);               %plot the vector y versus vector t
7 -   grid on;
8 -   xlabel ('Time t[seconds]');
```

Fig. A.8 A MATLAB script for generating and plotting a sinusoidal digital signal

actually does, the names of the authors, and the role of parameters and variables. This facilitates a good understanding of the script by other users.

Save the file in your own directory, for example under the name `sinus.m`.

You can run the script by pressing the green arrow button in the Editor menu, or by typing its name at the MATLAB prompt.

```
>> sinus;
```

We can also plot only certain segments of this sinusoidal signal. For example, if we want to plot only the upper half—given by the first 51 samples—we can use the command:

```
>> plot (t(1:51),y(1:51));
```

Let us now analyze the sampling process. We generated $N = 100$ samples from one period of the signal, with the total time duration of Td = 0.1 s. So our sampling period was Ts = Td/N = 0.1 s/100 = 0.001 s. The sampling frequency is fs = 1/Ts = 1000 Hz, meaning 1000 samples per second. This seems correct, if we consider that we had 100 samples generated in a period of 0.1 s.

Let us now keep the signal's parameters unchanged, but reduce the sampling frequency. For example, we will generate the same signal with a sampling period of 0.01 s, meaning that we generate only 10 samples per cycle.

```
A=1;                      % amplitude is 1
f=10;                     % frequency is 10Hz
t=0:0.01:0.1;             %generate a vector with 11 time moments
                          %time runs from 0 and 0.1 sec
                          %time step is 0.01
y=A*sin(2*pi*f*t);        %generate vector y containing the samples
                          %of the sinusoidal signal
plot(t,y);                %plot the vector y versus vector t
grid on;                  % show a grid
xlabel ('Time t[seconds]');    %label the x axis
```

Fig. A.9 An undersampled
sinusoidal signal

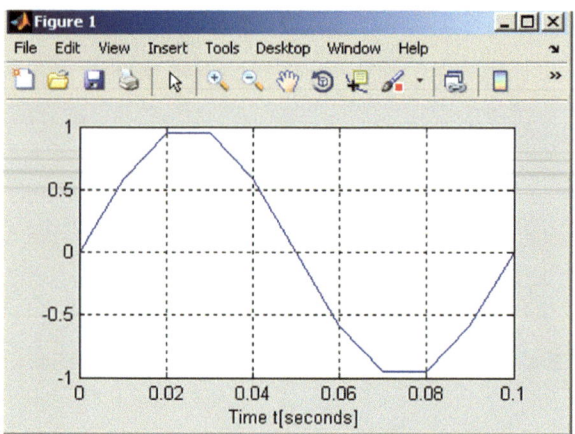

The resulted signal illustrated in Fig. A.9 is deformed and looks less sinusoidal. This is the effect of *undersampling*. This example shows how important it is to sample a signal with a high enough frequency.

Suppose we want now to generate a sinusoidal signal with a different frequency, say $f = 100$ Hz. Of course, we could retype the previous program and change the frequency and other variables that depend on it, but this process might turn to be error prone. A solution to this problem is to write a *function*. A function is a construction meant to perform the same action many times, each time with different values for the input variables, called *parameters*.

For example, we can build a function called `sinus_gen` (A, f, fs, Td) that will take as parameters the signal amplitude A, its frequency f, the sampling frequency fs, and the signal time duration Td and will generate a vector containing $N = Td * fs + 1$ samples of the corresponding digital sinusoidal signal. First, we open the script editor and we *declare* the function we intend to write.

```
function [s] = sinus_gen(A,f,fs,Td)
```

This declaration says something like:

Hi, I am a function. You can call me `sinus_gen`. When you call me, I need four parameter values, that I internally call A, f, fs, Td. I will do some magic and generate an output vector, that is internally called s.

Everything that follows a declaration creates the body of the function, explaining how to do the magic and generate this output vector. Here follows the body of our function. Note that all parameters have generic names, and there are no concrete amplitudes, frequencies, etc., involved yet.

```
function [s]=sinus_gen(A,f,fs,Td)
%this function generates and plots a sinusoidal signal
%with the amplitude A, frequency f, sampling frequency fs, and
%duration Td
t=0:1/fs:Td;              %generate a time vector named t
                          %time runs from 0 to Td sec
                          %time step is 1/fs
s=A*sin(2*pi*f*t);        %generate a vector s containing the sampled
                          % sinusoidal signal
plot (t,s);               % plot the signal against time
grid on;
xlabel ('Time [seconds]');
```

Type this body in a script and save it with the same name as the function, sinus_gen.m.

The function sinus_gen is now created and ready to be used. We can call it by using its name and this time some *actual* parameters $A = 1$, $f = 10$ Hz, fs = 1000 Hz, Td = 0.1 s. The magic of this function was to generate and plot the sinusoidal signal. The result plotted in Fig. A.10 looks the same as before, but it is generated in a more elegant way. The big advantage is that in no time, one can produce another graph of a sinusoidal signal with any other amplitude, frequency, or duration.

Fig. A.10 A sinusoidal signal generated by calling the function sinus_gen

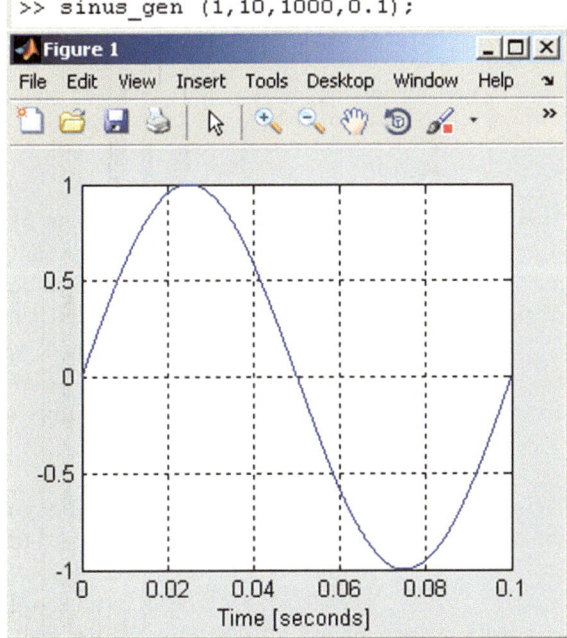

If ewe calls the function like this:

```
>> y = sinus_gen (10, 100, 8000, 2);
```

then besides the magic of plotting the signal, the samples will be stored in the vector *y*.

Exercise 3

Write a MATLAB function named note_gen (f, fs, Td) which generates and plays a note of frequency f, at a sampling frequency of fs, lasting for Td seconds. As an example, use this function to generate and play a 440-Hz A note for duration of 10 s. This should be possible with the command: note = note_gen(440,8000,10). You will need to use MATLAB's sound command to play this note. The sound command needs two parameters: a vector with the samples that should be played and the sampling rate. For example, if note is a vector containing a sinusoidal signal sampled at a rate of 8000 Hz, then it can be played through the PC loudspeakers using the following MATLAB command:
>> sound (note, 8000);

Experiment 2. Record a speech signal from the microphone

For this experiment, you need a microphone, for example the one embedded in your webcam. You should configure and test it first in Control Panel. You might, again, need to use headphones to hear the generated sound.

First, set the sampling frequency to 8000 Hz.

```
>> Fs = 8000;
```

Recording sound in MATLAB can be done by using an object of type audiorecorder. You will need to specify the sampling frequency, the number of bits per sample, and the number of channels. The default parameters are a sampling frequency of 8000 Hz, 8 bits per sample, and 1 channel.

For example, using the following command, you can create an object called rec, of type audiorecorder, with a sampling frequency of Fs = 8000 Hz, 16 bits per sample (type double), and the number of channels set to 1:

```
>> rec = audiorecorder(8000,16,1);
```

In order to acquire a sound of a given duration, you can use one of the methods of the object, called recordblocking. To record for 5 s, start the acquisition with:

```
>> recordblocking (rec, 5);
```

and speak a short phrase into the microphone after you pressed <Enter>.

When the acquisition ends, you will be returned to the MATLAB prompt (≫) again.

```
>>
```

You can play back and listen to the recording using:

```
>> play (rec);
```

If you expand the variable `rec` in the Workspace window, then you can see (in this example) that the length of the recording is set to 40000, which seems correct, because you have recorded audio for 5 s using a sampling frequency of 8000 Hz (samples per second).

To store the acquired samples into a numeric array, for example one called `speech`, you can use the following command:

```
>> speech = getaudiodata (rec);
```

You can see that the recorded speech signal is represented now with an array of double elements, with the length of $5 \times 8000 = 40,000$. You should also know that the sound is stored in MATLAB as a matrix, with one column per channel. That means that speech recorded as a mono audio signal will be stored in a column vector.

Let us visualize the audio signal which we have just acquired. The vector can be plotted by using MATLAB's plot() function:

```
>> plot (speech);
```

You can analyze this plot and decide to cut out a segment of this signal that looks "good" and deserves more attention. To do this, you can select a region of interest (ROI) or a *time window*. For example, plot the signal between the samples #10.000 and #32.000 using the following MATLAB command:

```
>> speech = speech(10000:32000);
>> plot(speech);
```

As an example, Fig. A.11 shows a recording of the word "one" being spoken three times in a row.

Fig. A.11 The time waveform of the word "one" spoken three times in a row

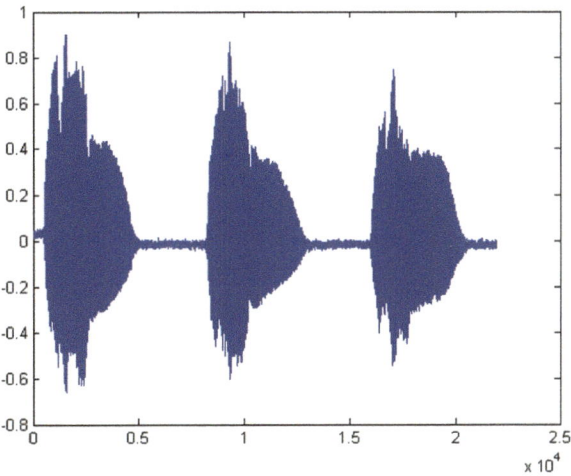

Exercise 4

Utter a certain word three times, and record yourself as you do so. Cut the
signal into three similar segments, and plot the resulting signals in a mosaic of
three windows—one window for each segment, placed one above each other—
using the MATLAB function `subplot`.

You have probably noticed that if you plot the waveform in this way, you have no
idea about the timescale. On the *x*-axis, you only see the index of the samples, but not
the corresponding time. You can convert the *x*-scale into a timescale, because as you
already know, the time interval between two subsequent samples is $\Delta t = 1/\text{fs}$.

```
>> speech = speech(10000:32000);
>> t = [0:length(speech)-1]/Fs;
>> plot(t,speech);
>> xlabel('seconds');
>> grid on;
```

Now, you should have a plot of the speech waveform, with a timescale in
"seconds" on the *x*-axis, as shown in Fig. A.12.

The audio signal can be saved into a file, called, for example, "one.wav".

```
>> filename = 'one.wav';
>> audiowrite ('one.wav', speech, 8000);
```

Fig. A.12 The same waveform but now with grid lines
and time on the *x*-axis

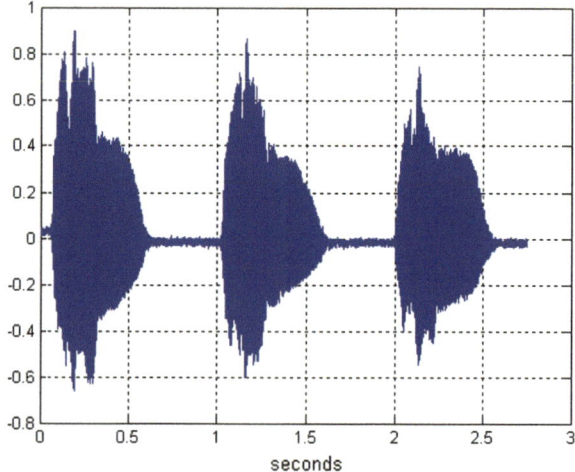

You can later ask for information about this audio file with:

```
>> audioinfo('one.wav')

ans =

              Filename: 'H:\Documents\MATLAB\one.wav'
     CompressionMethod: 'Uncompressed'
           NumChannels: 1
            SampleRate: 8000
          TotalSamples: 40000
              Duration: 5
                 Title: []
               Comment: []
                Artist: []
          BitsPerSample: 16
```

The recording can be read back from the file into MATLAB, using:

```
>> [speech,Fs] = audioread(filename);
```

As a result of this command, two things will happen. First, the samples will be stored in a vector called `speech`. Second, the sampling frequency used during recording, which is crucial to be known for sound analysis, is stored in the variable called Fs.

The MATLAB has a function called `sound`, which can play back a sequence of audio samples. This function needs two parameters: the sound vector and the sample rate. If you do not specify the sample rate, sound will play back using a rate of 8192 Hz.

You can now listen to the acquired speech waveform by using this sound command:

```
>> sound(speech,Fs);
```

Hopefully, what you will hear is exactly what you said during the recording a few minutes ago.

Note that the `sound` function is more powerful than another MATLAB function named `play`, because it can also play back sound using other frequencies. Next exercise will ask you to experiment with this functionality.

Exercise 5a
Try to record a sentence with a low sampling rate (undersampling), and play back the result. Observe and describe the effect. Explain why this effect happens.

Exercise 5b
Try to record a sentence, and then increase or reduce the playback rate and observe and describe the effect. Explain why this effect happens.

Exercise 5c

Modify your script so that the recording is played in reverse. You can search the Internet for a MATLAB function to reverse the sound vector, if you need to.

Experiment 3. Record a periodic signal from the microphone and analyze it

For this experiment, you will need an A440 tuning fork. Tuning forks are physical systems that generate sinusoidal signals. Make sure that the current microphone is the microphone embedded in your Microsoft LifeCam Webcam.

You have to use the tuning fork to generate a signal of 440 Hz. Use a sampling frequency of 8000 Hz. Start a recording of the signal for 8 s with these commands:

```
>> Fs=8000;  % sampling frequency is 8000Hz = 8000 samples  per
             % second
>> rec = audiorecorder(Fs,16,1);
>> recordblocking (rec, 8); %record a sampled signal during 8
seconds
```

Strike the tuning fork against your knee or table, and then hold it close to the microphone.

After 8 s, you will get the MATLAB cursor (>>) back.

Store the samples into a numeric array, called for example, y:

```
>> y = getaudiodata (rec);
```

You can plot this vector in a figure using this command:

```
>> plot(y);
```

Zoom into the signal, and plot only a short segment; you should be able to see that it looks quite periodic and even sinusoidal, as shown in Fig. A.13.

Fig. A.13 A zoom in the tuning fork waveform

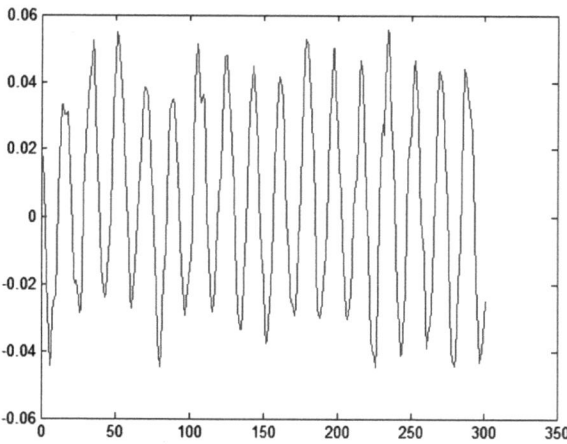

Exercise 6

Change the *x*-axis so that you can see the time in seconds, and then plot the acquired signal against the time axis again. Can you determine the signal frequency from this plot? Compare it with the known A note frequency.

Experiment 4. Acquire an image from a camera

Check that your camera is connected to the computer's USB port.

MATLAB has a toolbox called `Image Acquisition Toolbox`, which you can use to interface with a Webcam.

First, you can experiment by using a MATLAB tool called `imaqtool` that provides a way to interactively acquire an image. The corresponding MATLAB code will appear in a window. Watch these commands, and try to reproduce them later.

```
≫imaqtool
```

After you have experimented with `imaqtool`, it is time to write your own MATLAB code to acquire an image. First, we have to find information about the available image acquisition hardware. The command below returns information about all the video adaptors available on the system. An adaptor is an interface between MATLAB and image hardware.

```
>> imaqhwinfo

ans =

    InstalledAdaptors: {'winvideo'}
       MATLABVersion: '8.3 (R2014a)'
         ToolboxName: 'Image Acquisition Toolbox'
      ToolboxVersion: '4.7 (R2014a)'
```

The adaptor for our camera is called `winvideo`, so you can ask MATLAB for more information about that particular adaptor:

```
>> imaqhwinfo ('winvideo',1)

ans =

              DefaultFormat: 'RGB24_640x480'
         DeviceFileSupported: 0
                 DeviceName: 'Microsoft LifeCam Cinema'
                   DeviceID: 1
      VideoInputConstructor: 'videoinput('winvideo', 1)'
     VideoDeviceConstructor: 'imaq.VideoDevice('winvideo', 1)'
           SupportedFormats: {1x22 cell}
```

We can see that the default spatial resolution of the image is 640×480, and the image representation format is RGB.

You need to create a MATLAB object called `vid`, which will be associated with your camera.

```
>> vid = videoinput('winvideo',1);
```

Start the video object with this command:

```
>> start (vid);
```

This command triggers image acquisition, meaning that images will be continuously recorded and stored into the memory, until the system receives a command `stop(vid)`. The blue LED of the camera will turn on, which means that the acquisition is running.

If you want to see the images continuously acquired from the camera, you can use the MATLAB command `preview`.

```
>> preview (vid);
```

Now, capture your first image from the video stream:

```
>> im = getsnapshot (vid);
```

It is important that you close the video object properly once you are done with it, so that you can use it again without any problems. The best way to do it is like this:

```
>> stop(vid);
>> delete(vid);
```

You can satisfy your curiosity and take a look at what you have just acquired. The image is stored in a numerical array called `im`, and you can use the MATLAB function `imshow` to visualize it (see Fig. A.14).

```
>>imshow(im);
```

Fig. A.14 The acquired image

Congratulations! You have just acquired and visualized your first image using MATLAB. Maybe, it is a good idea to save this first image in a file, which you can (for example) call `test.bmp`.

```
>> imwrite(im, 'test.bmp', 'bmp');
```

In case you do not trust the system, you can retrieve it again and make sure that it has been adequately saved by asking MATLAB to display it.

```
>> im = imread('test.bmp', 'bmp');
>> imshow (im);
```

Finally, you can get some information about the image, by using the `iminfo` MATLAB command.

```
>> imfinfo ('test.bmp')
```

You can now analyze your beautiful image. Maybe, it is good to know that the origin of the coordinate system is in the upper left corner, as shown in Fig. A.15.

You can see in the MATLAB Workspace window that `im` is of the type <480 640 × 3 uint8>.

The image is a color image in RGB (red–green–blue) format. An RGB image is represented internally with a three-dimensional array. Each element is associated with one pixel in the image and represents the amount of red, green, or blue in that pixel's color. By default, each element of this array is represented with an 8-bit integer (uint8), with values between 0 and 255.

Fig. A.15 The geometry of a digital image in MATLAB

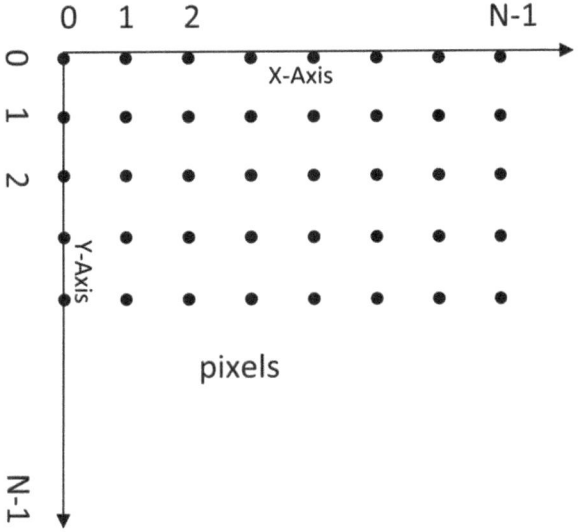

If you type:

```
>> size(im)

ans =

    480    640      3
```

you will see that `im` is indeed a three-dimensional array. MATLAB returns in this case three values: the number of rows, the number of columns, and the number of pages, saying that there is one plane or page, with the resolution 640 × 480 each, corresponding to a color (red, green, or blue). Using simple MATLAB queries, you can query the amounts of red, green, or blue in each pixel. For example, to obtain the level of green color of the pixel located in row 100 and column 200, you can type something like this:

```
>> im(100,200,2)
```

If you want to know all the three color values at that position, you could type this:

```
>> im (100,200,1:3)
```

But instead, you can use a very convenient MATLAB shortcut for listing all the values along a particular dimension, like this:

```
>> im (100,200,:)
```

MATLAB's response will then be as follows:

```
ans(:,:,1) =

  120

ans(:,:,2) =

  204

ans(:,:,3) =

  148
```

This means that the pixel at position (100, 200) has a color with the red component equal to 120, the green component equal to 204, and the blue component equal to 148.

You can also use the MATLAB command:

```
>> impixelinfo;
```

This will open a figure window, where you will see the coordinates X, Y and three RGB values of each pixel of the current image pointed by the mouse cursor.

Another useful tool in MATLAB is `imtool`. It allows us to display an image and perform various interactive operations on it. You can use it to analyze any image given by a MATLAB variable or by a filename. You can also just type `imtool` and then import an image variable from the workspace.

```
>> imtool;
```

A window will open, containing the image of interest. In the lower left-hand corner, you can see information about the mouse coordinates and RGB values for the currently selected pixel, as shown in Fig. A.16. You can also measure distances in pixels between points of interest, by using the ✎ function in `imtool` menu. For example, you could measure the side length of one of the six squares shown in the image.

Let us now generate a matrix $200 \times 200 \times 3$, filled with zeros. We can display the matrix as an image, by using MATLAB's function `imshow`. Can you already predict the result? Yes, you are right, and the resulted image is a black rectangle, because everywhere and in all planes the RGB components are equal to 0 (see Fig. A.17).

```
>> x = zeros(200,200,3);
>> imshow(x);
```

What will happen if we change x so that all of its first color plane (red) get filled with the value 255?

```
>> x(:,:,1) = 255;
>> imshow(x);
```

Fig. A.16 The `imtool` can be used to analyze a captured image

Fig. A.17 A matrix filled
with zeros is a representation
of a *black rectangle*

Then, we will obtain a pure red rectangle.

Exercise 7
Generate a square green image, change it to blue, and then change this blue
image to a red one.

One can also convert images from one image type to another. If you want to
display multiple images together, you should use the MATLAB `subplot` function. This function creates a mosaic of windows, in which multiple images or plots
can be displayed. Do not forget that a gray image is a two-dimensional data
structure, while an RGB color image is a three-dimensional one. The following
code sequence takes an image and converts and displays it in two formats under
each other: in RGB color and in gray scale.

```
>> im = imread('onion.jpg');
>> imgray = rgb2gray(im);
>> subplot(2,1,1);imshow(im);
>> subplot (2,1,2);imshow(imgray);
```

Conclusion. What did you learn during this laboratory tutorial?

- You became familiar with MATLAB.
- You acquired audio and image signals, and you performed some simple analysis
  of these signals.
- You connected real-world signals with their mathematical representation in a
  computer.

Troubleshooting

1. Some cameras return the image in a YUY format, instead of RGB. In this case, the image you will get when calling imshow is reddish. To fix this, you should give the following command, which will convert YUY images into RGB:

   ```
   set(vid,'ReturnedColorSpace','rgb');
   ```

2. Some cameras have a very high resolution (1024 × 720) and will produce the MATLAB warning "Image too large to be displayed."

To fix this, you can change the resolution of the image.

The resolution of images acquired from a camera using the Image Acquisition Toolbox is not directly set by MATLAB. Instead, it is dependent upon the video format of the hardware device. Each video format has a specific resolution associated with it. Once a video format is chosen, the associated resolution is used. As an example, if you have a "winvideo" compatible imaging device connected to your system, the following command returns more information about the available image acquisition hardware:

```
>> info = imaqhwinfo('winvideo')
```

In order to see a list of supported video formats for this device, type:

```
info.DeviceInfo.SupportedFormats
```

This results in output similar to what is shown below:

```
ans=

    'RGB24_160x120'        'RGB24_176x144'            'RGB24_320x240'
'RGB24_352x288'    'RGB24_640x480'
```

Select a video format and associate it with a video object when creating the object in the MATLAB workspace. For example,

```
obj = videoinput('winvideo',1, 'RGB24_640x480');
```

sets the video format of the camera to acquire RGB images at a resolution of 640 × 480.

Appendix B
Simple Traffic Light Recognition Using MATLAB

Aim. Traffic light recognition is an inherent functionality of any autonomous car. It provides more awareness and vigilance, with reaction times that are much better than any human driver could. The same functionality is featured in navigation assistants for blind or color-blind pedestrians. Basically, street images are continuously recorded by a camera, and a smart vision system recognizes a traffic light on it and subsequently detects the state of its lights.

The real problem is very difficult to solve. However, we can simplify the situation, by creating a model of a vehicle positioned at a fixed distance in front of a traffic light. For this purpose, an experimental setup can be built, with a webcam placed in front of a miniature, yet functional traffic light, as shown in Fig. B.1. Normally in a single traffic-light stack, there is always only one color lit, as it is shown in Fig. B.2. The problem we will try to solve here is to recognize the state of a traffic light by using MATLAB (Fig. B.1).

Approach. Different states of the traffic light stack are characterized by two features: the active light *vertical position* (Top, Middle, Bottom) and its *color* (Red,

Fig. B.1 The experimental setup used for traffic light recognition

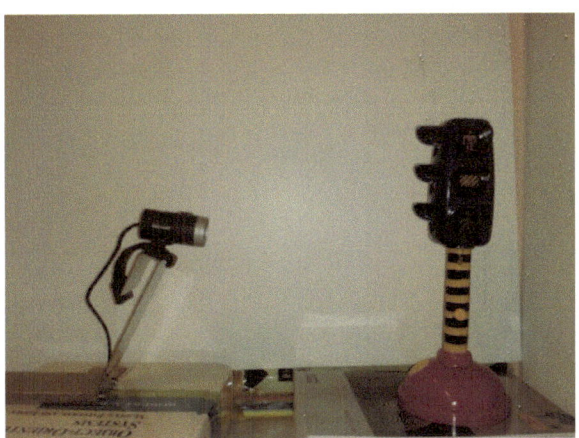

N. Silvis-Cividjian, *Pervasive Computing*, Undergraduate Topics in Computer Science, DOI 10.1007/978-3-319-51655-4

Fig. B.2 Images of a single traffic light stack showing three different states

Yellow, Green). The current traffic light state belongs to a set of nine classes, defined by all combinations of these two features as follows: states = {(Top, Red), (Top, Yellow), (Top, Green), (Middle, Red), (Middle, Yellow), (Middle, Green), (Bottom, Red), (Bottom, Yellow), (Bottom, Green)}. Of course, this is the general case. Different countries use different traffic light configurations. In The Netherlands for example, the traffic light can be only in three possible states as shown in Fig. B.2.

The plan is to start by acquiring an image of the traffic light and selecting a region of interest on this image, containing the three traffic lights. The next step will be to separate the active traffic light (segmentation) and finally classify it (recognition). The active light has a brighter color than the rest of the traffic lights, so this will be our BLOB. For segmentation, we will use all kinds of image processing techniques, including thresholding, morphological operations, and BLOB extraction. All this will be done by using the powerful features of MATLAB Image Processing Toolbox.

Step 1. Image acquisition and segmentation

First, we acquire an image from the camera named im, containing the active traffic light.

```
>> vid = videoinput('winvideo',1);
>> start(vid);
>> im = getsnapshot(vid);
```

We convert it to a grayscale image, im2, and consequently threshold it to obtain a binary image im3, shown in Figs. B.3, B.4, and B.5

Fig. B.3 The original RGB
image showing the traffic light

Fig. B.4 The same image
converted to grayscale format

Fig. B.5 The grayscale
image is converted to a binary
image through thresholding

```
>> im2=rgb2gray(im);
>> imshow(im2);
>> level=graythresh(im2)

level =

    0.4510

>> im3=im2bw(im2,level);
>> imshow(im3);
```

We can clearly see in Fig. B.5 the active light BLOB, colored in white. However, there is some white noise corrupting the image. Morphological operations can help here. By using `imtool`, we measure that this small, round noise object has a radius of ca 8 pixels. We segment this round object with a morphological opening, using a round structuring element of radius equal to 8.

```
>> im4 = imopen(im3,strel('disk',8));
>> imshow(im4);
```

The result of this opening operation is shown in Fig. B.6. You can see that the noise had been eliminated. Now, we can apply connected components labeling to extract the BLOB representing the active light (Fig. B.7).

```
>> [labels,numlabels] = bwlabel(im4);
>> vislabels(labels);
>> im6 = label2rgb(labels);
>> imshow(im6);
```

Step 2. Recognition

In the labeled image, the background is labeled with 1, the active traffic light BLOB is labeled with 2, and the traffic light body is labeled with 3. In MATLAB, we can query the properties of any labeled object with a function called `regionprops`.

Fig. B.6 The binary image after a morphological opening

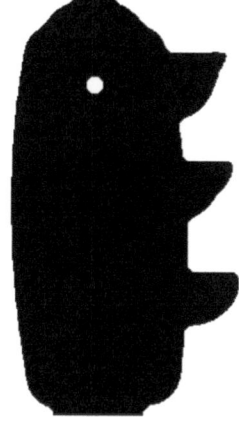

Fig. B.7 The result of connected components labeling. The active traffic light is BLOB #2

First, we want to determine the BLOB's position. To do this, we can query the coordinates of its center of mass or its *centroid*. By convention, the first element of the `centroid` is its horizontal coordinate (or *x*-coordinate) of the center of mass, and the second element is its vertical coordinate (or *y*-coordinate).

```
>> stats = regionprops(labels,'centroid');
```

stats.Centroid is a structure with three elements. We can ask their values by typing:

```
>> stats.Centroid

ans =

   19.4049  183.3723


ans =

   99     82


ans =

  205.8473  180.4848
```

We are interested in the vertical position of its second element, because our BLOB has its label equal to 2, as we can see from

```
>> y=stats(2).Centroid(2)

y =

    82
```

MATLAB answers us that the vertical coordinate y of our BLOB is equal to 82. To which class will this value belong? In order to classify this active light position, we analyze some traffic light-relevant images using the imtool MATLAB tool. We divide the traffic light stack image into three zones, as shown in Fig. B.8: Zone 1—Top with the Y-coordinate between 0 and 120 pixels, Zone 2—Middle with Y between 120 and 240 pixels, and Zone 3—Bottom with Y between 240 and 360 pixels.

This is in fact a rule-based classifier, using the following rules:

IF (Y > 0 and Y <=120) THEN position = Top
IF (Y > 120 and Y <=240) THEN position = Middle
IF (Y > 240 and Y < 360) THEN position = Bottom

According to these rules, our BLOB with Y=82 belongs to the class Top.

Next, we have to determine the color of this BLOB. We go back to our labeled image in and ask other properties of the BLOB object #2.

```
>> stats = regionprops(labels,'BoundingBox');
```

We want to extract a rectangle area around the BLOB, so we write:

```
>> rect = stats(2).BoundingBox;
```

By convention, this returned value, named rect, is a four-element position vector [xmin, ymin, width, height] that specifies the size and position of the cropped rectangle.

Fig. B.8 The traffic light image with the delimited *Top* (Zone 1), *Middle* (Zone 2), and *Bottom* (Zone 3) zones

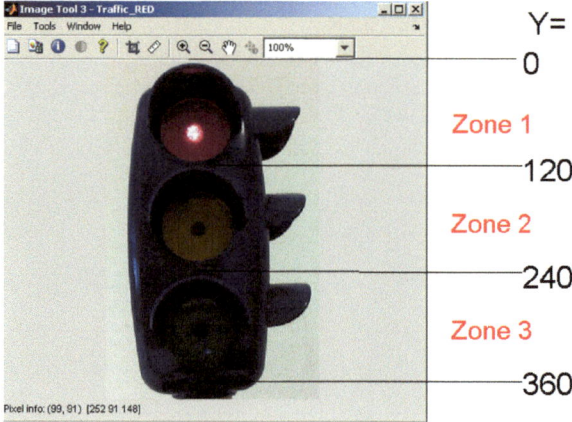

Fig. B.9 The rectangle containing the active traffic light

We go back to our initial RGB image `im`, and we select only that particular rectangle, containing our active traffic light (see Fig. B.9).

```
>> subImage = imcrop(im, rect);
>> imshow(subImage)
```

We cropped the image to a bounding box, and we have to classify its color to determine the color of the active traffic light. We adopt the following intuitive approach. We calculate the mean value of all RED plane pixels in this box. If this value is larger than 200, whereas the GREEN and BLUE mean values are much lower, then we classify this color as RED. This is in fact also a simple rule-based classifier, using, for example, for RED the following rule:

IF   (RED > 200)   and   (GREEN < 200)   and   (BLUE < 200)   AND (RED-GREEN > 50) AND (RED-BLUE) > 50 THEN colour is RED.

```
>> m_vector=mean(subImage(:,:,1)); %calculate the mean READ
>> m=mean(m_vector)

m =

   243.6055
```

We can see that the mean value of green is lower than 200.

```
>> m=mean(m_vector) %calculate the mean GREEN

m =
   173.8438
```

To conclude, we can classify this active traffic light state as:

Position = Top
Colour = Red

Finally, we can write a MATLAB function called `traffic_light_classify(im)` that takes as input parameter an RGB image containing the traffic light with one active light and returns the position of this active light, as being 1 (Top), 2 (Middle), or 3 (Bottom) and its color, as being red, yellow, or green.

```
function[position,colour]=traffic_light_classify(im)
position = 0;
im2=rgb2gray(im);
level=graythresh(im2);
im3=im2bw(im2,level);
im4=imopen(im3,strel('disk',8));
[labels,numlabels]=bwlabel(im4);
vislabels(labels);
% position classification
stats=regionprops(labels,'centroid');
y=stats(2).Centroid(2);   % the y coordinate of the BLOB nr.2.
if (y < 120) position = 1;
end
if (y > 120) && (y < 240) position = 2;
end
if (y > 240) position = 3 ;
end
% now the colour classification
stats=regionprops(labels,'BoundingBox');
rect=stats(2).BoundingBox;
subImage = imcrop(im, rect);
imshow(subImage);
m_vector=mean(subImage(:,:,1));
RED_Mean=mean(m_vector);
m_vector=mean(subImage(:,:,2));
GREEN_Mean=mean(m_vector);
if (RED_Mean - GREEN_Mean > 50) && (RED_Mean > 200)
    colour = 'Red';
end
if (GREEN_Mean > 200) && ((GREEN_Mean - RED_Mean) > 50)
    colour = 'Green';
end
if (RED_Mean > 200) && (GREEN_Mean > 200)
    colour='Yellow';
end

end
```

We can test this function on a traffic light image with the red light on.

```
>> im = Traffic_RED;
>> [pos,colour]=traffic_light_classify(im)

pos =
     1

colour =

Red
```

The same with a green light:

```
>> [pos,colour]=traffic_light_classify(im);
>> pos

pos =

     3

>> colour

colour =

Green
```

Finally, we test it with an active yellow light.

```
>> im=imread('traffic_yellow.bmp');
>> imshow(im);
>> [pos,colour]=traffic_light_classify(im)

pos =

     2

colour =

yellow
```

We conclude that our function works well for all three possible cases.

Index

A

A* algorithm, 35
A/D resolution, 21, 22, 25
Acceleration, 16, 24, 33, 75, 86
Acceptance testing, 157, 171
Accidents, 9, 48, 129, 141, 152, 153, 160
AC motor, 42
Activity diagram, 143, 148, 149, 170
Activity recognition, 120
Agile, 131, 142, 164, 166
Alias frequency, 22
Aliasing, 22, 25, 26
Amplitude, 18, 29, 30, 78, 80, 82, 84, 90, 106
Analog signal, 20–22, 24, 43, 77
Analog to digital converter (ADC), 28
Artificial neuron, 112, 127
Automatic insulin pump, 135–137, 139, 141, 142, 149–151, 161
Automatic speech recognizer (ASR), 102, 103, 110
Autonomous car, 10, 42, 47, 48, 55, 98
Autonomous vehicle, 45, 48, 151, 153
Averaging digital filter, 88, 90

B

Back log, 143
Band-pass filter, 88
Band-reject filter, 89
Bayes rule, 117, 118, 122, 127
B formal language, 140, 157, 170
Binary image, 26, 65–68, 70, 100, 101, 115
Binary large object (BLOB), 70
BLOB extraction, 70, 72
Blood glucose, 134, 139, 160
Blood glucose concentration (BCG), 133, 135, 151

Boundary value analysis (BVA), 158
Brightness, 19, 25, 26, 55–59, 61, 72
Brightness adjustment, 19, 56–58, 61

C

Calibration, 40
Calibration table, 41
Calm computing, 9
Camera, 9, 10, 20, 48, 55, 144
Cepstrum, 106
Classification, 12, 55, 93–95, 97, 100, 101, 104, 105, 107–109, 111, 112, 114–119, 122, 125, 126, 168
Classification accuracy, 115, 122
Classification algorithm, 107
Classification error, 122
Classification system, 94, 97, 126
Close-loop control, 44, 52
Closing, 36, 40, 68
Colour, 26, 28, 30, 48, 85, 95
Colour resolution, 26, 28
Colour RGB image, 11, 26, 28
Concept of operation (ConOps), 136, 169
Condition-action rule, 40
Conditional probability, 117, 122, 127
Confusion matrix, 123, 124, 126, 169
Connected components labeling, 72, 73
4-connectivity, 70
8-connectivity, 70
Continuous signal, 19, 20, 28
Contrast enhancement, 72
Controller, 1, 8, 9, 28, 31, 36, 39–43, 47, 50–52, 134, 135, 137, 141, 146, 163
Correlation, 63, 64, 66, 72, 73, 110
Cost of defects, 154
Cut off frequency, 88

© Springer International Publishing AG 2017
N. Silvis-Cividjian, *Pervasive Computing*, Undergraduate Topics
in Computer Science, DOI 10.1007/978-3-319-51655-4